from Martha

This Is Nature

This Is Nature

Thirty Years of the Best from
Nature Magazine

Selected and Edited by
Richard W. Westwood
Editor, Nature Magazine

Illustrated by Walter W. Ferguson

Thomas Y. Crowell Company
New York • Established 1834

To the late Edward Alexander Preble, noted field naturalist and associate editor of *Nature Magazine*, who wrote:

THE LOVER OF NATURE

To the nature lover the universe constantly pours out its wealth. Daily he gathers the fruits of seed sown in the beginning of the world.

For him no season is dull, for each is successively absorbing: In spring he is entranced by the awakening of myriad forms of life; summer reveals the maturity of all creation, autumn brings the fulfillment of earlier promises; winter lulls life to sleep, with its assurance of the resurrection.

All weathers are one: The rains of spring nourish all nature; the heats of summer mature and ripen its fruits; the frosts of winter give rest and peace; in all he rejoices.

Each day is good: In the morning life awakens with him; through the noon it works; the peace and quiet of evening shed their benediction upon him.

He knows no dull moments; he seeks not to hurry time. If he be delayed, he may discover something never before seen by man, and his impatience is forgotten.

His youth is filled with the joys of discovery; in middle age the marvels about him hold his interest undimmed; he awaits old age with calmness, for he is one with the universe, and is content.

All the stories in this book originally appeared in *Nature Magazine* and are reprinted by kind permission of the authors. In addition, "The Wit of a Red Squirrel" by William L. and Irene Finley appeared in *Wild Animal Pets*, published by Charles Scribner's Sons. The photographs in "A Box Turtle Lays Her Eggs" by Lewis V. Kost are copyright by the author.

Library of Congress Catalog Card No. 59-11386
Manufactured in the United States of America
1 2 3 4 5 6 7 8 9 10

Introduction

NATURE PROVIDES one of the most exciting of human experiences—discovery. This is the theme in this book. While man has left few geographical frontiers to explore, he can always turn to nature for its myriad surprises. He can share with the inquiring naturalist and writer the thrill of discovery of truths "more fascinating than fiction."

During thirty-six years as assistant editor, managing editor and editor of *Nature Magazine,* we—the editorial we—have read more nature articles than perhaps anyone else. Certainly we have read more unpublished—and unpublishable—articles than anyone we can imagine. But an editor fondly hopes that the words that finally find their way into imperishable type on the pages of his magazine are the best that have come to his hand, or the writing of which he has encouraged, or the use of which he has been able somewhat to embellish.

To choose a half-hundred "best" of the articles that have been published involves a revaluation of past editorial judgment. It is also an interesting, sometimes humbling, experience, requiring a review of nearly 25,000 pages of the bound volumes of the magazine, starting with the first issue in January, 1923. Indeed, it is rather frightening to realize that, figuring conservatively, the editor in preparing issue after issue has read 15,000,000 words, most of them at least four times in the progression from manuscript to final printer's proof. He has now of necessity reread many of these words.

In arriving at the selections for this book it quickly became apparent that the some 125,000 words here presented could be no more than *some* of the best. Indeed, the material chosen as a basis from which final selection was made would provide four or five volumes this size, all of them, in this editor's opinion, worthy of republication.

Selection has, therefore, been largely on the basis of variety, both with regard to the phases of nature covered and differing literary approaches to it. Through the years each issue of *Nature Magazine* has sought to express the aims described for it as the official spokesman for the American Nature Association—stimulation of interest in all phases of nature and the outdoors and furtherance of conservation of the great natural resources of this country. These were the goals set by the founders, the late Charles Lathrop Pack and his son, Arthur Newton Pack.

Conservation—militant and independent —has been a basic tenet of the magazine. With regard to wildlife, emphasis has been on a knowledge and appreciation of all forms of animal life as essential to conservation thought and action. We believe that this theme is also inherent in the selections here provided.

Contributors to *Nature Magazine* during these years have been refreshingly varied. Indeed, in the field of nature the author occupies a position of somewhat more intimate relationship to his readers than in most publications of general distribution. He shares enthusiasms with other enthusiasts; he enjoys a rapport born of a common interest with those who read what he has written. Thus our contributors have included such accomplished naturalist-writers as Dallas Lore Sharp, Edwin Way Teale, Donald Culross Peattie, Alan Devoe and John Lindsey Blackford; such eminent naturalists as David Starr Jordan, Vernon Bailey, Edward A. Preble, W. L. McAtee, and William Beebe; and an army of unsung amateur writers and enthusiasts. With the layman particularly, and often with the scientist, the editor has found it necessary to lend such talents as he may possess to achieve the popular touch and to realize the literary standards that the magazine has sought to attain. We hope that some of the selections on the pages that follow reflect such collaboration.

One compensation that an editor derives from his labors is to be found in the friendships he has formed with those who have written for him. Some of these are personal; more of them are through correspondence alone. Because of the limitations that lie between the covers of a book, it has been impossible to recognize more than a few of his writer-friends, although not from the lack of will to include many more.

Finally, we hope that the material here presented will reach many who will draw pleasure from and find inspiration in these selections, as have many thousands of readers of *Nature Magazine* through the years.

RICHARD W. WESTWOOD
Editor, *Nature Magazine*
Washington, D.C.

Contents

This Is Nature

So Long, Voyageur!

Gerald Movius

WHEN THE SPRING FLIGHTS of Canada geese steered north above our place, my wild gander, Voyageur, was reminded of faraway places I hoped he had forgotten.

Voyageur could not fly, and it hurt me to see him try. I had found him, keel-up, in the weeds along the coulee bank the previous autumn. I was ten years old. He was badly wounded; more dead than alive. A month's rest in our woodshed and a diet of chicken mash put him on his feet again, but one wing dragged and he walked lopsidedly.

He could barely scramble to the top of the straw pile, and there he would stand when the honkers passed, his good wing flailing his side, yearning for his kin to notice him. Always before, their clarion voices had smothered his calls, but that one time they heard him.

The flight veered and detached a small task force that wavered downward for a closer look. Their voices took on a sharp note of distress, and the flight echoed it. All they could see was Voyageur and a small boy, in stocking cap and mackinaw, who wished that somehow the great gray birds could help their earth-bound fellow down below.

Then they were gone, for there was nothing they could do. And Voyageur was hushed. His wing beat slower and slower as he watched the dark skein fade into the fabric of the rose and golden dawn. His head drooped in his torment of helplessness. After that he paid no more attention to the wild geese than did our chickens. It was as though he had decided to make the best of things; to become a part of this new life.

The books say that Canadian honkers are haughty and aloof. Voyageur was as sociable as a collie pup and as talkative as an old parrot. He was under my feet at chore time, stropping his neck against my overalls and, in sudden bursts of affection, shoving his bill into my hand and pretending to bite.

Voyageur liked everybody, especially such infants as then adorned the place. The baby chicks used his back for a sun porch or an obstacle in their games of follow-the-leader. Turkey poults, whose rattle-headed mothers left them straggling in a sudden fall of rain, could depend on Voyageur for emergency shelter. When Vinegar and Mustard were absent on important social matters, Voyageur baby-sat their kittens, and he mourned the accidental death of Mustard's kitten more than Mustard did. I found him with his long neck stretched protectingly across the limp little carcass, making sorrowful noises deep in his throat.

The honker is monogamous and mighty fussy in his choice of bride, but we hoped Voyageur would mate with one of our domestic geese and father many broods of hybrid goslings. The offspring of a honker and a barnyard goose is called a "mongrel." It is about the finest eating this side of Olympian banquet halls, and the railroads in those days snapped them up at fancy prices. Mongrel geese cannot reproduce themselves. They are sterile, like the mule.

If Voyageur would co-operate, I figured my fortune was made. Our virgin geese were willing. They were drawn to him like moths to a candle. In his lean and elegant presence our lumbering foreign ganders looked like stodgy louts. Voyageur was a symphony in black, gray and white, and you got the idea of a young clubman turned out for a full-dress wedding.

Tulip's affections were his for the asking. Tiptoe trailed after him with languishing air. Teresa fluttered every feather if he so much as brushed against her. Voyageur ignored their blandishments.

I tried penning him alone with Tulip. But Voyageur sulked in a corner and whacked Tulip's head with his bill if she came within range.

He appeared to have resolved on a life of good works and monastic meditation. Then he astounded everybody by bringing home a bride of his own selection, a little Pilgrim goose from the Hathaway place a mile up the road. She was shy about the proposition, but he urged her ahead of him with his bill, gabbling reassurances.

Voyageur must have done his courting at the coulee where all the waterfowl in the neighborhood cavorted, and he had chosen well. The Pilgrim was svelte and demure, and her frock of light gray and white feathers put you in mind of a Colonial lass. The Hathaways demanded and got five settings of chicken eggs in exchange for their bird, and I named her Priscilla.

She chose an old barrel for a home, and I furnished the nest with a glass goose egg to keep them happy while I snitched her eggs as fast as she laid them, setting them under accommodating broody hens. The last ten eggs Priscilla was allowed to keep for herself. While they were incubating no stranger could get within yards of the barrel without inviting Voyageur's wrath. He was a changed bird, barely civil even to me.

It was then he discovered that his wing had healed. He had gone down to the coulee for a hasty dip and must have thought he heard Priscilla call him. He *flew* back, hurtling into the yard as easily as if his wing had never been damaged.

He landed with a bump, shook his head in surprise at his own achievement, examined the wing as if he had never seen it before—and burst into an ecstasy of gabbles. He danced on his toes with both wings aloft, raced to Priscilla and chucked her under the chin with his bill—then came running to me for my admiration, pulling at my overalls and thrusting his bill into my hand. His splendid eyes glinted with excitement.

From that time on he flew all over the neighborhood. It could portend only one thing—Voyageur would leave in the fall. Sure, I could clip his wings. But he was too happy. Voyageur with a crippled wing had needed me. Voyageur with two good wings needed nothing except his freedom. I had made too much of him for my own good, I guess. He was about the first living thing I could truly call mine. I hated to see the summer end.

Voyageur and I were in the yard together when I heard the pipes of the first southern flight. His eyes were restless, and he quartered the sky to mark the course. His body trembled. He took a running start and launched himself upward. I said to myself: "So long, Voyageur! So long!"

Priscilla took it with serenity at first. In their months together he had flown off for hours at a time, but now, when night came, she was uneasy. In two days she was a sick bird. We had had geese before who went into declines when something happened to their mates. Priscilla, though, to make matters worse, was alone in her anxiety, for she had formed no social attachments with our other geese. Her goslings no longer needed her. She moped and rejected food.

But both Priscilla and I had underestimated Voyageur. Within three days he was back. The wildness was gone from his eyes. The tug of his ties with Priscilla had surmounted the impulse to join his own kind. The instinct of devotion was stronger than the migratory urge. He was completely himself once more, getting in my way at chore time and showering attention on Priscilla, who bloomed into health again.

It was the season of fun for our waterfowl. The cares of family life were over for the year. The Indian summer sun warmed the coulee water, and there were fractious young geese and ducks for the oldsters to whack over the head when they were too saucy. Voyageur reveled in the life. It was also the hunting season, and I could hear the shotguns in the early morning hours. Now and then a goose would falter from the V formation overhead, struggle desperately to keep aloft and then spiral to the ground.

I was glad Voyageur stuck to the safety of the coulee, which was sternly posted as out of bounds to hunters. That was why I could hardly believe it when I heard the slam of a gun so close to our place; and the scream of terrified geese. There was a cold, sick feeling in my stomach as I ran to look. On the opposite side of the coulee a man was running the other way. You could tell by his clothes he was a city dude, and not one of our people.

Priscilla was dead. Voyageur was unhurt. The hunter must have been aiming at him. Frightened at having killed a domestic goose, he had legged it away.

Voyageur was crouched in the grass where Priscilla had crawled. Her feathers were soaked with blood. His long neck rested across her, and I remembered the kitten he had mourned. This time he was silent and his eyes were glazed with truly overwhelming misery.

I buried her in decency and honor, and Voyageur watched. As I tamped the last shovelful of dirt on the small grave he ran to me and thrust his bill into my hand, as he had done so many times, whimpering like a grieving dog. Overhead the honkers piped, and Voyageur looked up. I knew what was going to happen. He was telling me goodbye.

"So long, Voyageur!" I said. "So long!"

This time it would be "So long" forever. There was no Priscilla to lure him back. There were only the sky and the muted voices of his own breed—and the northern wind that nipped at their sterns and urged them on to the winter resting grounds.

And then he was gone to join the distant flight. The sunset blazed as night crept in on purple prairie land.

The Story of the Baby Opossum

Carl G. Hartman

IN SOME RESPECTS the opossum is the most remarkable animal in America. It is the only marsupial or pouched animal of the New World; the kangaroo and other near relatives all live in Australia. The pouch of the female is a fold of skin stretched around eleven to fifteen milk glands on the lower abdomen in a region corresponding to the cow's udder. The pouch may be closed by ring muscles much as a tobacco sack may be closed by pulling the string; in this way the tiny babies may be guarded against cold and other dangers. Shelter, warmth, and food the opossum babies find in this admirable contrivance of nature designed for the care of her children that are born younger and in most respects less developed than any other mammal babies in the world. It is this early birth that astonishes both the naturalist and the casual observer of nature's ways.

No wonder, then, that strange traditions have arisen about the generation of the opossum. One story has it that the mother blows the babies into the pouch from her nostrils; another notion is that the young come directly out of the nipples that are in the pouch. How the opossum develops, is born, and reaches the shelter of the pouch can be easily told today, since the interesting details have recently been discovered. We are, moreover, fortunate in being able to present an actual picture of an opossum egg photographed in the living state soon after it was removed from the animal. For, like every other animal, the opossum too comes from an egg. The reader can see a picture of the egg soon after it comes from the ovary and later the embryo itself while it is developing into the baby opossum ready to be born.

To understand the opossum egg, which is extremely small, comparison should be made with the hen's egg. In the middle of the hen's egg is the yolk; this is the egg proper, much enlarged because of food stored up for the developing chick. Around the yolk there is a layer of albumen or egg-white—more food and some water. The whole is surrounded by a shell membrane and a hard calcareous shell; one can notice the shell membrane in a hard-boiled egg, from which it is easily peeled off after the shell is cracked and removed. The tiny opossum egg has a shell membrane but no hard shell, for it is not "laid" like a hen's egg but develops in the delicate uterus inside the body. Under the shell membrane there is a thick layer of albumen, as clear as a dewdrop. The egg proper is in the center. It is so small that 170 of them laid side by side like a string of beads would be required to make an inch; a thimble, small as it is, is big enough to hold half a million. The whole egg with the egg white is of course larger. From such a tiny speck, just visible to the unaided eye, an opossum ready for birth develops in 12½ days.

At first the egg itself is a single cell. This soon divides into two, four, eight cells and so on. The cells arrange themselves into a hollow sphere or vesicle. This grows and becomes very thin-walled and filled with liquid, a most delicate, beautiful structure —like soap bubbles or fragile fairy balloons blown by a magician. They are indeed more than magical—they are nature's products and hence more wonderful than fairy tales can conjure up. They are living things. What miracles take place in them in the course of a very few days!

When the vesicle is the size of a poppy seed the place where the embryo opossum is about to start its development is indicated by a round disk of cells which are thicker than the others. This round disk becomes pear-shaped when the vesicle is the size of a mustard seed; and a line appears running lengthwise in the pointed end of the pear-shaped area. This is the signal for the embryo to start its development, for there is, up to this point, not a trace of an embryo opossum—the egg has only been getting ready for this event. Yet six days have already been spent in this preparation out of the 12½ days which nature allows for the whole process. In other words, in 6½ days after the embryo proper starts its development it must be well enough developed to be born into the world and take its first journey, the journey into the pouch for food and shelter!

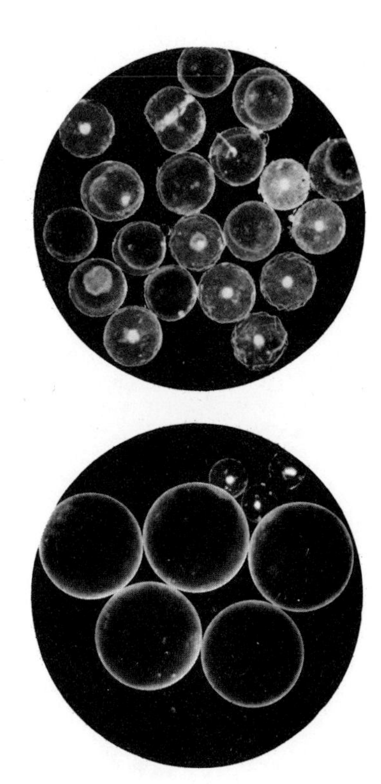

Top: *Vesicles and undeveloped eggs at 96 hours.* Bottom: *At 5 days, vesicle is poppy-seed size.*

The first organ to make its appearance in the opossum, as in the chick and all other animals, is the brain—it comes in front of the streak in the pear-shaped area. The opossum develops on the surface of the liquid-filled sphere or vesicle just as the chick develops on the surface of the yolk, which is semisolid in that case. Soon the body form takes shape and as it needs more room it dips down into the hollow vesicle. The vesicle grows to accommodate the larger embryo and it also becomes provided with blood vessels with which to come into close relation to blood vessels of the mother to get food therefrom and give off waste. But there is never an elaborate sys-

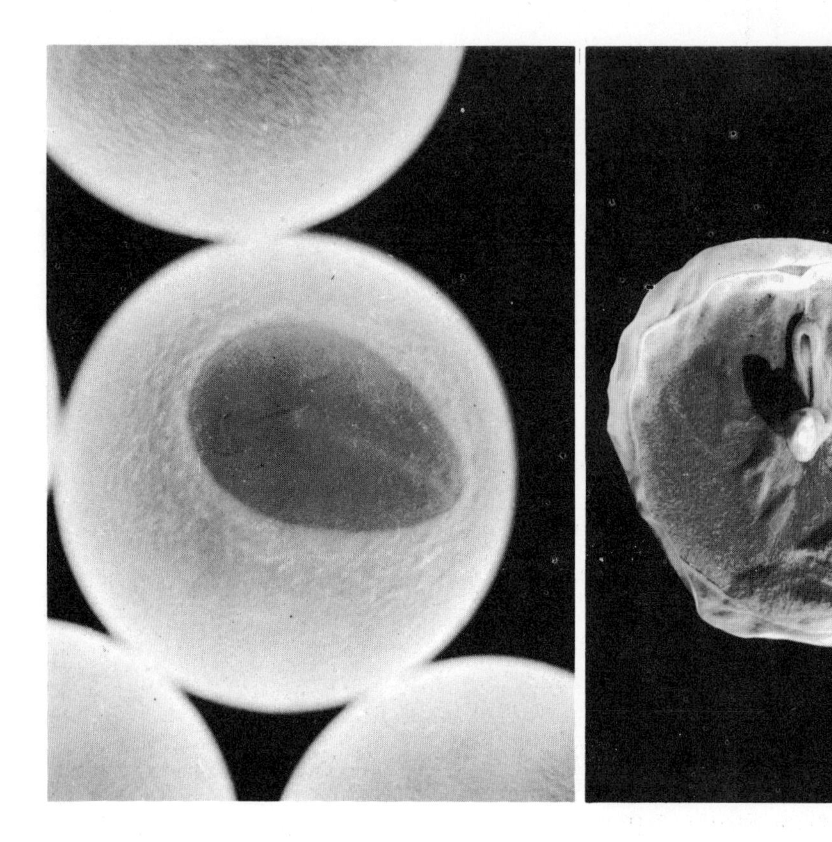

Above, left: *The size of a mustard seed at 6 days, the embryo will be born 6½ days later. It is at this time that a line begins to appear in the dark portion of the egg indicating that the embryo is ready to develop.* Above, right: *Here is the embryo at a further stage of development, within its vesicle and supplied with blood vessels. It is now beginning to take on the shape that presages the arrival of the baby.*

tem for getting nourishment from the mother for long; hence the baby opossum must the sooner find its food outside the body, namely its mother's milk. So small are the opossum babies at this time that a litter of eighteen, if you can imagine it, may rest secure in a teaspoon. Such a whole litter weighs one-fifteenth of an ounce—270 opossums, living, breathing, digesting animals together would weigh one ounce. They are less developed than mouse babies, which themselves, as every boy knows, are blind, helpless bits of pink flesh. One cannot speak of such babies as "seeing the light of day" when they are born, for opossum young do not have their eyes open for the seven or eight weeks that they are in the pouch attached to the teats—and well must they hold on for their life depends on it.

How does so poorly developed a baby reach the pouch and find the teat, for this it must do or die? It had been formerly supposed that the mother

The mother opossum's pouch, where the 3-week-old litter is carried.

caught the young in her lips and placed them in the pouch and on the nipples. That's the story one finds in many nature books still. But this was a mere guess that happened to be proved wrong like so many other wives' tales.

If you will examine the picture of a newly born opossum you will note the mouth and the nostrils surrounded by a peculiar "muzzle." The front legs and feet demand special attention, for they are highly developed and provided with sharp-hooked claws, while the hind feet are mere buds or pads. The facts are that when the baby opossum is born it crawls into the pouch by itself, and it is for this first journey that it has the well developed front feet. I saw it do this with my own eyes. It travels with a hand-over-hand motion like the stroke of a swimmer. It moves about until its muzzle touches the nipple and then it takes hold and, believe me, it continues to literally "hold on for dear life" for nearly two months.

At two months the young have a fine coating of hair, their eyes are open and lips completely separated. They are now cute and interesting as they scamper about on the old one, holding onto the mother's rich fur, as she lies basking in the sun on a hollow log that constitutes their den. Or at night when she prowls around for food for herself and her family they hang on tenaciously lest they be brushed off by passing shrubbery. In another month they hunt food for themselves, but still for some time like to have mother about for protection and perhaps for some instruction in the ways of life, for many problems of food-getting must be solved.

An Owl in Our Chimney

Harriet Burkhart

ONE NIGHT in mid-October, as I was preparing for bed, I heard a rustling noise in my bedroom fireplace. Absently glancing in that direction, I met the large-eyed gaze of an *owl!* He was clinging to the inside of the fire screen, with pinions wide and ear tufts prominent—a gray phase eastern screech owl.

As I approached my unexpected guest, he retreated to the back of the fireplace, where he immediately assumed the typical owl attitude of defense, throwing himself back on his wings exactly as though they were arms, freeing his talons for action. He also started snapping and clicking his beak with as much menace as such a diminutive predator could muster, while puffing out all his feathers to make himself look as formidable as possible.

By the time I got my camera and flash, the visitor had settled down on top of the logs, where he remained with eyes stubbornly squinted while I tried a couple of exposures. When my daughter tried to pick him up, however, he flew to the top shelf of the bookcase and perched on top of the books like Poe's raven, hunched over so that he could watch us. Presently, by dint of much scrambling, the owl managed to wedge himself into the small space behind the books, where he spent the next hour with only the very tips of his "ears" visible. If anyone came into the room, however, the big eyes quickly came into view above the books, and solemnly watched what was taking place.

Meanwhile I got out the proper size of band and pliers—for what bird bander would pass up such an opportunity!—and put on gloves for good measure. But our visitor proved to be much more tractable than the only other owl I had handled, a young barred owl I raised after its parents were killed. So I decided to try one more picture, this one on a lower shelf of the bookcase, where there was a niche for our guest among the books. He had trouble getting a foothold on the slippery enameled surface, but soon settled back in the corner and sat for his portrait with great aplomb, watchful but not unduly alarmed. Even the flash made him blink only once or twice.

In fact, I was the one who lacked confidence when it came to getting the stiff band around the thickly feathered tarsus. The band looked impossibly small. I have no pliers with a hole large enough to take a size 5 U. S. Fish and Wildlife Service band and close it in a perfect circle. So I had to use an ordinary pair of pliers with extreme caution, so that the band would neither overlap nor bite into the feathers. The owl lay quietly in hand during this procedure and afterwards actually seemed to enjoy gentle stroking of his head and back, for he closed his long-lashed, feathered eyelids and relaxed, leaning slightly against us. He also readily accepted and swallowed small pieces of raw beef liver. I think he was probably very hungry, for I am sure he had spent the day sitting unobserved in the fireplace. Several times during the preceding night I had heard noises to which I had paid scant attention, since I, like most country dwellers, am well accustomed to white-footed mice in my waste baskets. How long he had been in the chimney I have no way of knowing, but the miracle is that he was able to get down into the small fireplace at all, with the damper partially closed.

About midnight we installed the little fellow in the barn in a large rectangular cage, in which we had placed a piece of gnarled driftwood. He lost no time in perching, sitting slim and tall. In the dim light his yellow eyes opened wide, with the pupils large and dark, very different from the huge, limpid, brown eyes of a former occupant of that cage, the baby barred owl. I wondered again, as I have so many times, whether the barred owl is still alive, for around the little lake resort where I live owls are far from popular. They are the innocent victims of stupid prejudice on the part of not only the summer people from the city but many of the local residents, who are actually alarmed if owls hoot close by in the woods at night. The innumerable unfortunate superstitions that have grown up around owls through the centuries are responsible. It is astounding that these old wives' tales are still believed in this enlightened age, but many people really believe that owls are harbingers of misfortune, or even of death.

The next morning, when I tried to feed the screech owl before leaving for the day, he kept his eyes as tightly shut as his beak. Plainly he had no wish to be disturbed at that hour, in broad daylight, and did not touch the raw ground beef I left in his cage. I discovered that even when his eyes seemed to be closed he could still see, for his head turned to follow me when I circled the cage. But in the early evening, when I tried another feeding, the owl was again wide awake, extremely alert, wary and active. He turned his back to me, spread his amazingly wide gray wings like a mantle, and then brought his head completely around, facing me in that disconcerting contortion so natural to owls. This time he objected, with beak and claw, to being handled, but took his raw beef all the same.

When I put him back, he resumed his nimble maneuvers around the roomy cage, until, in order to examine more closely the intricate and beautiful barring of his wings, I turned the beam of a flashlight directly on him. He quickly threw out both wings and quavered one soft, clear note of thrilling tone quality—in pitch a perfect C, the one above middle C on the piano. Once again he made this exquisite sound before I went on up to the hayloft to set mouse traps in the hope of catching a proper owl meal. I knew that owls swallow small animals whole and later eject from the mouth the skin, bones, teeth, and other indigestible portions, all done up in neat little packages. In the case of the barred owl I found that this process takes several hours, and only once in a whole summer's observation did I actually see him bring up a pellet from his throat one day while I was feeding him.

The next day, with the help of a young friend, I tied a string to the bird band and set the small owl in the crotch of an oak sapling at the edge of our woods for the final pictures. Only once or twice did the bird make any attempt to take off, and then flew sluggishly. (I have since learned that all screech owls are slow fliers, which is one reason they have to hunt by night. They can see perfectly well in the daylight, but I did notice that this owl always squinted the eye toward the sun, making it impossible for me to get outdoor pictures with both owl eyes fully open.) The owl's flight was, of course, noiseless because of the tapering of all the flight feathers into a hairlike fringe, which offers a minimum of resistance to the air. Chickadees are audible—almost noisy—flyers compared to owls.

By this time word had gotten around to a number of my former Junior Auduboners that I had an interesting visitor, and five or six of them, of assorted ages from eleven to fifteen, appeared on the scene, two on horseback with a collie dog in tow. Pandemonium promptly ensued. Genghis Khan, one of two Siamese cats I tether on clotheslines because of the birds, went to the top of a Norway maple and had to be retrieved before he hung himself. The only calm individual in the whole gathering was the little screech owl. He seemed to accept all situations like a philosopher, sitting unperturbed on the shoulder of one of the boys, while the only girl present fed him raw beef liver. He ate eagerly and seemed to swoon with pleasure when she stroked him. The children were interested in the fact that, like all members of the owl family, this one had a facial disc, although it is not nearly so prominent and facelike as the pale one of the barn owl, for instance. I could well believe, watching the small owl with all these youngsters, what I have so often heard and read—that screech owls are easily tamed and make delightful pets. This is certainly not true of all owls. Our baby barred owl never became really tame, although he did come to tolerate our attentions in the course of time.

By this time the other Siamese had caught a chipmunk, although on the leash. I put it in the owl's cage, not knowing whether he would tackle such an overwhelming offering, but wanting to give him one really satisfying meal before I turned him loose. Screech owls ordinarily eat small creatures, such as mice and shrews, insects, snails, crayfish, reptiles, etc., with only occasionally a small bird. The screech owl itself sometimes serves as a meal for one of the large owls, I have heard.

When I returned an hour or so later in the early evening, the owl was holding bloody shreds of the chipmunk's flesh gripped tightly in his talons against the driftwood perch. He was also rocking a little from side to side and crooning contentedly to himself six notes in a definite pattern. The song—for such it certainly was—started, like the call note I had heard before, on the C above middle C and in the same long, sustained quavering whistle. But now it was followed by five shorter descending *chromatic* notes—the A natural above middle C, G sharp, G natural, F sharp, and F natural. Over and over he repeated this song, with scarcely opened beak and slitted eyes. Presently he raised the whole thing two tones, to E natural instead of C.

I sat in the dusk beside the owl, entranced by the beauty and strangeness of the song, and wondering how this little singer could possibly have deserved the harsh, inappropriate name of *screech* owl. As for its scientific name, *Otus asio naevius*, what a name for one of the smallest and most lovable of our North American owls! It is not even especially descriptive, since the first two words have the same meaning—one in Greek and the other in Latin—horned or eared owl, of which there are several other species. The third name, *naevius*, signifies having a spot, mole, or blemish, of all things, and must be intended to refer to the many lovely streaks and other subtle markings that make up its plumage. But whatever his name, of one thing I am sure: I shall never forget this particular little owl and his engaging and endearing ways. May his tribe increase!

Lucky Bugs, and Others

Edwin Way Teale

STEP ON A CRICKET, and it will rain.

Release a fly buzzing along a windowpane, and it will bring you good luck.

Catch the first butterfly you see in spring, and bad luck will follow you all the rest of the year.

Count the spots on a hibernating ladybird beetle, and you will find a dollar for every spot you count.

If a honeybee circles around you, a letter is coming.

If a butterfly alights on your shoulder, you will receive new clothes.

Such are half a dozen of the innumerable superstitions that have been linked with the insect world. In all countries and all ages, these small, familiar creatures have been considered as connected in some way with misfortune and good luck. "Lucky bugs" and "soothsayer insects" are numerous in folklore. The commonest of everyday insects, at various times, have been supposed to have supernatural effect upon the weather and upon the fortunes of mankind.

Dream of ants, one superstition of early England has it, and you will be either happy and industrious, move to a big city, or have a large family. Whenever a stone has been overturned and an ants' nest revealed beneath, the stone must be replaced carefully, according to another belief, or bad luck will follow.

One early fall afternoon, I was plodding down a winding forest trail close on the heels of a Maine guide. Suddenly, my guide stopped. He pointed to a wasps' nest, hanging low among the bushes.

"We're going to have a mild winter," he assured me. "When wasps build their nests high, the snowdrifts are high. But when they build them near the ground, the winter is mild and snowfall light."

This belief is a weather-superstition that is accepted in many places. The fallacy lies in the fact that the wasp colony does not overwinter and hence it matters not at all to it how deep the snow drifts. A few fertilized queens hibernate outside the nest and all the workers of the colony die in the first freeze.

Wasp-lore contains other odd superstitions besides this belief of the Maine guide. In central Europe, girls used to place a piece of paper from a wasp nest in their clothing. This was considered an infallible charm that would make their suitors love them the more. Such insect paper was also prized by old people who believed that spectacles cleaned with wasp-nest fragments enabled them to see better. Clay from a mud-dauber's nest, at one time, was held in high repute as a cure for boils. Such nests were treated with respect by housewives in some European countries because it was firmly believed that the woman who knocked down a mud-dauber's nest would shortly thereafter break all her dishes.

To the credulous, the actions of butterflies often have been matters of great concern. On a summer's day, if a butterfly found its way through an open door into a house, superstitious housewives believed that they soon would have a lady visitor and that she would be wearing a dress of the same color as the insect. Seen in late fall, a butterfly was considered a harbinger of early cold. On the other hand, when a mourning cloak was observed flitting about a woodland glade during a February thaw, the insect was regarded as bringing news of an early spring.

When a summer butterfly settled on the head of a young woman, the fact was accepted as an indication that she would have a new sweetheart. If one of these insects alighted on a person's hand, he was sure to receive unexpected money in the near future. Yellow roadside butterflies, clustered about a mud-puddle, were always skirted carefully by children who had heard the old folklore belief that disturbing such insects was the equivalent of "losing a pot of gold." And who would take such a chance?

Those night-flying relatives of the butterflies, the moths, usually have been linked with somber superstitions. In many parts of the world, white moths have been thought to be the returning spirits of departed friends and relatives. In middle Europe, it was said that moths bewitched the butter by flying over the milk-pans or by crawling into the churns. When a moth singed its wings in a candle flame, its misfortune was considered to foretell sickness or dire calamity in the household. Electric lights downed this superstition.

The children of moths and butterflies also have their place in the realm of these curious beliefs. When a woolly bear caterpillar was seen hurrying across an open space, it was taken for granted that winter was close behind. By examining the width of the central band around its body, the gullible believed, the severity of the coming cold could be determined.

Superstition says that stepping on a cricket will bring rain.

Among the English hop fields, farmers always used to pay close attention to the chrysalides of certain anglewing butterflies. Golden dots appeared on the sides of these chrysalides. When the dots were large, the hop-growers went about their work confident that the crop would be big and their profits proportionately large. Measuring worms, seen looping along a man's clothing, were often said to be measuring him for a new suit. When they were seen on a woman's hand, they were getting the size for a new pair of gloves. In some regions, the actions of the measuring worms were viewed with foreboding. They were thought to be taking measurements for a shroud.

Foreboding has been a frequent attitude toward commonplace actions in the insect world. Leaf miners, those small larvae that eat out curving and looping tunnels within the tissues of leaves, were formerly viewed with superstitious dread. The markings they produced were thought to be the signatures of evil spirits. Similarly, the "W" formed by the thickened veins near the tips of the wings of the seventeen-year cicada has been looked upon as a warning of coming "war, want and woe." And, when a swarm of honeybees settled upon a rotten limb, the fearful and credulous people in some of the counties of England accepted it as an indication that there would be a death in the family.

Honeybees—so mysterious in their actions and for so many centuries closely associated with man—have been linked with a host of superstitious ideas. These curious misconceptions cover a wide range and include such oddities as the following: A beekeeper must never count his hives or the insects will languish. No one can own more than ninety-nine hives; as soon as the number reaches 100, all the bees will die. If bees alight on a baby, it is an omen that the child will be eloquent. A stolen swarm never thrives. Bees never prosper at the home of a quarrelsome family. Bees are idle or unfortunate in time of war. At midnight, on Christmas Eve, the bees hum in a particularly musical manner in special celebration of Christ's nativity.

In several parts of the world, it is believed that the bees must always be informed of important news events. Beekeepers, in certain parts of England, used to inform the inmates of the hives whenever a political change or a declaration of war occurred. Unless the insects were taken into their confidence in this way, the apiarists believed, they would not thrive. When the master (sometimes any member) of the household died, one of the family was delegated to knock on the side of each hive and repeat: "The master is dead! The master is dead! The master is dead!" If this ceremony were neglected, the bees would fly away. In pioneer America, the same idea prevailed. Whittier's poem "Telling The Bees" is based upon this age-old custom.

In other ways, bees have been treated as members of the family. At the time of a marriage feast, the Breton peasants, in France, always dressed their beehives in red. When a death occurred in the family, in certain regions of England, black crepe was placed on the hives, or a stick, painted black, was thrust into the ground beside each hive. For generations, it was the custom in one English village to give the bees a formal invitation to every funeral.

A few years ago, in a small town in northern Florida, I encountered an insect superstition that was new to me. A boy of about twelve assured me that a praying mantis could cause blindness by "spitting tobacco juice in your eye." He even declared that he had heard of a boy in a town twenty-five miles away who had lost his sight in just this way. Thousands of miles away from the Florida town, across the Atlantic, French children believe another—equally unfounded—idea about the praying mantis. They call the insect The Soothsayer. When a child is lost, the mantis—if it is lifted

The cicada was believed to be a prophet of disaster. When credulous persons saw the "W" formed by enlarged veins in its wings, they took it to foretell "war, want, woe."

from the ground—will stretch out its forelegs and point the way home. Similarly, American farm boys, for generations, have interrogated daddy-longlegs to find out the direction strayed cattle have taken.

Years ago, as a child on my grandfather's farm in the dune country of northern Indiana, I used to hear a curious superstition about houseflies. If you kill one fly, the saying went, ten more would come to its funeral. Another odd item on the list of fly lore of that period was the belief that a fly buzzing about your face indicated that a stranger was anxious to meet you.

Ever since the days of Aristotle, people have been imagining untrue things about the small masses of white foam seen clinging to grass and weeds in early summer. Throughout Europe, they have been thought to be "frog spit" or "cuckoo spit." In reality, they are produced by small, soft-bodied immature insects that live within the protection of the froth until they reach their adult, winged stage. The foam protects them from the sun and from their enemies. A superstition of the South, accepted by many people, is that horseflies hatch from the masses.

During winter months, insects of various kinds are thought to bring good luck to many people by entering dwellings for hibernation or for protection from the cold. A cricket in the house is considered a lucky portent in many parts of the world. To hear one of these insects chirping after a person has gone to bed is believed to foreshadow extra good fortune.

Curiously enough, one of the most beneficial of our insects has been looked upon almost universally with superstitious dread. Superstition has it that dragonflies doctor snakes and even that they are evil spirits sent by Satan to plague the world. This is at wide variance with the truth. Dragonflies are, in reality, valuable friends of man. They catch and consume immense numbers of troublesome gnats and mosquitoes. Such facts are overlooked by superstition which, in the case of the dragonfly and the other insects—as in the case with everything else, is based on another foundation than the truth.

The Trees that Walk to Sea

Walter Henricks Hodge

ALONG SOME of the sheltered beaches and shoals of Miami's Biscayne Bay, and fringing the many island keys that lead southwesterly to Key West, one can glimpse some of the most unusual among trees. These are the mangroves—"the trees that regularly walk to sea."

No forest is more weird or grotesque than a so-called "mangrove swamp." It is nature's original Jungle Gym. Each mangrove tree is surrounded by a mass of curious prop roots, which grow down from the main trunk and lower branches, tying them firmly to the soil. Submerged regularly by the tides, these roots often become encrusted with oysters, hence the unusual but true tales of plucking oysters from trees. Ropelike air roots, as well, often dangle from the upper branches, eventually penetrating the tidal mud or marl below. This strange combination of living stilts enables the mangrove to "walk"—over an extended period of time, to be sure—straight into the sea.

Mangroves are really tropical trees and cannot endure killing frosts. It is the warm Gulf Stream that protects Florida's mangroves. However, farther south on the Peninsula, especially from Cape Sable to the Ten Thousand Islands area, mangroves really come into their own. In fact, Florida can boast of more than a thousand square miles of fringing mangrove swamps. But tens of thousands of square miles of mangroves inhabit the sea margins elsewhere in the tropical world, from the Caribbean borderlands to Africa, and from there across the Indian Ocean to the myriad islands of the vast Pacific. During World War II, many American servicemen came face to face with mangroves the hard way, storming through these almost impenetrable thickets as a part of amphibious assault on the insular strongholds of an entrenched enemy.

The name "mangrove" most properly pertains to trees of the mangrove family, the Rhizophoraceae. One or more species of this family occur in nearly all mangrove swamps wherever they are to be found. Other trees, quite unrelated, mimic true mangroves in habit, grow with them in these seaside swamps, and by these tokens are also called mangroves. The commonest true mangrove of Florida and the Caribbean is the red mangrove, *Rhizophora mangle*, but there are other familiar American species such as the black or honey mangrove, *Avicennia nitida*, and the white mangrove, *Laguncularia racemosa*.

Mangroves and mangrovelike plants share the unique habit of being able to thrive even though their roots are submerged in sea water, whose salty brine is notoriously lethal to most land plants. Prolonged flooding by fresh water is sufficient to kill most trees by suffocating the living tissues of the root. Regular daily flooding by salt water is another matter, and trees growing in such a medium are in exactly the same situation as the sailor with "water, water everywhere, but not a drop to drink."

Although surrounded by water, with roots bathed in it almost continuously, mangroves are continually "thirsty" for the fresh water that they require. Like desert plants, they are threatened constantly by drought. But this is not desert drought where there is no water. The drought experienced by mangroves is what scientists call "physiological drought." Water is present but, because of its heavy salt content, it cannot be imbibed by the roots of the plant. All the curious structures associated with mangroves are related to these extreme conditions of life found at the sea margin. Like desert plants, mangroves conserve moisture in special ways. For example, the attractive green leaves are wax-covered and thickened, and under a microscope

they would show much similarity to the leaves of desert plants.

The abundant stilt roots of the common red mangrove have a double purpose. They anchor the tree firmly on the unstable, shifting mud of tidal areas, and they also may act as a sort of living air-hose, permitting gaseous interexchange to the underwater parts of the roots. Believed to have a similiar air-catching purpose are the curious, asparaguslike "pneumatophores," which rise from the submerged horizontal roots of some mangroves.

The problem of reproducing their kind has been beautifully resolved by the mangrove fraternity. Think of the job of planting a seed on mud flats that twice daily are washed bare by tidal water. The red mangrove has solved this problem. Instead of sowing seeds, this tree sows seedling plants! Seeds dropped into the water would float away, or, at ebb tide, would have no time to germinate. A seedling plant, with roots pre-formed and already growing, has a better chance of getting a root-hold in the shifting soil.

Watch what develops from the attractive clusters of yellow, star-shaped flowers. First to appear are curious fruits like small green pears. Instead of simply ripening and falling, the fruits hang on the parent tree for months. Within, the single seed is already sprouting, eventually to push out a thick tap root needed to attach the young plant to the soft mud below. The spearlike root is beautifully adapted for plummeting into the mud when the time comes for the youngster to be separated from its parent tree. At that time the seedling may have attained a length of twelve inches or more, although a fruiting tree usually shows seedlings in all stages of germination. Like those animals that bear their young alive, plants whose offspring are produced as germinating seedlings are termed "viviparous." Mangroves are good examples of such plants, and a single tree may produce 300 viviparous seedlings during a single season.

With extraordinary luck a seedling mangrove may fall to become successfully anchored in the mud below. However, in most cases, although fitted for just such a thing, the seedling will land in water and be carried away by the tide. But the young mangrove is noted for its ability to take long ocean voyages and still retain its viability. During the fruiting season, the flotsam and jetsam of tropical seas may be laden with such arboreal voyagers. Many are driven ashore by wind or tide. Five hundred and twenty-eight seedlings were counted on a 500-yard-long strip of beach at St. Petersburg, Florida, following a single storm. Floating seedlings gradually become waterlogged. The heavier root tip is the first to sink, and so, as it is washed into shallower waters, the seedling is in the proper vertical position to strike rapid root. The stimulus of touching ground apparently sets the root into active growth, and the growth of the seedling thereafter is unusually rapid. An East African mangrove seedling is reported as growing twenty inches in as many hours, a rapidity of development surpassed by few other plants.

Like miniature "Kon-Tikis," mangrove seedlings have been rafted across the oceans to found new colonies on far distant shores. Long before the voyages of Columbus, or any of his predecessors, red mangrove seedlings had conquered the Atlantic. Because of its propensity for travel, the common red mangrove is found on both sides of the Atlantic, while closely related species range widely from tropical East Africa to the far Pacific.

Mangroves are the original reclaimers of land. At the same time, they serve as nature's own breakwaters, protecting the sheltered shorelines of the tropics from the relentless sea. Because of the incessant restlessness of the tides and the profligate productivity of mangrove trees, seedlings are continually being floated across new shoals, bars, or mud flats as quickly as they form. Striking root, these juvenile pioneers act as reconnaissance patrols, in time enabling the main mangrove forest to migrate farther seawards.

As the tiny treelets grow, their developing prop roots interlock and entangle in such a way as to act as "catch-alls" for sediment, floating debris, or shifting sand. Adjoining thickets of pioneer trees soon grow together to form larger ones, and eventually wooded islands appear. With a continuing accumulation of detritus, land is built up, ground on which other trees, and even man or land animals, can pioneer. Engineering projects have taken advantage of the soil-holding ability of mangroves. When the present Overseas Highway to Key West was laid down as a railroad by the Florida East Coast Railway, mangroves were planted to protect the railroad ballast from the erosive action of the sea. That this original undertaking still stands after nearly half a century is ample proof of the help given by these strange trees.

Starting first as a low thicket, mangroves, under favorable conditions, may eventually develop into tall, pole-straight trees. In the tropics, especially, mature mangroves often attain a height of one hundred feet with trunks two to three feet in diameter. Quite naturally trees of such dimensions are of commercial value. The hard wood of the red mangrove is exceedingly durable, being resistant to both insects and decay. Thus it is often used as piling, as well as in local construction, and as a readily available source of firewood. Since early times Moorish seafarers have regularly carried mangrove poles in their sailing dhows from East Africa to Arabia for new building purposes.

Today mankind finds mangroves of greatest economic use as a source of tannin to convert his crude animal skins into leather. The first record of the use of mangrove bark for this purpose dates from the year 1230, when Moors on the coast of Arabia noted that this bark would tan leather. In the eighteenth century it was found that West Indian leather made from the bark of the red mangrove was superior to the oak-tanned leather of England. Nowadays mangrove bark extract is prepared in nearly all the widespread places where these littoral trees are found—in Madagascar and Mozambique, Tanganyika, Borneo, Indonesia, India and Panama. Unlike the sources of most vegetable tannins, which are rapidly being depleted, mangroves still exist in seemingly inexhaustible numbers, and so the use of their bark will undoubtedly continue to grow. Living as they do on the inhospitable tidal borderlands where they are almost completely free from competition with man, mangroves may be spared the intensive depredation usually associated with his interest in an economically important plant.

On the sheltered margins of tropical seas, mangroves will undoubtedly continue to occupy their unique niche in nature's scheme of things, feeling the eternal pulse of the tidal currents, bearing their young alive and launching them in the water at their feet, and all the time "walking" continuously, if imperceptively, on their curious, stiltlike roots out to sea.

Musky

Mari Sandoz

WHEN Father drove his buckskin ponies out of the valley and left us alone on his new homestead, twenty-five miles from the rest, I kicked a loose sod as nonchalantly as I could. My brother James spit into the dust. Father was a frontiersman, a locator and trapper. Staying alone in the wilderness of sandhills and rattlesnakes meant nothing to him. But I was only thirteen; James younger. Before Father was out of sight we ran to the shack for the twenty-two rifle and climbed to the top of the south hill to look around.

During the hot days of August we saw scarcely a cowboy. Mostly just meadowlarks, grouse, perhaps a dun coyote against the morning hillside. There were no near neighbors so we spent our time hunting in the hills and the drying swamp of the valley over the hill north, or watering the few scrawny cabbages in the lower corner of the ragged breaking about our shack. Now and then we saw a rattlesnake under a tilted sod, found coiling tracks about our shallow-dug well, or caught the faint smell of dead things that clings to the haunts of the diamond-back. I knew about rattlers. I had been in the hills once before, alone with Father, the time he was struck on the back of the hand by one. He shot the swelling off with his pumpgun and collapsed into the wagon. With the buckskins' unfailing sense of direction I got him to help. But I still dreamed about that day, especially here in the pitch-piny shack with holes for windows and the door; sleeping on the ground, in the center of the breaking.

One night I awoke in a cold sweat, the blood pounding in my ears. Something scaly and cold moved slowly across my neck. I had to let it, and every moment I expected the punctures of fangs from a flat, arrow-shaped head.

I listened. There was not a sound. Even James, rolled in a blanket a few feet away, seemed not to breathe, as though already dead. And somewhere in the dark was the cold body, the poised head. The blackness of the room began to shimmer in fiery spots, pressing down, choking me. At last I had to breathe, and with the sound of a

ripsaw through the stillness. There was no movement anywhere. Nothing except the faint smell of dead things.

Two feet away was the lantern, and matches, and along my arm lay the warm barrel of the rifle. But these things were as nothing—for somewhere, near my face, near my eyes, perhaps, was the cold, scaly body of a snake. A move and there would be a whirr, a strike. Suddenly the darkness went spotty again. I was already bitten. My arm was numb, cold. It was spreading.

Then something cold touched my cheek, not piercingly, as with poisoned needles, but daintily, as the lick of a black tongue.

From there on I don't remember much, except that I lay tense and unmoving for as long as it took to build up all the layers of the earth under me. Gradually I became conscious of someone whispering.

"Mari, Mari"—very softly.

It was James, but I dared not answer. For the thing that had touched me had not moved away. When my brother's whispers veered from fright to horror, I answered, out of the far corner of my mouth. So we lay, listening, our ear drums almost splitting. But there was nothing to hear except the faint sound of quarreling water birds in the swamp, the occasional deep call of the thunder-pumper, the sudden sharp howl of a coyote on a knoll. At that there was a soft, swishing sound at my ear and then nothing more.

Daylight came and at last the familiar things took form—the stove, the homemade table, the bench, finally the ridges in the dirt floor and James' drawn, frightened face. Cautiously I lifted my blanket. Nothing. But there, between us, were many tracks as of a finger drawn back and forth in graceful curves on the rough ground.

We slipped into our shoes and before dressing looked about the shack, even upsetting the cowchips from the fuel box. At last we settled down to breakfast.

Suddenly James made the queerest noise, dropped his fork, and ran to the corner where our old broom stood. A black, flattish tail and a brown, furry bunch showed on one side of it and on the other side a bit of dark nose and whiskers. James jerked the broom away. Cowering in the corner was a muskrat, two-thirds grown, pulled together into a shaking lump of frightened brown fur. So that was the cold tail that trailed over my neck; his whiskers, not a snake's tongue, had touched my cheek. We leaned against each other in foolish relief and laughed until the little fellow scurried away under the wall, where he had probably been all the time we were looking for him. But he soon was back behind the broom.

By dinner time we had Musky, as we called him, eating before us, nibbling with his bright yellow teeth at the thick roots we dug for him in the swamp. When we spoke to him he stood up tall and sniffed but returned to his food.

By evening we had put up a sod pen about three feet high, with the top link of our stovepipe, which kept blowing off anyway, buried in the ground for a burrow and a nest from a rat house in the swamp in the far end. We built a little pond lined with alkali mud and fringed it with rushes, cat-tails, and arrowheads. But Musky ran back and forth, trying to get out.

"Let's let him go," I suggested, halfheartedly, because our backs ached and our hands were blistered.

About dark he let James push him into the stovepipe with the spade handle, but only a little way. After all, we couldn't tamp him into his hole as you would soil about a post.

Before we rolled up in our blankets we took the lantern out but couldn't find Musky. The next morning he was gone; nothing left of him but a hole between the sods. We were suddenly very lonely and a little angry, too, at his lack of appreciation. James walked through the browning marsh grass to our dried out water-hole, calling "Musky, Musky." I fried pancakes.

And then while we ate he came out from behind the broom. Our enthusiastic reception frightened him into a lope through the doorway but we headed him and drove him back into the house. Once more he settled behind the broom, his bright eyes watching. After an hour or two of apparent neglect he sallied forth to smell at the bit of pancake we dropped for him.

Musky was curious and liked to explore the legs of the table, the stove, the chipbox, standing up and reaching as high as he could with his queer handlike forefeet. Once he stuck his nose against the hot ashpan I lifted from the stove. He gave a sharp little squeak and loped away to his broom, wiggling his nose. There he rubbed it with his paw and looked at me from hurt eyes. The next morning he was gone.

"You went and let him burn himself!" James complained.

"Aw—can't he learn to keep out of the way?" I demanded in sisterly resentment. But I spent several hours searching for tracks like the insertion on my Sunday petticoat, a strip of graceful curving like ribbon in the center. That was his tail. The regular, dainty little spots on each side were the tracks of his feet. But the wind had rippled the surface of the sandpass leading to the swamp. I gave it up and went home to put the shack in order. We were expecting Father. James took the twenty-two and went out alone, pretending to look for game.

And then all at once Musky was in the doorway, wrinkling his nose in the air. Satisfied that he was welcome he slid in and plodded to his corner. He was round as a ball, his sides sticking out like a bloated cow's. For the first time he let me pick him up. He even snuggled down in my arms and went to sleep. There was a scabby place on his shoulder, with a little dried pus, probably an old battle wound. From this came that dead smell I caught the night he trailed his tail over my neck and pushed his whiskers gently against my face. I sopped the scab with a solution of carbolic acid and let him sleep curled up in the corner.

That evening Father came, with Jule, our eldest brother. We tried to coax Musky out to nibble crumbs but he was shy and aloof. Probably not hungry. Anyway he took one look at the newcomers and scurried to the door.

"Head him off!" Father ordered, but Musky slipped between my awkward feet.

"Oh, now you let him get away. His hide is green yet but he'd bring fifteen-twenty cents."

James and I looked at each other. Of course our trapper father would look at it like that. Jule took the lantern out but came back alone.

"We'll set a trap for him. He may come back," Father said over his pipe.

There wasn't much we could do. Remonstrances were out of order in our family, but a little subterfuge was not. When the rest were in bed I slipped out and listened. It was September, chilly, and the rattlesnakes holed up for the night. So I slipped through the breaking. Down at the lower edge of the garden plot I heard a soft gnawing that stopped every time I moved. Probably Musky in the cabbages. I sat down and called softly. The noise stopped completely and after a long time I felt something like fluff along my stocking and a cold nose against my hand. He let me carry him to the house and put him into an empty nail keg. There he was, a round, brown ball, when I crossed the frosty yard the first thing the next morning.

By the next evening we got permission to snap the number one steel trap set along the door. Father decided he might as well wait until the fur was prime.

That day he tacked in the windows and hung the door. Jule tried to make friends with Musky but the little chap's affections couldn't be forced. When our impatient brother tried to make him nibble at a root as he did for us, Musky bared his yellow teeth and snapped them on Jule's finger. He almost died for his daring. James rescued him and ran away, the frightened little head buried under his arm. When we were alone again he learned to trust us almost as before. He still slept behind the broom and foraged about the room at night, his long digger nails making a loud noise on our new floor. On cold nights he snuggled in at James' feet. Sometimes he tried trailing along when we went hunting but he couldn't understand this climbing the towering sandhills and after the first pitch he usually gave up and plodded back to the cabbages and the sod corn or waited outside the door until we came to open it.

Musky made few noises with his mouth. Once or twice when I stepped too close to him he gave the funny cry of the day he sniffed the hot ash-pan. And once when a coyote howled daringly close to the house he cried like that outside the door and scratched frantically until we let him in to be safe in our companionship.

He was less and less interested in the roots we brought from the swamp, preferring to chew on the loose nubbins from our corn fodder or on a bit of cabbage. Snow fell. Musky's fur got thick and close and grayer, but still a little shaggy, not glossy as that of his kind in the cold swamp. He got fatter and softer too, and when Mother came down with the household goods and the babies she found him in the cowchip box behind the stove.

"Out you go!" she commanded. "No, I won't have animals like that in my house. Couldn't you catch a badger or maybe a skunk or two?" She chased Musky out into the dark with the old broom that had sheltered him so often. It was sad.

But the next day we found that he had made a nest behind an anchor post of the windmill set up on the new well that took the place of the old spade-dug hole, now covered with a few boards and hay so the children wouldn't fall into it. Musky seldom came to the house after that but he got his cabbage hearts and his corn, and he drank at the chicken trough. And often I was scolded for spending my time scratching his jolly soft sides and pulling his fat cheeks when I should have been minding babies. Sadly I gave up my free ways of the last few months. My *Wanderjahr* was over.

But James was loyal and even Jule fed Musky now and then. Father scratched his beard and laughed as he told us, prophetically, how much he would get for the hide.

When winter was upon us we carried home sacks of hay and, with manure over it to generate heat, made a house for Musky. He trotted out to the chicken coop to eat and drink and, while the rooster was suspicious, the hens ignored him. But somehow he seemed a little neglected and sad now. I hoped he would make the break and run away, not to the north swamp, however, for Father was chopping into the freezing rat houses and setting traps.

Then one day as I poured steaming water into the frozen chicken trough, Musky didn't come. I hadn't noticed him for several days. Neither had the boys.

"Now you let him get away," Father said, but even he didn't seem to be so very sorry.

The winter was cold but short and February brought a fine thaw with snow-water running. It washed away the hay from the old well and Mother decided it must be filled. Something floated about on the surface. We dipped a bucket under it. Musky. The call to water had become too strong.

His hair was slipping and so we buried him in the dead cabbage patch. James almost cried for this foolish little Musky who deserted his fine swamp and his gay fellows for a corner behind an old broom, some cabbage hearts, and two stupid children. And I didn't share James' boyish fear of shedding honest tears.

The Mighty Little Flea

George S. Fichter

I HAD OUR HOUSE all to myself for a few days last summer. My wife and children had gone to visit the grandparents. Even Hambone, the neighbor's dog, quit making his daily visits.

Then, one evening as I sat reading the paper, I felt my legs being bombarded by tiny pellets. Now and then there were sharp, stabbing pains, so I bent down to have a look. As my daughter would have put it, the "joint was really jumpin'." For there, before my eyes, a black swarm of little bodies bounced around on the rug. I had uninvited guests. Fleas! I dusted the house with a potent insecticide, locked it up, and joined my wife and children at the grandparents. I knew why we had fleas. Hambone, our boxer dog friend, ordinarily played host to them. In his absence, they had turned to me.

Flea problems were not new to me. Several years ago I taught zoology in a small university in the mid-West, and telephone calls from flea-troubled, near-the-campus residents came every season.

"I'm embarrassed to tell you this," was generally the way the calls began, "but we have fleas. They're all over our house."

"Do you have a pet?" we always asked—and the answer, invariably, was an emphatic, "No, we don't, and that's what makes it so odd. You see, we did have a dog, but he died several weeks ago. Never in all the years he was here—and he had the run of the house—were we bothered by fleas. Now our house is filled with them. It's so strange. . . ."

But it was not strange, really. Dog fleas like *dogs*, not humans, and roughly half of the fleas will be plump little females, each of which lays hundreds of eggs during her lifetime. Not in any particular place, nor all at one time, but here and there and now and then as she crawls about in the dog's hair. The eggs tumble out freely, and are scattered when the dog shakes itself or jostles as it moves about.

Five to six days later, a tiny, maggot-like white larva squirms out of each egg. Legless and with no eyes, the hairy raveling inches its way along by using the stiff bristles on its body to get traction, and it stays well out of sight, hiding in cracks between floor boards, in crevices of the dog's bed, or in seams of upholstered furniture. There, it gorges on an unsavory diet of organic scraps and dried feces from adult fleas.

Within two to four weeks, if it has found plenty of its kind of food, the wriggling larva measures about a quarter of an inch long. Then it spins a cocoon of fine silky webbing, produced by glands in its mouth. Bits of dust and dirt that adhere to the moist outside of the small, white capsule make it blend perfectly with its surroundings. After a week of quiet rest, under ordinary circumstances, an adult flea kicks its way out of the cocoon and goes hopping off in search of a dog. If none can be found, the hungry flea has no choice but to change diets.

So a few weeks after a pet has died or has been moved to new quarters is a likely time for fleas to begin making themselves obnoxious in their old host's haunts. They bite voraciously, sinking their stilettolike mouth parts into skin and tapping a flow of blood. Then they pump out the red fluid ravenously, and, if left undisturbed, they eat until their little abdomens are round and reddish.

Vacationers who pack Fido off to the kennel or take him with them are sometimes greeted at the door on their return by a hungry horde of these vampirish little insects. Fido seldom gets blamed. Why should he? He has not even been home! So when they summon a pest control man, they will tell him that their house is overrun with sand fleas. It sounds cleaner.

Actually, the abundance of little animals that greet the homecomers is an accumulation of Fido's fleas that have hatched during their absence. Fleas can live for two months or longer without food, but at the end of that time they are hungry enough to emulate Shakespeare's valiant flea, and feed "on the lip of a lion." Worse, they become much more numerous during the first day or so, since a fair percentage were still in their cocoons while the house was quiet.

Do not be deceived into thinking that, because you see only a flea or two on your dog, he does not have more. Fleas do not make a habit of flaunting themselves. I know a man who de-fleas his dog several times a year. One day, a month or so after the dog's regular treatment, he saw a single flea scurrying from one forest of hair to another under the dog's collar. There were obviously too few fleas there to be bothering the dog, but he decided to take a census anyhow. So he spread some papers on the floor, and then gave the dog a dusting with DDT.

Dazed and drugged fleas bobbed up like corks in a stream of water. When they stopped dropping, he had sixty-eight little brown bodies on the paper. Yet his dog, relatively speaking, was clean and well cared-for. It does not take long for a family of fleas to make themselves at home and become numerous enough to hold reunions.

On a dog that keeps one hind leg constantly digging at a flea bite while it gnaws industriously at another, the total flea population may run into the high hundreds. Raw openings resulting from the bites of the fleas, and the retaliating bites and scratches by the dog, are open avenues for all kinds of skin infections. And the fleas themselves, transferring from dog to dog, take with them tapeworm eggs and a variety of other vermin.

I have seen fleas seething—literally millions of them—on the dry, dusty floors of livestock barns. Pigs, especially, harbor fleas in abundance; but, oddly enough, fleas do not bother sheep. Instead, when fleas burrow into the sheep's wool, they get so hopelessly entangled they cannot get out.

Few warm-blooded vertebrates are exempt from these bloodsuckers, however, and some species of fleas even inhabit the polar regions, snug and warm in living fur coats. The little insects also are found in the tropics, and during the Second World War were introduced to isolated islands of the Pacific which, until then, had been free of fleas. In temperate regions, fleas are most bothersome during the warm summer months, overwintering in their cocoons if they are outdoors, but carrying on life as usual on pets indoors.

So far, entomologists have identified more than 1400 species and subspecies of fleas. Specialists in the study are called siphonapterists (Siphonaptera, which means "tube without wings," is the name of the insect family to which fleas belong), and they quip that they started in the business "from scratch." For more than half a century, the scientific flea center of the world has been the Tring Museum, at Hertfordshire, England, where Nathan Rothschild, son of the famous banker and financier, made a lifelong hobby of collecting and identifying fleas. Now his collection is a part of the British Museum, although still maintained at Tring, and is presided over by flea authority F. G. A. M. Smit.

My personal interest in fleas was so whetted by their invasion of our house last summer that I set out searching for, of all things, a flea circus. I found one on 42nd Street near Times Square, in New York City, and I decided to visit it.

A flea circus is as portable a live-animal act as you could possibly conceive. Professor Roy Heckler, the operator, carries his entire ensemble in neat cases, inlaid with mother-of-pearl. There the fleas are bedded down comfortably in separate compartments with white wool and cotton blankets. Fifteen fleas are always trained and ready to perform. Three or four times as many are on reserve status. Those that are working get a full meal twice and sometimes three times a day; understudies are fed less often. And the feeding, if you are not squeamish, is another convenience. The Professor simply bares his arm and puts his herd out to pasture on it. Fleas—and his are human fleas—are not hard to please as long as they are able to maintain their steady diet of blood.

Fleas, the professor explains to his audience, should not be disdained as ignorant. It requires an average of three weeks for a flea to graduate from its course of training as a full-fledged performer.

In the real life drama, fleas play the role of villains, for they are vectors for all sorts of pestilence. Tapeworms, tularemia, murine typhus—all can be transmitted by fleas. But the most notable malevolence to their credit is their syndication with rats in the spread of bubonic plague, a disease which has taken, over the years, a toll of some 150,000,000 people.

Fleas play their part on the team by passing the plague from rat to rat, and from rat to man; for the moment a sick rat dies and its body begins to cool, its contingent of fleas deserts it and goes looking for a new, warm home. Choice of a human being is generally fatal to the human.

Fleas are greatly flattened from side to side, an adaptation that makes it easy for them to slip through thick, close growths of hair. And hair is their trademarked habitat; so much so that in police circles, nowadays, shaggy juvenile sideburns are referred to as "flea ladders." Some fleas, like those infesting dogs, are decorated with short, stout bristles, directed backward so that they do not hamper the flea in moving forward, but give him a good support to lean back on. Typically, too, fleas have a hard, shiny exterior, so slick and polished that even if you do get your hands on one you will have a hard time holding it.

But their most remarkable feature—their ability to jump—prevents you from keeping them in sight for long, once they get out in the open. They have the reputation of being the most accomplished jumpers among insects, and have been credited with jumps more than seven inches straight up and more than thirteen inches horizontally. This, it is often pointed out, is comparable to a man leaping over the Washington Monument. But it is seldom explained that the flea's jump, while phenomenal, is not much more than you would expect of an insect with powerful jumping-legs. Like other joint-legged creatures, their muscles are attached to give them highly efficient leverage, and their feats of power and strength really are no strain.

Some fleas do not jump well at all compared with the human flea, which is credited as the most agile. Female chigoe fleas, which live in the tropics and occasionally stray into our own South, pick a host and then stay by burrowing under the skin. Their fertile abdomens swell with eggs, and the surrounding area becomes infected. Sticktight fleas, or tropical hen fleas, hang on too. But most fleas move about freely from host to host, preferring one particular kind of animal to another, but settling for blood wherever they can get it.

With fleas our close companions for as long as man has been on earth, it is natural that all sorts of cures for infestations have been recommended. Pliny, the Roman, advised collecting the dirt from beneath your right foot when you heard the first cuckoo's call in spring, and then sprinkling it in your bed and about your house. In England, you were told to keep your windows closed and your doorway swept on March first, the day fleas were supposed to return after winter. And there is a fable about the wise fox that backed into the water holding a bit of moss on his nose. When his fleas had all scurried to it to keep from drowning, the fox ducked under and let the moss drift away, carrying the fleas with it.

Today, fleas may be controlled. Tight doors in modern houses, powerful vacuum cleaners, easily washed bedding for pets have all made it easier to prevent having a persistent flea problem. If such a problem arises, you have powerful, recommended insect killers, like DDT, chlordane, lindane, dieldrin, and others. But these poisons should be used carefully and according to directions, and do not be surprised if they fail. Fleas, like flies and other insect pests, quickly build up a resistance to many chemical killers, particularly when the same chemical is applied to successive generations.

To make certain the job is done right, you can always call for help from an experienced, bonded pest-control expert. Make sure you get one who uses more potent materials than the operator who was grilled by the lady who had called him to take care of a problem she was having with clothes moths. She wanted to know if his insecticide would harm her food, kill her plants, or ruin her furniture—so the badgered fellow blurted out, "Lady, what we're planning to do to your home won't even hurt a flea."

A Motherly Knight in Armor

William Beebe

THERE ARE three things of the sea that have been delineated by man more than any others—dolphins, mermaids, and sea horses, and there are three things about which we know almost less than any others—sea horses, mermaids, and dolphins. I am sure that five thousand years ago some Egyptian or Chinese or nonunion stone mason of those days was daubing or hacking out an attempt at one or the other, and I know right well that at this very moment a young artist in a garret is drawing an original design of a pair of dolphins or sea horses with their tails entwined. I have awakened in a guest room where four walls revealed unending rows and columns of sea horses—so awful that I had to leap out of bed to avoid counting them and calculating how many more there would be if the window space had been filled in.

I really believe we know more about mermaids than of dolphins or sea horses, for there is a splendid freedom of imagination which is engendered by uncertainty of the existence of anything—a freedom cribbed and confined by knowledge of actuality. Our medieval ancestors believed much more in mermaids than in other marine organisms, and I am sure that if a mermaid and a sea horse appeared for the first time at the same instant I should be much the more astonished at the latter.

My initial experience with a sea horse in Bermuda was from the point of a *lusus naturae* rather than as *Hippocampus punctulatus*. It was the first point of call of the *Arcturus* and we anchored at St. Georges in an afternoon's downpour of rain. I stayed only a few minutes on shore, went to a drugstore and bought the first thing I saw—a dried sea horse covered with gilt paint. Had I left it, its future would probably have been to collect dust on the whatnot of some parlor, instead of which it performed a nobler function—that of a leavening climax after many hours of intensive investigation, when, in a sudden burst of amazement, Will Gregory saw a golden sea horse lying amid the scarlet and ebony treasures from a mile-deep haul in the Sargasso Sea. This achieved successfully, it was thrown overboard and as it sank into the depths of mid-ocean, I knew that the slow disintegration even of a dry and gilded sea horse would bring nourishment and joy of life to a host of diminutive scaven-

gers, and then I remembered that my shilling was still on its way from one Bermudian hand or pocket to another, and I was pleased with the destiny of my first sea horse.

If we keep on thinking mermaid hard enough we will probably come across something not unlike such a lady and much more wonderful. Things work out that way quite often, as in the case of the sea horse. When Aristotle and the poets of classical Greece wrote of Hippocampus they had in mind a wholly mythical sea-monster, a dragon, half-horse and half-fish. They thoroughly believed in this piscine centaur and so there soon swam into their ken a half-horse and half-caterpillar, and Hippocampus being only imaginarily "preoccupied," as our taxonomists would say, it naturally fitted the new natatory reality. Medicine evolving slowly out of witch doctors and magic, and museums not yet having come in, any creature as strange as a sea horse would, in those early days, be considered from the point of view of drugs. So we find attributed to it a marvelous list of panaceas. If I had only had a library of early chirurgeons on the *Arcturus* and a little more faith I would not so readily have consigned my dried sea horse to the deep, but would have burned it and consumed its ashes in wine and thereby have guarded against pains in the side, or, had I taken it merely mixed with water, my canker and leprosy would have been alleviated. Best of all, had I stirred my Hippocampus ashes with oil of marjoram or liquid pitch and rubbed it on my bald pate a glorious head of hair would have resulted.

We may laugh at these prescriptions of old, but what except a feeling of shame shall we cherish toward an elaborate volume of seashore life, printed in the late 1920s, which states that Hippocampus is a primitive ganoid, that it lives to be a century old, and that it inhabits depths under great pressure! Before we ever smugly deride the ignorance or credulity of our ancestors let us stop a moment. To appreciate to the full a sea horse we must make ourselves believe that we are the first to discover it.

We require a sea horse, so we send out a motor boat and pull a small dredge slowly through some of the growth of eelgrass in Bermuda's Castle Harbour. One, two, three or no sea horses may result, but usually we find at least one of the curious little beings lying quietly in the mass of trigger-fish, shells, grass, seaweed, and mud. He is as helpless as a prostrate knight in armor. I lift him and gently wash the mud out of his fin—mane I was going to say—and then let him slide down the submerged ways of my fingers and he is launched in a fresh aquarium. He rights himself—not like other fish, but vertically, turns his eyes from left to right, and glides slowly away. He seems to have no visible power of propulsion, but it is the invisibility of an airplane propeller—the fin on the back has become a dim, thin haze, its endless rippling web pushing back against the resisting water. The aquarium is a narrow rectangle and the sea horse traverses one long side, then a short end, and rests. And this first journey drives home a simile that needed just such an impetus; much more than the head of a horse, our Hippocampus resembles the knight of the chessboard, and his first move in the aquarium has been a knight's move—two squares ahead and one to the right.

It is well, however, to get rid of the horse idea altogether, and watch and learn to like our fish for himself. I put in a branch of seaweed and the long tail feels for it and coils about it with the grip of a chameleon. The next person who comes up to look cannot at first find the sea horse—he has begun to lose his identity. As we watch, this continues—he shifts from dusky brown to a pale neutral color and then again to dark, this time green, and Hippocampus is fairly within the protective cloak of seaweed sanctuary. He has gone vegetable and has taken upon himself the easy load of seaweed dangers and the very considerable advantage of algal immunity. I reach down and gently swing the weed back and forth, and still another trick is sprung—the little creature sways both body and head loosely to and fro in rhythm with what to him are the swells of ocean. On the tips of the knobs and spines of his armor are numerous, long bits of frayed-out filaments, and these wave about and importantly disguise his zoological reality.

So here we have the sea horse and his niche in the world, balanced and weighed in the scales of life and death and found on the whole good. From snout to tail he is encased in bony jointed rings—one ring to each vertebra, and while it slows him down almost to a snail's pace, yet it serves to protect him from small predaceous crabs and other enemies. To carry about such a complete armor requires delicate adjustments, one of which is a large swim-bladder filled with gas just sufficiently buoyant to hold him in hydrostatic equilibrium. If, through accident, his inner balloon is punctured and the merest pinpoint of a gas bubble escapes, gravity seizes upon him, he sinks helpless to the bottom, there to remain until his wound be mended, or until Nemesis comes along on legs or fins.

Even for the sea horse in perfect health and strength there are waiting scores of hungry mouths armed with great cruel teeth that would crush him like a nut. Against these he builds up the seaweed defense—of haunt, color, pattern, shape, movement, and in addition he even has an unpleasant odor—or to water creatures, taste. His tail fin—most valuable of all for progression—is gone and instead he twines like a tendril. His life is lived at lowest output of energy, a semisessile pseudocrinoid of sorts, almost, we might think, on the way to the fixation of barnacles. But this is not degeneration, it is adaptation to a safe environment, and as we go on to study Hippocampus we realize that he need have no envy for the swift herring or the voracious dolphin.

It would seem that in the matter of food our sea horse must desert the quiet, patient elementalness of seaweed, and dangerously revert to fish activity. But here again nature has worked out a most ingenious plan. For such a vegetative existence little nourishment can be needed, yet we have a carnivore that must have food. Resting on a frond of weed in the aquarium is a tiny crustacean, one of the untold myriads that inhabit all the seas in the world. The sea horse has also seen the copepod, but he wishes to keep me under surveillance as well. Slowly he swims nearer and nearer, and peers ahead with the comic intensity peculiar to shortsightedness. He turns sideways, and now the approach is still slower and he accomplishes two things simultaneously—one eye is cocked forward, gazing steadily at his victim, the other is twisted far back, never leaving our person. It was fair disconcerting and rather disturbed my own concentration. He throttled down his little push propeller to lowest speed, and the slowness of his advance began to approach the rapidity of the growth of his seaweed. Then he went into reverse, with no change that I could detect in fin ripples, and I looked and found that the copepod had vanished. I was certain that it had not swum away, the sea horse had made no snap or bite in its direction, and I was completely confused.

It was a long time before I had another chance to be in at the death after a sea horse's stalk and this time I knew rather than saw what happened. It was in a small hand aquarium and against the glass floated a score or more of fish eggs that had come in with a surface haul. I was lucky enough to get a flat-field eight diameter hand lens in position without causing the sea horse to shy. I watched without a wink and I saw the mouth of Hippocampus open wide, whereupon one egg after another simply was no longer where it had been an instant before. A flicker—and I knew that an egg had been sucked with amazing speed from a distance into the tube mouth, but my senses were too dull, my rods and cones too human-slow to register such bullet speed. Then the reason for it flashed upon me and I saw how, even in its pursuit and capture of living prey, the sea horse still plays the role of a vegetable. The cheek of this fish is formed of one large bone, the opercle, and is fastened by strong muscles directly over the gill-openings. There are no clogging gill-rakers or teeth or tongue, so that a sudden lifting of this great pair of valves induces a mighty influx of water, sufficient to drag with it at lightning speed any living creature in the path of the waterspout.

I have never seen the courtship of sea horses, but it is described as most amusing, the marine stallion shaking his head and moving swiftly around the female. I was about to pen some light, casual phrase about all that was lacking was to have him paw the water and neigh, when I came across an account, which, as so often happens, made considerable sense out of a meaningless joke. For it is recorded that by cunning movements of the lower jaw the little fish can produce a loud snapping that increases in volume and frequency as the season of courtship approaches. They have even been known to call and answer one another when confined in separate aquariums.

We might reasonably suppose that now we had exhausted the little bag of life tricks of a sea horse; that it remains only to record that the eggs are deposited and hatched, the young grow up and the eternal cycle starts another turn. But we are only at the beginning. Hippocampus is to prove that for sheer interest the last fact may be first, that a psychological reverse may make all physical shifts seem trivial, that what would be abnormal in ourselves has become usual and general in sea horses, and (what in science is almost a truism) that to the most dramatic phenomena we can often ascribe no primary reason or ultimate value.

We left the male sea horse doing his best to charm his mate, curvetting about, rippling his mane, snapping his jaws. The climax comes when she approaches and the two little creatures, rearing high, meet in midwater. By the rules of sex throughout the ages, at this moment the eggs should be fertilized, but apparently the race of sea horses is bound by no rules. At the moment of contact, one or several eggs pass from the ovary of the female out into the water, and by some instinctive bit of magic are slipped into the orifice of a pouch, which, like the pocket of a kangaroo, is suspended in front of the male. What we mistook for evidences of an unusually heavy meal is something far otherwise. Again and again the female swims up, and egg after egg is produced and passed between them. So our generous male was wooing not only for marriage but for the custody and care of prospective children. The last egg is tucked away and without a "Cheerio" or backward glance, the bride turns and swims off, to the work or play or meditation on life which occupies a lady Hippocampus—I know not, after this amazing, ten-minute honeymoon whether to call her maid, wife or sea horse widow.

Also without a thanksverymuch, or even a well-merited sigh of envy of his more fortunate brothers in the world, our sea horse —etymologically a woman—swims off on his life's path, with his pocket full of the hope of the next generation of sea-pasture equines.

If it is true that the eggs require four weeks to develop, then a fathom or two down, among the eelgrass and seaweeds of Castle Harbour, a certain sea horse was courted, married and deserted on a Saturday night, the sixth of June. On the second of July we seined him off our bathing beach. As he glided gracefully about the aquarium I saw he was a horse of unusual beauty. He was full grown—one hundred millimeters from snout to tail—or, less impressively, four inches. His color was a brilliant sea green, darkened on the back, but the cheeks, chest and pouch were aglow with this beautiful shade; his eyes were blazing gold, cut foursquare by lines of alabaster; his neck was arched and proud as that of a thoroughbred Arab horse. The pectoral fins were long and widespread like wings, and the graceful body gleamed with a host of white dots, streaming out into constellations or concentrated into galaxies —good reasons all for calling him Pegasus.

His pouch was unusually distended; now and then, even when he was quietly resting, the emerald surface was troubled, quivered, and was quiet again. I returned frequently to the tank and watched him time after time make the circuit of the glass and back to his resting frond. He was restless and gave no time to feeding. His eyes kept turning, twisting, sometimes in rhythm or often independently as if they belonged to a span of horses. So I left him at midnight, slowly gliding on his rounds.

The following day, at ten o'clock, I saw the first sea colt break from the paternal stable and rush across the aquarium. I chivied it into a narrow glass and watched it carefully for a long time. Its activity was prodigious and its position was ancestral. Never for more than a moment did it rear into a true sea horse posture, but was usually outstretched with tail trailing and head bent at only a few degrees, reminiscent of some pipefishlike forefather. Its heart beat vigorously and the great dorsal fin and the lower pectorals fanned the water and sent it swiftly ahead. The tail was the most amazing portion of its anatomy; it coiled and uncoiled, stretched and drew back, but especially it lashed from side to side. More than any other movement of fin or head or body, this lateral stroke was characteristic. When it wished to attain ultimate speed, it was by lateral wriggling, and when it began to resent and be enraged at the constant bumping of its nose against the glass it twisted its tail into a veritable corkscrew, then undid itself and with the greatest ease astonishingly entwined the tip around its own snout, neck and fin. Now and then it opened its tiny tube mouth, and the short, broad hyoid bone would bend downward in an absurd resemblance to a very blunt, second lower jaw.

At four o'clock two more young sea horses slipped out of the opening of the pouch corral. This was distended and throbbing with life—the pressure and struggles of little heads and bodies being plainly discernible on the surface as intermittent dimples and bulges. A few minutes later a loud cry arose from my watcher and an instant after, with my hand lens, I was at the aquarium.

The parent Hippocampus had taken a firm grip with his tail around the branch of a sea fern near the bottom and was swaying back and forth with head drawn in and the body and pouch pushed far forward. As I watched, the body was drawn back, and then, every muscle being brought into play, his whole being again strained forward. The upper third of the pouch, which usually shows as a deep fold down the middle, was now distended to the full, and in the center was revealed a small round orifice. As the pouch reached its utmost distention, the opening enlarged slightly and with a convulsive movement there was ejected a mass, a mist, a whole herd of young. They were thrown into the world in the shape of a rounded ball, which, like a smoke-ring or a bomb from a firework, held together as it moved rapidly upward and obliquely forward through the water. Only when it began to lose impetus, ten or twelve inches away, did it spray out into long streamers and scattered blobs of infant Pegasi. From the moment of slackened paternal impulse the individual sea horse motes assumed individual activity, swimming, twining their tails around themselves and one another, lashing out from side to side for all the world like diminutive crocodiles. With all this casual, indirective movement there was a steady stampede of each successive herd toward the surface; a scientist would describe it as positively phototropic.

Five more parental ejections took place before the pouch was empty, and the fourth and fifth were both still ball-like, revolving slowly upward, while the earlier ones had spread out into a subsurface film of frisking young Hippocampi.

The pouch did not collapse as I expected it would, but for another half hour was only slightly shrunken. Yet the last of the young had emerged—three hundred and six in all. This was the end, and in the morning the parent's pouch was indistinguishable and the green color had given way to a suit of dark brown, starred with white and faced with yellow-green. And father and young were doing well.

The story was once told and has been repeated many times of how the young sea horses return, at the approach of danger, to their father's pouch. It is a charming idea but is quite untrue. There is no bond between offspring and parent once they are shot out of his pocket, and their instinct to swim up to the surface and toward the light is wholly unlike his ideas of a proper trajectory—which is down and among the protective fronds of seaweed. In addition to this the opening of the pouch closes tightly immediately after the multiple births, and precludes any readmission.

There is no doubt about the interest which the life of a dolphin must hold, and I am sure that the way of a mermaid in the sea would inspire a best seller, but for charm, for quiet success in life and for sheer unexpectedness of mating, incubation and birth the sea horse has no equal. As to the questions that arise: How did this intricate and reversed relationship first come about? Why does the female hand over her eggs? Why does the male parent shelter and incubate them? Why—I can only answer, I don't know.

The Turbulent Life of the Sand Bug

Robert Cushman Murphy

STEP INTO the wash of the surf on a sandy beach during midsummer, and you may find yourself startled by the semblance of a hundred half-seen whiskered faces peeping up from the bottom. Then, within the twinkling of an eye, the curtain of seething water streams back to sea and blots out the vision. By the time the torrent of gritty foam has gone, leaving the wet slope bare, there is no sign of life. Was it fact or fantasy? Before you can investigate further, the wrack of the next breaker swirls up, and the bottom is again lost beneath a foot of froth.

Now change your position a few paces along the beach. Stand quietly where you will be ankle-deep when the swell is half sucked back. Once more, "as through a glass darkly," bristly visages stick out of the surface of the sand that a moment before had seemed bald as an egg. Where the streaming is swiftest down the incline, you may even see the rotund bodies behind some of the faces torn from their anchorages and whisked pell-mell toward deeper water, only to vanish magically as soon as they touch bottom. A mad and riotous life it is, whipped and rolled and mauled by waves that never cease.

What are these teeming creatures? Rocky coasts, we know, swarm with kaleidoscopic life, but any naturalist will tell you that the lower strand of sandy beaches and the waters inside the outer breakers have no great variety of beings large enough to catch the eye. Rather, this joint strip of earth and brine forms more of an ocean graveyard than an environment for the living. Yet we now see that at least one astonishing animal fills the sand in numbers beyond imagination, however much its way of life may hide it from the casual observer. The mysterious beastie is the sand bug, a crustacean, technically known as *Emerita talpoida,* which might mean—if zoological names may be said to mean anything—"the mole-shaped one who has served out his time." Whatever their name or antiquity may be, the sand bugs, as Professor Leidy once remarked, are as thick in their habitat as currants in plum pudding!

The sand bug has a range tens of thousands of miles in length and ten yards—or it may be only ten feet—wide. Those you find along the shores of other oceans than our own North Atlantic may be first or second cousins of the kind that dwells on the beaches of the Carolinas or Fire Island or Cape Cod, but you would need a very dull book and a lens to tell any of them apart. To all intents, one and the same *Emerita* occupies most of the world's temperate and tropical coasts, except those of Europe. In many places, such as India, Madagascar, Peru, Florida, and California, the sand bug has been used from time immemorial as food for men. Indeed, it was by watching Indian fishermen on the broad shining strands of Peru, where the creature is known as the *mui-mui*, that I first became acquainted with it, long before I learned that it frolicked practically in my own dooryard on Long Island. But wherever you find it, its bailiwick is always in sandy beaches sluiced by waves from the open sea, and it leads the most turbulent life of any denizen of the great waters.

Now, for the sake of prying more deeply into the ways of this odd little neighbor of our bathing beach, let us scoop deeply with both hands under the backwash and run ashore. Plop the load down on dry sand, and a half-dozen or more of the sand bugs may roll out, either to lie still as though dead, or to scuttle off backwards with the movements of miniature war tanks, quickly orienting themselves to a course down the slope. If the spot is level, or even inclining slightly away from the water, they may appear puzzled for a few moments. However, under such circumstances, another reaction quickly takes the place of the one affected by gravity, for the tiny tanks will presently turn themselves and head, or rather "tail," directly for the ocean. A little experimenting with the stranded victims will prove that their primary directional responses, when they find themselves out of water, are two, and that these are more or less balanced one against the other. The first of them is geotropic, or related to slope; they like to run downhill. The other is phototropic, or related to the source of strongest illumination, that is, to the glare of the sky above the sea. Either of these instinctive responses would tend to save their lives if they chanced to be cast high and dry. But a sharp slope away from the water fools them and poses a problem. In this case they soon demonstrate that the geotropic reaction is stronger than the phototropic; they forget the bright sky off shore, alas, and follow their weight downhill in a direction which will do them no ultimate good.

On dry sand they are creatures of the surface, and must grope their way as best they can toward the water. But if you place one of them on sand well wetted by the last wave, you may at the same instant say "Goodbye!" You will just have time to see the sand bug tip up its snout and vanish hind-foremost, leaving scarcely a dimple to mark the spot. "Sand mole" would be a more appropriate name. In a quart glass jar filled with water above three inches of sand, one of them will swim and tunnel its way to the bottom within a second or less.

The females of the North Atlantic sand bug are about an inch in length, the males a third smaller. During August most of the females carry under their tails orange egg-masses, in some of which developing embryos are visible. The smooth, rounded carapaces of the creatures are of a sandy color, tinged with pink. Their bodies are shuttle-shaped, and when snugly folded up they show rather less in the way of protruding members than a "blimp." All appendages, in fact, tuck away securely, leaving a perfectly streamlined exterior, but each pair has, nevertheless, its special function in locomotion and feeding. Thus while the hindmost are stirring the sand and scooping it outward, during the burrowing process, other jointed limbs are pushing and paddling the body into the hole it makes as it goes. While excavating, the sand bugs always work against the prevailing current, with the useful result that each runoff of the waves leaves them facing seaward as they stand nearly upright in the sand, with only the eyes and antennules

exposed. Ceaseless activity is necessary for retaining their positions, for with each wave the topmost layer of sand is transformed into a fluid and every solid object near the surface is undermined. Their existence is like that of a trapeze acrobat who never stops performing.

The inefficient-looking eyes of the sand bugs, mere spots at the ends of threadlike stalks, must serve their purpose well in warning their owners of shadows or of large opaque dangers such as curlews, or gulls, or men. Certainly the tufted faces withdraw, and leave no trace, within an instant after you have darkened their hiding places.

Little neatly-folding doors of the mouth parts and anterior limbs of the sand bugs, protected further along their edges by bristly hairs, serve to keep the sand out of their mouths and gullets while the incoming wave is bearing up their next meal. Up to this point they remain shut as tight as a chest. But as the water starts back, two long curved flagella, lined with hairs like the feathery antennae of a moth, are whipped out from within the doors. It is these structures that give the sand bugs their bushy-snouted appearance and that also make the tiny V-shaped ripples in the sand which, in tranquil weather, may give the first inkling of their presence. As the water rushes through the finely fringed flagella, microscopic organisms, both plant and animal, such as diatoms, radiolaria and foraminifera, are entangled in these fish nets. Then, in the calm moment while the wave is out, the nets and their contents are drawn once more behind closed and locked doors, and during the subsequent inrush of the surf the happy sand bug scrapes off and swallows its meal.

The active life of the creatures is, therefore, the brief period of the backward wave, when they hang on for dear life with one set of appliances and gather in their subsistence with another. During the less devastating influx of water that follows, they find opportunity to enjoy the fruits of their toil. Like the human heart, the sand bugs take all their rest between beats. Swimming, burrowing, or perambulating, moreover, they go through their existence tail-foremost. A *posteriori* beings they are, indeed, for they may be said to reach every conclusion backwards!

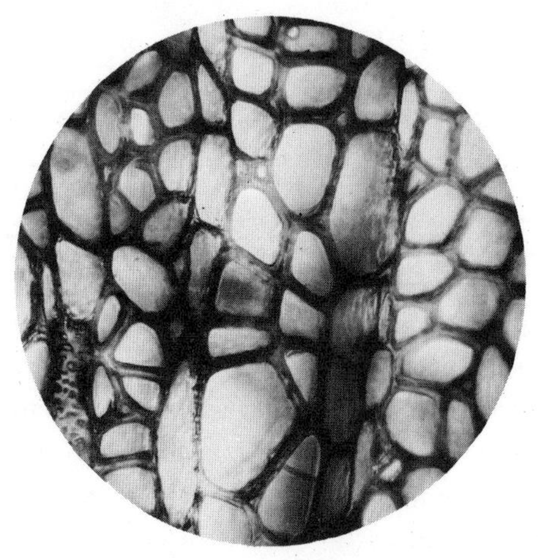

Cross section of tobacco root.

Scales of painted lady butterfly.

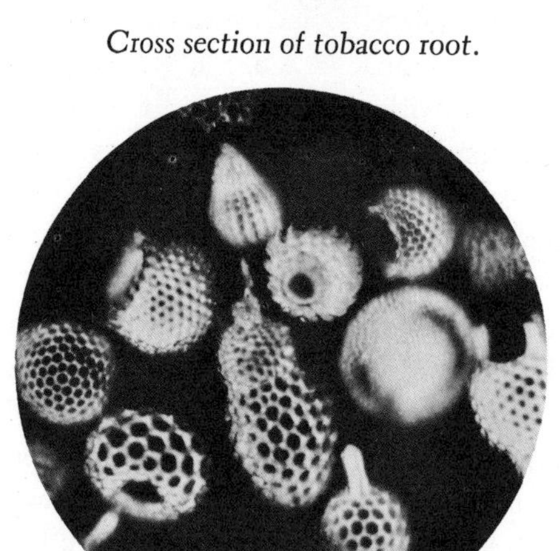

Radiolaria.

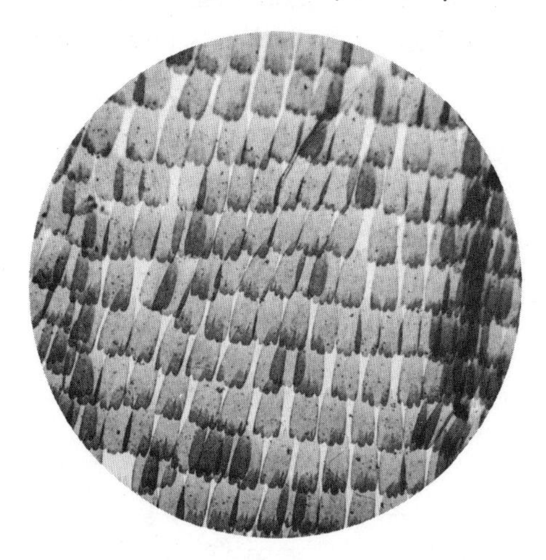

Wing scales of the emperor moth.

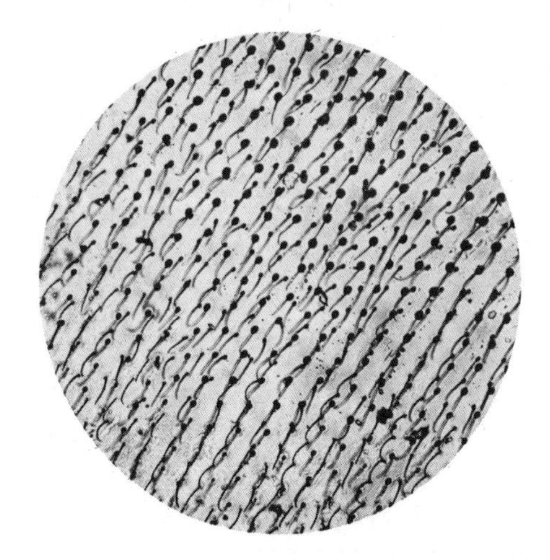

Wing hairs of a blowfly.

Down feather of a hummingbird.

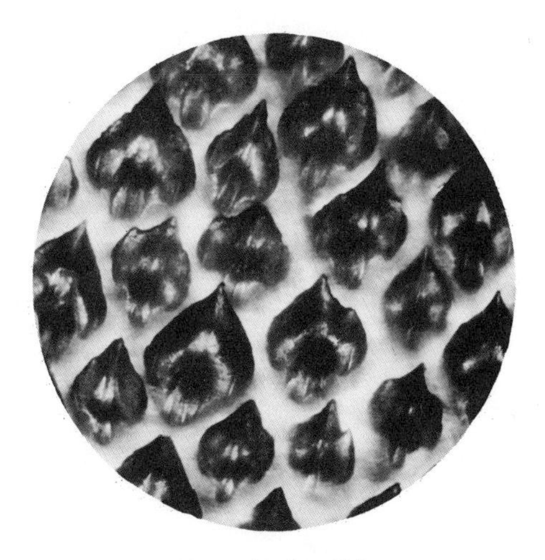

Skin of a dog fish.

Eggs of the large white cabbage butterfly.

Hairs of vapor moth caterpillar.

Eggs of a pig louse.

Hidden Beauty

PHOTOGRAPHS BY DOUGLAS F. LAWSON

THERE ARE, all about us, many examples of nature's mastery of beauty in design. Fully as much is hidden from the naked eye and revealed only through the magic of the microscope. English photographer Douglas F. Lawson went exploring in this field, and made a series of photomicrographs. There is a temptation to make a quiz of these pictures, but it is unlikely that many people would recognize the sources, and most of us would be completely frustrated by such a quiz attempt. Those who wish to try to identify the subjects may do so by forcing their eyes to stay away from the captions.

Mothers of the Wild

Alan Devoe

HIDDEN in a hedgerow, in the fragrant summer dusk, I had twice seen a cottontail rabbit come hopping cautiously to the same spot among the tall grass stems. On our first meeting she had remained there, invisible, for nearly an hour. The second encounter was shorter, but long enough to make me positive about the guess I had made. There must be a nest of baby rabbits there.

But how could there be? After seeing the rabbit's first stealthy visit, I had crossed and recrossed that area of the field, staring at every foot of ground, but found nothing.

Now, marking the point with my eyes and never losing sight of it, I again began slowly combing the tall grass. Suddenly, in the dim light, I saw a tiny stir of motion, as if a patch of earth beside a tussock had moved. I bent down. What had seemed to be only a bit of grass-grown earth was actually a tiny, soft, felted blanket. Gently I lifted the little coverlet. Tucked under it were four rabbit babies.

I had learned mother rabbit's secret. The blanket was a quilting made of her own fur and matted wisps of grass. Every time she left her youngsters in the nest after a feeding, to go off through the summer fields on her own errands, she pulled this warm, soft covering over them, leaving them perfectly hidden and secure against the evening chill.

This practice is only one of many wonderful devotions and ingenuities by which mothers of the wild bring up their little ones. Baby mammals are born in all sorts of situations—caves, burrows, hollow trees, nests made as cunningly as birds'. Whatever the circumstances, the wild mother has the mother-wit to give them the special care they need, and a mother-love that lights the world of woods and fields with one of its loveliest radiances.

Nature's simplest nurseries are "built-in" ones; the body pouches of animals called marsupials. Kangaroos belong to this category. So does the koala, nature's real-life teddy bear. So do opossums. Marsupial babies are born incredibly tiny. A big kangaroo stands man-high and may weigh 200 pounds; but some of mother 'roo's little ones at birth are only an inch long. An opossum's baby is as small as a bee and weighs only two grams.

Tiny and undeveloped as they are, marsupial babies instinctively head for the nursery pouch. The mother watches intently, ready to give a fondly helping nudge. Sometimes she licks a smooth path across her fur to make the way easier for her tiny traveler. With her brood safely cradled—a single baby in the case of kangaroos, a family of as many as eighteen for mother 'possum—she uses special muscles to pull the pouch securely closed.

As baby marsupials grow up, their mothers use many protective ingenuities for their care. When "Joey" (as Australians call a kangaroo youngster) is old enough to leave the furry nursery periodically, and hop along beside Mother, any sudden appearance of a pursuing enemy sends him diving back head-first into the pouch. He rights himself, peeps out, and Mother instantly takes off on a jouncing race to safety. If the hunter is gaining, her one thought is for little Joey. Dodging for a second into underbrush, or behind a boulder, she furtively flips him out. Then she leads away the enemy, mile after bounding mile. Only when she is sure she has shaken off pursuit does she come back circuitously and rescue her charge from his hiding place.

When mother opossum's babies' nursery days are over, she ensures their safety by carrying them as passengers on her strong, furry back. The bright-eyed, sharp-nosed little fellows hook their chins over her backbone and hang on tight to her pelt. Sometimes she arches her long tail over her back and lets the children wind their little tails around it. This educates them in the use of a prehensile instrument that will mean a lot in their opossum lives when they are old enough to leave her and shift for themselves.

Mother koala, dweller in treetops, sometimes 150 feet above ground, also carries her single offspring pickaback. She has a special problem when the time for weaning comes. Koalas live exclusively on the strong, pungent leaves of eucalyptus. To enable baby koala to make the transition from milk to this adult fare, the animal mother uses one of the strangest physiological processes in Nature. Temporarily her body makes a sort of eucalyptus "pap." She produces this unique baby food only for a month or so, only every two or three days, and only at a special time in the afternoon.

Animal mothers that do not have "built-in" nurseries make many kinds of nests and dens to give their babies security. But some species, because of their ways of life, cannot provide such a birthplace and must resort to methods all their own. A mother bat arranges her childbirth by hanging upside down by all four feet and spreading her wings and body to make a receiving cradle for the youngster. While her baby is still small and helpless, she carries him everywhere with her on her flights through the darkness. He holds tight to the fur of her breast with his milk teeth.

Water-dwelling animal mothers, like aerial ones, have special childhood problems. Mother porpoise's technique has been observed and filmed within recent years by scientists at the Marine Studios in Florida. She gives birth to her baby under water. This is fraught with danger, for porpoises are air-breathers. The mother must be sharply alert and act with instant promptness. The scientists have found that she frees her baby from his birth-cord and launches him into life on his own with such amazing speed that he shoots to the surface and is breathing air within ten seconds of birth.

Mother gorilla builds a suitable tree-cradle of leafy boughs, so located that father gorilla can keep it constantly under watch from a shelter he constructs at the base of another jungle tree nearby. But all sorts of other animal mothers, down to very small ones, are just as painstaking, each in her way.

Mother polar bear tunnels out a nursery in the snow; perhaps at the foot of an iceberg. At the end of the snow tunnel she scoops and shapes a comfortable cub-room, as secure against the arctic blasts as the inside of an igloo.

Mother coyote takes over the abandoned burrow of a badger, woodchuck, or some other digging animal, and renovates it especially for her babies' needs. She cleans it out and enlarges it, and equips it with an air-hole that provides cross-ventilation.

In fashioning underground nurseries, even such small mothers of the wild as meadow mice and gophers are scrupulous about constructing special "sanitary rooms." Animal children are trained early to obey the law of cleanliness. I have dug up many nurseries in which various four-footed little ones have started their adventure of life—snug little rooms lined with leaves, made soft with fur. To find a messy one has been a rare exception.

One of the most delightful nurseries is the work of the common white-footed mouse. Mother mouse gathers fine grasses, rootlets, shreds of soft leaves, strips of pliable cedar bark. Working and reworking the material, fluffing and kneading it, she weaves an almost perfectly spherical ball. At one side she leaves an opening just large enough for her to squeeze in. Darting in and out, she performs innumerable turnarounds, hollowing a cozy chamber in the center of the ball. She lines it with the softest materials she can find, bits of moss, wisps of plant down. The finished nest is at last given a final extraordinary detail—mother mouse makes a door-stopper. In bitter weather, or when she is away from her babies, this tight little plug of grass is inserted into the doorway, closing it against any intrusion of foes or weather.

Bringing up animal children involves a constant round of motherly attentions. Feeding, washing, sanitary care in early babyhood—these are by no means all. Few animal mothers are able to wean their offspring as effortlessly as mother koala. This was impressed on me the first time I had a fox den under observation.

When the four cubs seemed old enough to be graduating to solid food they would gather eagerly around their mother, pawing and pestering, every time she arrived home with game. It struck me that she was a hard-hearted, selfish sort of mother, for she always seemed to bolt the morsels herself. Careful watch with binoculars revealed what she was really doing. She would tear apart the prey she had brought, chew it carefully to eliminate indigestibles, and then with a quick gesture scatter it on the ground for the youngsters.

A heroic chore that falls to the lot of many animal mothers is the task of moving the family. Squirrel mothers, delicately sensitive to impending weather changes, often decide they must leave a frail old hollow tree when they sense a bad storm coming. One by one the youngsters are picked up, mother squirrel slinging them upside down under her chin, gripped by their stomach-fur in her teeth, and the difficult transfer is made to a new and safer location, perhaps at some distance from the first site.

Cat mothers of all kinds usually carry their children by the napes of their necks. When a mother bear must transport her cub she uses a peculiar method that looks alarmingly dangerous. She seizes the young one's entire head in her mouth. Somehow she is so gentle that she does not harm the baby.

Young animals must learn life. Instincts must be perfected, native skills brought out, and a whole outdoors education imparted in the brief days before they go on their own. Animal mothers are responsible even for imparting many lores that we may imagine to be inborn.

Grown-up seals seem as at home in the water as do fishes, but baby seals, born on the rocky headlands, have to be taught to take to the water and swim. Pleading, persuading, enticing, mother seal generally ends up by *pushing* her reluctant young one adrift. Mother otter, too, must induce her offspring to learn the art of their "native" element. She often resorts to motherly trickery. With a youngster on her back, she swims out quietly into the channel of a stream and then suddenly submerges.

Mother flying squirrel must push Junior off a tree branch, to get him to learn gliding. Mother bear cuffs her cub to teach him to come when she calls. Mother deer butts and bunts lessons in quietness into her fawn. Mother cat boxes her kittens' ears for slowness and inattention in the art of mousing. (Kittens are not mouse-catchers instinctively, they must learn it from Mother. Naturalists find that kittens raised without a mother to train them do not recognize mice as prey. They often make friends with them, and sometimes are afraid of them.)

Animal mothers use endless devices in teaching and training. Harsh discipline is the rarest of these. Chiefly they teach by drawing their youngsters into creative play. Mother lioness twitches the tip of her tail, inducing her children to pounce on it. Mother raccoon flips frogs and crayfish to her young ones, on evening excursions by the brook, letting them make a game of what will later be serious business.

Perhaps the most moving of all such devotions is the superb courage of mother animals in giving protection.

I have seen a mother woodchuck, when a farm dog was pawing furiously at her burrow to dig out the babies from the nursery, throw up barricades of earthworks as fast as the big, powerful dog could dig. Down would go one barricade. Within seconds she would have flung up another. Then another, another, another, yielding the tunnel only inch by hard-fought inch. I thought her heart would burst, but it was the dog that grew exhausted first, and left, defeated.

I have seen a tiny chipmunk mother stand firm against a weasel, rearing up on her hind legs, boxing, lunging, snapping, until the most implacable killer of the fields and woods had enough. I have seen a white-footed mouse mother, smaller than my thumb, whose nursery in an old bird-house I had inadvertently disturbed, make six laborious trips, within two feet of me, carrying her babies one by one to safety. She was fairly shivering with fear; but there are things even in a mouse's world that are greater than fear. Five times she came back to the endangered nest, almost under my hand, and rescued every baby of her brood. For conversational purposes we speak of valor that is like that of a tigress with her young, or a she-bear with her cubs. Actually that blaze of heroic devotion burns in every mother of the wild, even the least.

Uncle Hoiman

Helen Ellsberg

UNCLE HOIMAN and his adhesive-toed relatives educated and delighted us for an entire summer.

Uncle Hoiman was a tree frog, or *Hyla,* who spent the long summer evenings clinging to the outside of our kitchen windows, devouring the gnats and smaller moths that swarmed against the pane, attracted by the light within. When his friends and relatives saw how he was living off the fat of the land, they too left their hunting grounds on leaf and bush and clambered up the slippery glass. We sometimes counted as many as eight at a time clinging by their tiny, suction-cup toes, happily diminishing the gnat population.

Uncle Hoiman came by his unusual name in a roundabout way. One day our three children were spending an afternoon at the public playground. They made the acquaintance of a young man from Brooklyn, about six years old, who worked hard at putting over the idea that he was a very tough guy.

"My Uncle Hoiman," said the lad proudly, "has only got four toes, becuz one of them got shot off."

Sister stopped swinging. "With a gun?" she asked incredulously.

"Sure with a gun."

"Did he do it himself?"

But we never found out who shot off Uncle Hoiman's toe, for just then a burly man came up and bluntly and profanely removed the small braggart. We never saw him again, but for some reason the incident of Uncle Hoiman and his missing toe stuck in the children's minds, and the subject came up frequently for several days afterward. They had never heard a Brooklyn accent before, and they accepted the name "Hoiman" literally. They never thought of it as being the same name as "Herman," the boy who delivered our milk.

It was about this time that Sister was surprised one evening to see a tiny tree frog on the kitchen window. We all gathered around to watch him.

"Look!" I said. "One of his toes is gone on one foot."

"Like Uncle Hoiman," said Sister, and the twins laughed.

We watched him off and on until bedtime, but he still clung there, snapping at the swarming insects, and apparently enjoying a hearty meal. In the morning he was gone. But that evening, after the lights had been on for a while, Sister cried,

"Look! There's Uncle Hoiman again!"

And sure enough, it was the same little frog with the missing toe. From then on he was known as Uncle Hoiman. All through the summer we looked for him every night, and he rarely disappointed us. Even after window-pane gnat-hunting became a favorite hyla pastime, and the parking space was becoming rather crowded, the children would climb up on their chairs and look over all the visitors until they discovered Uncle Hoiman.

He was obviously no ordinary tree frog. He was a personality, a pioneer and an adventurer. So far as we ever knew, he was the first hyla to learn that there were gnats upon the lighted windows, and after he disappeared, no other hyla has appeared there since.

At first we could not find him at all during the daytime, but finally, tired of commuting from a bush, he made his home in a recess in the window ledge, carefully turning himself the exact green of the house paint, so that he was practically invisible. Here he spent most of his time.

The children's fondness for the little hyla increased when they discovered that he liked to have his back scratched. Frequently, during the daytime, when amusement lagged, they would decide to see if they could find Uncle Hoiman. If he was not in his nook on the window ledge, they would set out forthwith to annoy all the tree frogs on the place trying to find him, which they often did. Around the house they would go, lifting up the hydrangea hylas, and the rose-bush hylas, and the hyla who lived among the gladioli, looking for Uncle Hoiman with his missing toe. If they found him, they would pull blades of grass and scratch his back, while he blinked and arched his back contentedly.

One day it was necessary to repair the window where he spent most of his time, so I gave him to Sister, telling her to take him away where he would not get hurt. For some reason, instead of putting him on a shrub, she put him in a weather-beaten old box, dropped in an aphis-infested rose branch for him to lunch on, and put him in the garage. That evening I heard a heated argument in the garage.

"That isn't him! Uncle Hoiman is green!"

"It is too him! I put him in here this morning—see, there is his foot with the toe gone."

"Let's show Mother."

So I was called out to see what had happened. There sat Uncle Hoiman in a corner of the little wooden box, turned the exact color of the weather-beaten wood. So I explained to them as best I could about the phenomenon of protective coloring. I had told them a little bit about it before, but it had never registered. Now, seeing it before

their eyes, it became something marvelous.

"I liked him better green," said a twin.

"Oh, he'll turn green again as soon as you put him back on the green ledge, or on a leaf," I reassured him. "You remember, that one we saw on a strawberry leaf this morning was dark green just like the leaf, so we could hardly see him."

"If he sat on a strawberry, would he turn red?" asked the other twin.

"No," I laughed, "I'm afraid his repertoire of colors is limited to brown, gray and green."

They put him back on the window pane so he would not be late for his evening meal, and, sure enough, next morning there he was in his little nook, matching the house to perfection once more.

When the weather was damp, or a rain imminent, Hoiman and his friends would burst into song. Other frogs may croak, but the hylas' pipings are so musical, no one could possibly call them croaks.

Another thing that set Uncle Hoiman apart from the other hylas was his penchant for big-game hunting. We never saw the others eat anything except gnats and the tiniest of moths, but Uncle Hoiman would take a chance on anything that flew within the reach of his sticky tongue. We all had a good laugh at him for his gluttony one night when he grabbed a miller almost as big as he was. He got its head in his mouth all right, and by a series of gulps, most of its body, but there was evidently no more room inside, for he could not get the wings down, and there he sat, with a wing protruding at each side of his mouth like bristling side whiskers, giving periodic futile gulps, while the children shrieked with laughter at his weird appearance, although they felt very sorry for the moth. Finally he turned and crawled down off the window pane. It was a dark night, and we never learned what he did about the moth—whether he finally got it down, or gave up.

Uncle Hoiman was probably closer to death than any hyla who lived to tell it. One day when the children were playing in the garden, I heard such screaming that I rushed to the door in alarm, expecting blood or broken bones. They met me with grief-stricken faces.

"Mother, Mother, come quick! A great big snake just caught Uncle Hoiman! Hurry, hurry!"

They seized my hands and we ran to the garden where, sure enough, beneath a cucumber vine, a snake was devouring our wee pet. He had caught him by a hind leg, and it was obvious that in a few moments, Uncle Hoiman would be only a slight bulge in the snake's middle if he was not rescued at once. The "great big snake" was a garter snake about eighteen inches long, but the way we all pounced upon it with sticks and stones, anyone would have thought we were battling a boa constrictor. We ruined the cucumber vine, but we also ruined the snake, and when he was limp and lifeless we set about the delicate task of extricating Uncle Hoiman—and it was Uncle Hoiman, all right, for the feebly kicking protruding hind leg was minus a toe. Gently and carefully we pulled him out. For a moment he lay limp and apparently lifeless, and then it dawned upon him that he was free, and he gave a feeble, lopsided hop, just managing to reach a cucumber leaf, where he clung, halfheartedly, his golden eyes dull, his little sides heaving. Sister picked him up gently.

"Poor little fellow, he's nearly scared to death! I guess anyone would be who was nearly swallowed by a snake. I'll put him in the little box again until morning. Maybe he'll be all right then."

Personally, I expected him to die, he looked so limp and utterly done in, but in the morning, there he was in the corner of the box, once more turned a weatherbeaten gray, his eyes glistening in the sun, seemingly as fit as a fiddle. So Sister put him back in his little window nook, and that night he was back on the window pane, snapping at gnats with his usual gusto.

But we saw him only a few times after that. The first cold winds of autumn came with driving rains that beat against the house and ran in torrents down the window panes. One by one the hylas disappeared and settled down for their long winter sleep.

With spring's first balmy days, the tree frogs began to sing, and the children began watching for Uncle Hoiman to appear on the window. But he never came, nor did any other hyla. Whether he ran afoul of another snake, with no humans to come to his rescue, or whether he left us for larger and gnattier window panes, we never knew. But without Uncle Hoiman to lead them, the conventional hylas dropped back into the old ways. They lived comfortably among the shrubbery, dining upon aphids and occasional unwary flies, but days of bright lights and high living were gone.

In the Language of Birds

Paul H. Fluck

BY INVENTING the ladder of evolution, naturalists have tried to draw the animal kingdom to scale with human beings. Some have been criticized for placing *Homo sapiens* upon an exalted pedestal, and arranging the lesser creatures in ascending positions. But this is not quite true, for when the various schemes are examined, every builder of these pyramids has placed the birds atop another pyramid, which has as its base the reptilian kingdom. Birds occupy, in this zoologic setup, a place akin to man's. There they sit, astride their own pyramid, much as we, the greatest of the primates, sit upon our own.

If we accept this zoologic ladder of our own making, we should expect to find, within the bird, the master developments of the reptilian kingdom: the highest intelligence, the best development of limbs and digestion, as well as a highly developed voice. The all-important flight feathers are only the glorified scales of slippery, crawling things that lived in prehistoric swamps. The mellifluous voice of a thrush is only a step removed from the shrill of the hyla shrieking in the ditches on a spring evening. In this way things have been arranged in the filing cabinet of science.

Let us see whether, among the cackling and the warbling voices of the bird world, we can find the rudiments of a language. Let us see if we can recognize, in these varied notes and vocal ejaculations, any resemblance to the vocal communications that make it possible for man to occupy his place at the top of the pyramid of primates.

Can a bird speak? Do birds converse? Is there a language of birds?

The first question cannot be simply answered by pointing at a parrot or a magpie, and saying, "Of course they can." Such imitations are far from speech as we know it. Speech must be more than an imitation; it must carry with it the power of representation, and the essence of intelligent understanding of its own meaning. "Polly wants a cracker" can hardly do that.

To learn the speech of birds, their words and their meaning, it would be well to do as we advise those who attempt to master a foreign tongue—"Go live with a foreign family." But it is difficult to live with the birds. Furthermore, it is difficult for birds to live with us. And with the mere passing acquaintance of distance, it is not easy to learn much about the language of birds. We may hear a crow "caw," a mourning dove "coo," or a robin sing, but we learn little about their speech in this way. In fact, we learn so little that we have come to believe that they are quite dumb, and that they have no power of speech at all. Nothing could be farther from the truth.

Although, in some parts of the world, chickens scratch about in the floors of dwellings that are not much more than pig sties, it is hardly possible to simulate such conditions in the United States, if one is not to be visited by a representative from the Board of Health. But it is possible to maintain a small bird within the walls of a modern home if one is willing to submit to certain embarrassments and minor destruction. Fate may some day send an injured bird, or a young, uncared-for fledgling, into your home.

Most of my observations were made from such a bird—Saucy, a tame bluejay, that an injury kept from her normal home in the tree tops. She lives in an ordinary house, where the beautiful spangles of this vivacious creature flash from cellar to attic as she attends to every household duty, for she has the run of the establishment. She sleeps in her master's bedroom, in an old canary cage, and feeds herself from the table at meal times, when she enters into conversation in her own understandable way. Much worth-while knowledge has been garnered from this intelligent bird.

To begin with, Saucy knows her name and comes when she is called, just as any dog runs to its master. This, you will say, only proves that she understands our language. And it does. But Saucy does more, she actually speaks, not in nouns, verbs, and adjectives, but in a way, and a language, of her own making; for Saucy arrived in my home as a tailless baby bird that could hardly have acquired bluejay habits under more than very primary conditions. Surprisingly enough, Saucy has learned a sign language, which she intersperses among her vocal calls, and, by means of this combination, she manages to convey quite well what she has to say.

Let us take the simple matter of "Yes" and "No." Saucy can say both of these words, with and without emphasis. Her voice, within my aural range, makes no sound when she answers my questions, but

she answers them decisively, and effectually, with the sign language that she knows so well. "No" is simply a matter of flying swiftly away. "No" is not only signified; it is carried out with decision. Ask Saucy if she wants to go to bed, in daylight, then try to coax her near her cage. She may be sitting on it, but the mere mention of the word "bed" will send her flying at top speed into another room, where pursuit is useless as long as the word "bed" is used. But as evening approaches Saucy shows a different feeling toward the same three-letter word. "Bed" is then acceptable; she flies over to her cage, and hops through the door that I hold open. She sits upon her perch, and goes to bed. This is her way of saying "Yes," but she has no bird word for it. "Yes" is altogether an action, just as "No" is an action. This is exactly the way a human infant, a dog, or a lipsticked Juliet signifies "Yes" and "No," for compliance and agreement seem to be the most efficient primitive ways to answer verbal questions in the affirmative.

Sign language plays an important part in the language of birds, just as it does in the language of primitive people. Sign language, moreover, is a language. With it we manage, as do the birds, to convey our own ideas to the consciousness of others. With it we speak as deaf mutes speak, but we speak, nevertheless.

I prove a hundred times a day that Saucy understands my language. She answers me by using the sign language that she finds so effective. I tell her that I am going to steal her peanut from under the newspaper, and before I can move a muscle she is on me, tearing and pecking at me with all of her unusual strength. I tell her that I am sorry, and she stops at once. She sits on my finger, twittering soothingly. I tell her that she is a "bad bird" and, like a bad boy, she will sass me from the top of the door. She will even make a pass at my ear, or muss my hair, by way of protest. I tell her to get her "breakfast," and she flies into the kitchen at any time of the day to shovel mouthful after mouthful of sugar down her greedy throat. "Breakfast" and "sugar" are synonymous to Saucy. I ask her for a "button," and if she is in the right mood, and thinks that I intend to do right by her prized button, I get a button, not a peanut, or some other trinket such as she collects by the bushel. I stand on her rug, the wooly hiding place for her treasures, and my heel will bear the marks of her bill for several days. She asks me to move my clumsy feet, in sign language of the most effective kind. So much for the sign language that both Saucy and Sitting Bull have used to advantage.

But how does Saucy *ask* questions? Perhaps she wants to attract our attention because we have forgotten, and locked her in the bathroom. She whistles, just as the paper boy whistles to attract our attention on Monday, when he comes to get his money. She has a cheerful, informative whistle to warn us not to step on her in a dark hallway, or otherwise to let us know where she is.

There are times when sign language is inadequate to explain the urgency of her problems, and then Saucy resorts to a variety of different vocal sounds. She chirps a mournful note when she has been forgotten, or when no one has bothered to turn the light on for her. She repeats this dirge-like note over and over again. It is a sad sound, and Saucy is sad when she makes it.

If you talk to Saucy, tell her nice things such as how pretty she is, or suggest scratching her belly, she will twitter and chirp, fluff her feathers and strut, just like any flattered blonde. If I am in some other room, I can tell that Saucy is being complimented by someone, just by hearing that twittering. Listen to a female starling, or an English sparrow, while the male flits about in flattering and complimentary flight, and you will hear the same twittering that inflates the chest of my bluejay.

Defiance is another matter. Saucy is defiant, as are all bluejays. No bird has a more valiant tradition than the jay; he is the bravest of the brave and the most fearless. Saucy screams in our faces, and returns time after time to attack us if we as much as move one of her precious peanuts, or some other prized possession. She speaks a defiant language if we give her a reason —and a hearing.

Bird happiness is especially vocal. I often wonder if the beautiful songs that we associate with the mating season are not just happy songs, due to the complexion of the weather, the season, and the abundance of the food supply. The length of the day may play an important part in this singing, for on long days a bird has ample time to find its food and play.

Humor plays a part in bird life, as well as that of man. Birds have a genuine sense of humor. Saucy will steal every cracker from a plate, and then return to mock us when we notice that they are missing. She will snatch a diamond ring and fly speedily to some hiding place. Then she will return to watch us, cackling meaningly when we demand the priceless heirloom. She will not tell, and she gives us the "Ha Ha" in her own sweet way, for she loves to play a joke. Often, when we enter a room, Saucy will not be in evidence. She has ducked into a corner to hide, and she expects us to look for her. When we do, she will come out of her hiding place, using a series of short bows and whistles that say, "See, you couldn't find me."

When the jay is downright cantankerous, the mere word "goodbye" will make her change her behavior. If she is stubborn and refuses to perform for her audience, we just say "Goodbye, Saucy," and Saucy will carry out her act, or obey a command. She will let us have a peanut that she has been hiding in her throat, or cough up a "bobby-pin" that straddles her wind pipe. She will let go of anything to prevent us from leaving her alone. "Goodbye" is the word we always use when we lock her up, so "Goodbye" gets results when we use it.

Speaking to a pet bird is practical, and that goes for almost any bird. Animal trainers know the value of speech in training animals, for there is little doubt that speech is better understood by animals than we have ever suspected. Birds may speak a universal language, as well as a specific one. The big green parrot that preens itself in the window next door can interest Saucy, although she cannot duplicate the parrot's hooting and cackling. A scream of defiance from the parrot will promptly bring one from Saucy. She reflects the humor and the disposition of her neighbor quite well, although they speak a different bird language. A bluejay, in the forest, can alarm every bird or animal within earshot. It is nature's warning siren for her hard-pressed creatures.

It is a human failing, and not the fault of birds, if we do not understand them. Their language is simple, for a large part of it is pantomime, and is not wanting in decision or variety. Flight activities, fluttering, swooping and the whistling of wings, I am sure, may have definite meanings. We should not allow our ignorance of bird language to lower our estimate of bird attainments, any more than we should underestimate the accomplishments of a foreigner speaking to us in his language, the only language he has ever learned, even though we are untutored in it.

It's a Little Dog's Life

Arthur H. Carhart

THE CHUNKY, buff-gray burrowing squirrels of western prairies that sat erect beside their tunneled homes barked excitedly at the early explorers. Because they barked, someone called them prairie dogs.

Lewis and Clark gave them a truer name when they encountered them, in 1805, in western South Dakota. They called them the "barking squirrel." But even before this expedition's official report was made, the dog name apparently was in common use.

In a footnote to his *Journal*, October 24, 1806, Zebulon Pike, then pushing westward in Kansas, wrote: "The wish-ton-wish of the Indians, the prairie dogs of some travelers, or squirrels, as I should be inclined to denominate them, reside on the prairies of Louisiana in towns or villages, having an evident police established in their communities."

The Indians' "wish-ton-wish" is no more related to the canine family than to zebras or polar bears, but he still remains the prairie dog by popular name.

By any name, sitting upright, flipping his stubby tail as he barks danger warnings, he has been a symbol to travelers that they have reached the place where the West begins. As recently as five years ago, tourists could see "dog towns" beside main highways. Today one must search wide acres to locate one of these communities.

What is happening to wish-ton-wish should not happen to any kind of dog.

Irrigation that turned semi-arid lands into cultivated fields blotted out many dog towns. Federal agencies in organized campaigns have poisoned multiple millions. The late Vernon Bailey, noted wildlife authority, has reported that forage consumption of 256 prairie dogs equals that of one cow. Stockmen begrudge the little animals the range food that otherwise might be eaten by domestic stock, and literally millions of acres of dog towns have been cleared of the last inhabitant by systematic poisoning.

Added to all attacks by man, epidemic disease has swept into many prairie dog areas. Within one season thriving towns have been eliminated entirely as the plague struck.

This lively, interesting little native is a highly social but rugged individualist whose activities and antics always have lent character to the prairie landscape. Man's de-

mands may blot him out, but cannot dim his interesting personality.

The prairie dog family is divided into two groups. The white-tailed species are mountain dwellers, sometimes establishing small colonies as high as 10,000 feet above sea level. Because they do not gather together in so densely populated communities, they have a better chance of survival than the other division of the family.

The town-dwelling, black-tail types live on the plains. They are so socially minded, and so bent on maintaining community life, that when part of a town's residents are wiped out, survivors draw together and reorganize their settlement. Thus bunched, they are vulnerable to recurrent attacks until all residents are gone.

The family and community life of the prairie dog is well organized. Family units live in their own home, and it is their castle. When danger threatens, a dog from another burrow may dive into a neighbor's tunnel and be tolerated. But let him intrude under other conditions and he is an interloper. Even if he be larger, the householder will oust him, and drive him away in a furious, chattering attack.

The dog home is a tunnel that descends directly to a point six to ten feet underground. From here the tunnel slants upward at an angle to the nest room, which may be only a foot or two beneath the ground surface. This construction makes it difficult to flood out a burrow. Pike states he had one hundred forty kettles of water poured into a dog hole with no results.

Burrows of the plains towns usually are built on flats where cloudburst storms occur. To fortify their homes against flooding, the prairie dog family builds a circular earth wall around the entrance, sometimes as much as eighteen inches above ground level. Each armful of moist earth added to this fortification is firmed by the prairie dog, using his blunt snout as a battering-ram, with all the force of his bent body back of each thrust.

The building of the "chimney" around a burrow is prompted by instinct. A prairie dog pet, reared without contact with others of his kind, was taken to Maine, and allowed the run of the home grounds. Just as if he were in a western dog town, he built the earthen dike around his hole, using his head to tamp it into a solid wall.

The earth mounds serve as lookout points. Prairie dogs are credited with cutting down tall weeds near mounds, so the view may be unobstructed in all directions.

During the two active periods of the day, between sunrise and midmorning, and from four to sundown, a fat sentinel always is sitting up on a mound. When he barks an alarm, the others gallop clumsily to a burrow mound, sit up, and join the chatter. If danger comes too near, they dive into their burrows and for a period lasting from thirty to sixty minutes none are in sight. Then one reconnoiters, sees the cause for alarm is past, gives the all-clear signal. In a few minutes the whole town is alive again, gathering food, digging burrows, building mounds, or playing like kittens. Even during the midday siesta, a dog or two will be on watch to warn others of approaching enemies.

Another type of defense against invasion is loose earth in the tunnels. When he is driven into the farther corridors of his home, the head of the family makes certain all the family is in quarters, then he plugs the hole with an earth barrier.

Each inhabited burrow has a "dodge tunnel," built to one side of the main one, about a foot beneath the entrance. Here the boss of the family hides until he appraises the threat that sent him into his burrow. The dodge tunnel serves as an outer guard room for the tunnels and rooms beyond.

Each family usually maintains three burrows, although they live in only one. The others are used for refuge and other emergencies. Field men working on rodent control projects have filled all holes in a town at nightfall. At daybreak the next morning, one in three of the plugged holes is dug out. By evening the other two have been put in order. This has been a means of estimating the number of families in each town and the total population, based on the average family of a half-dozen residents in each home burrow.

The young, usually four or five in number, are about one-third grown when their parents bring them to the surface in late May. For several days the youngsters are not allowed to stray far from the burrow's entrance. When the alarm signal is given, they are herded toward their doorway by the parents, and sit there, like stubby little pegs, with mamma and papa beside them.

"I don't know what the old lady says to the kids," remarks Donald Spencer, of the Fish and Wildlife Service. "But when she gives the word, they streak into the entrance like mad."

When caught while very young, prairie dogs make fascinating pets. The Spencers reared one, and he was given quarters in their basement. When he sought company, the little dog would come thumping up the stairs, run into the room, squeak and wait for attention. If he did not get it, he would rush to the portieres between living and dining rooms, give them a jerk, swing on them, drop to his haunches and sit up, watching Don Spencer. If this did not succeed, he would rush at Spencer, grab the cuff of his trousers, and tug.

"I always played with him when he wanted to play," Spencer says. "He was just as determined not to play if he didn't choose to. If he didn't want to frolic—well, I didn't want to tangle with those teeth of his."

In their northern range, in Montana and the Dakotas, prairie dogs hibernate. In New Mexico and Arizona, they come out of their burrows on sunny winter days to frisk and feed. They do not store winter food, and where they do sleep through cold days, the fat they store in their small bodies as fall approaches carries them through to spring greening of the prairies.

Several myths about prairie dogs persist. Old plainsmen often saw snakes and burrowing owls enter holes in dog towns, and spun the yarn that the three species made up a strange family. Owls do use abandoned burrows, and when a rattlesnake slides into a dog hole, he either is running from danger, or on his way to feast on a young member of the family.

Another myth, that prairie dogs always dig to water, is equally untrue. In areas where the first ground water is several hundred feet below the surface, and no water above ground, moisture required is secured from the plants they eat. In emergencies, they have been observed chewing holes in desert cacti in search of moisture. That is an old explorer's trick and the dogs may have shown it to desert travelers.

Because he is actually a squirrel, a clean animal, the prairie dog is good eating. If anyone talks of prairie dogs, you generally hear the old story of how they were shipped east in early days as prairie squirrels and, for a little while, were on menus as a delicacy.

Two homesteaders had gone broke in western Kansas. They had turned to eating prairie dogs in last resort, and found them excellent. They began shipping them as a unique type of wild game meat and their business was flourishing until a disgruntled railway employee exploded their venture.

"Squirrels!" he said. "They're prairie dogs!"

The dog name did it; the meat markets would peddle no dogs.

When stationed in Lubbock, Texas, a few years ago, the Don Spencers staged a dinner that had the potential of not making friends but definitely influencing people. They had often eaten young prairie squirrels, and wanted to prove how palatable these might be.

The dinner was dressed up with candlelight and all the other trimmings. The meat dish was served a-la-king. Guests had repeated helpings of the delicious food. Then Spencer brought in a whole roasted prairie dog, and disclosed what they had been eating.

"It didn't set well with some guests," he admits.

During the drought the Navaho Indians faced a decision about their prairie dogs. The flocks of sheep had eaten the grass down to the roots. The prairie dogs were eating the roots. To protect their flocks, the dogs had to be eradicated. But at that moment the prairie dog was a main source of good food for the tribe. It was a difficult choice to make. The need for protecting the flocks tipped the balance against the dogs, and poisoning campaigns began.

Western range and ranch men consider the prairie dog an enemy. When towns and their populations become so numerous they are almost continuous over large areas, the loss in forage can become serious. While each dog may eat only 1/256th of what a cow requires, a few hundred thousand on the range can consume tons of forage.

A quarter century ago, Grant County, New Mexico, had a third of its area covered by dog towns, with an estimated population of 6,400,000. Northern Arizona was one continuous dog town; it was difficult to be out of sight and hearing of these barking squirrels. Western Texas and other States contained areas as thickly populated as northern Arizona. Then drought years accented the conflict for forage between livestock and the dogs, and mass war hit the wish-ton-wish towns.

Poisoning and epidemic have done their grisly work. To find a prairie dog town today, watch the cheery, scampering play, the industry of the community, the manning of the watch-tower mounds, one must search wide stretches of country. Like the bison, which has found last-stand refuge in national parks, the prairie dog may have sanctuary there. But in other areas he faces liquidation.

If you watch along the highways as you drive toward the Rockies, looking for a prairie dog town where the sentinels cry out the news that you are entering the historic West, you will not have the barking squirrels to welcome you. Already they have all but vanished into history's realm and the storied West of the yesterdays.

The Baron of Cowfoot Lake

Ben Hur Lampman

NOW THIS POND in the cottonwoods, you must know, was amber as very old honey, so that none might be sure of its depth except the fishes themselves, or the herons that came. For Cowfoot Lake, as it was called by courtesy, made a brew of the fallen foliage of autumn, throughout the misty winter, the welcome spring and midway of summer's self. And amber it must remain until the river rose to sweep it clean again. It was, in fine, one of those minor dependencies of the bottoms, which have the great stream for godmother and must wait her gift. The mink knew the pond, and now and again an otter hunted it from bank to bank, and swans had been seen there. It was loved of willows and woodduck. More particularly it was the province and demesne of its overlord, and a testy baron he was, by all accounts.

And on this day of which one speaks—in late June, it was, and with morning no more than waking—the Baron was especially brief of temper, as he lay at his station in the tangled roots of the willows, the bold eyes of him striving to pierce that darkly golden water. He was motionless, as though in dream, this broad-flanked fellow, and the pugnacious dorsal fin was smoothly folded, the pectorals momently at rest. But the aggressive thrust of the lower jaw, that never belies the temper of the bass, seemed more than ever predatory. For though he was lord of Cowfoot, from willow to sedge, he had ruled it so harshly in the interests of appetite that its scant store of smaller fishes was all but gone, and his heavy paunch was lank beneath the dark indistinct lateral stripe. A large-mouthed bass of the bottoms, ten pounds in weight when Providence was kind, and by a whim of Providence the only fish of his species held in the cottonwood pond. Above him, from that curious silver that was the surface, vapor arose in drifting phantoms—and mellow and sad from the river a distant steamer called through the murk. Yet where he sulked all was soundless with an amber silence.

You are not to suppose his moodiness wholly a matter of hunger, since in this respect he was as staunch a philosopher as any savage. When choice fare dwindled he took what offered, and with a rush that would not often be denied. And beyond question he would have starved with stoic grace, if starvation had been decreed. No, to his mind, or to his instinct, there was something amiss with the season, and that which he lacked and longed for was the invasion of the bottoms by a swollen river—whence he might escape the pond to expand his gills in turbid snow-water, and be off to elsewhere, cruising, seeking, a shadow at the feet of the flooded cottonwoods, a sounding splash at sunset. And between this desire and that, the one for adventure and the other for food, he was as grumpy a bass as ever twirled a caudal fin. He was as gruff as an earl with the gout.

Do not be regretting that the water was of this singular hue, precisely that of spiced metheglin, since you may be assured that you could not have seen him, were it never so clear, when he slipped forth from the willow roots and went in search of breakfast. That is to say, if you had caught a glimpse of him under the most favorable of circumstances you would have seen no more than the wraith of a fish—visional, pallid, so like the green depths as to be of them, save for the dark band on his flank. Why, you might never have known that you had glimpsed him, but would have gone away thinking of those tricks that sun and shadow play in a pond. As for this Baron of ours, he was in scarcely better case, because in the bright dusk about him he could see no more than a fin's thrust in advance of his eager jaws. But he knew a thousand and one secrets that we shall never know, and these made ample amends. Indeed, this tinctured water was of some advantage to him, for if he could not see he could not then be seen. He drifted stealthily, and, as he drifted, with an eye to the pale surface, to the tips of the trailing willows, to the dim bulk of snag and sunken skiff, he was thinking ever so resolutely. And this was what he was thinking: "Frog." No more than that. "Frog." For frogs make commotion, and it is good to strike at them.

But Rana the bullfrog, who hunched in the spatterdock pads, was by no means an oaf, for all his lantern jowls and his air of complacent stupidity. Ordinarily he was uncommonly alert and prudent—yet June hath a way with a frog. All splendidly splotched in green and gold, with fugitive colors mingling, the better to match the spatterdock and its shadows, he sat there and throated the lyric of his kind. A very lovely song it was, too, for any who had ear for it, and if you were bemused with the vicinage. It is betwixt and between the bellow of a melancholy bull, for which he is fittingly named, and the round blaring of a boat's whistle. Why, sirs, it is such a sound as may not, must not, proceed from a frog, and yet in spite of all doubting it does. And Rana, singing to his portly lady, and listening with heart aflutter, and singing once again, quite forgot the dread overlord of the pond—forgot all else save June. Almost he leaned to listen . . . and listening seemed to hear her ponderous plashing in the drenched willows. Whereat the foolish heart of Rana leaped, and he with it, and together they woke the quiet water, and there he sprawled, listening. Yet a tiny thrill of terror nipped at his nerves, and he answered it with one strong stroke of the fat hams and webbed feet. The stroke sped him in from the depths and over the shallow, safely to the bank, and there he crouched in a heron track.

Behind him the surface dipped to a spinning eddy, lune-green at its heart, and there was a flash of the Baron's burnished scales as the bass missed his strike. Up sprang the huge fish, on that angry instant, high above the pond, with dorsal fin erect and threatening. When he took water again the cottonwoods echoed the splash. A faintest fragrance wafted shoreward, as of flowers and spices, for this is the fragrance of the bass. (If you choose to smile here, as you may, listen to Izaak Walton as he discourses of the English grayling: "And some think that he feeds on water-thyme and smells of it at his first taking out of the water; and they may think so with good reason as we do, that our smelts smell like violets at their being first caught; which I think is a truth.") Now here is something curious concerning Rana, and greatly to the credit of his prudence. No sooner had he gained the little flat of drab mud, whereon the heron had signed its foot, than he ceased to be green and golden and became burnt umber and sad slate. The Baron, cruising onward, no longer thought "Frog."

As he cruised he came to the drove of carp, that know nothing of want so long as there is rich mud to be had. With dour eye he saw that they were amber as the pond itself, and fat as no fish save the bass have any right to be. He cleft the drove with his passage, and the carp swerved to either fin with stolid grace, fearing him not at all yet yielding him his due. They rose to the surface in his wake, twenty round mumbling mouths in a ring, to feed on some light drift scorned of bass. Yet somehow he was aware that the carp, too, were impatient in their slow, phlegmatic way for the summer flood . . . to browse on clover blossoms in the sunken pastures . . . how odd a preference. And he passed on, quite forgetting them, and before him the mottled sculpin burrowed deep into the silt, and behind him a brilliant sunfish, no larger than an elder leaf, crept shining forth from the rushes and rose to a floundering gnat. It drew near to midmorning and the light in the pond was like nothing so much as suffused gold, with a hint of copper in it. Had it not been for hunger this pond, one believes, would have grown drowsy.

The Baron was conscious of a huge appetite, and a dull anger, as he rested just beyond the spit of sedge that thrust into the pond. The sedge was flooded at the roots, but in its mazes the water was far too scanty for his bulk. And there the sun had warmed a nursery for larvae of many sorts, and sundry swart sticklebacks lurked, and possibly a striped perch or two. Certainly there were tadpoles to be had if he but could come at them, the black tadpoles of the wood frog, which wakens from sleep and is about its mating long before Rana the bullfrog has stretched his heavy limbs and risen to blink and bellow. Yet if one mustered all his patience and lay quietly beside the sedge, it might be that some incautious morsel would venture over the depths—and so be lost to the nursery. Patience. This shadowy hunger waited.

It appeared that ink had been spilled in the sedge, until a broad blotch of it quite darkened the water. But it did not diffuse itself, this darkness, this odd ebony, and the border of it fluttered constantly. You would have been astonished to see it move swiftly, fluently, to the right, lengthening as it moved, then shaping itself anew into a rough circle. And twice you must have looked, and nearer, before you perceived that many tadpoles made it, and that each one of them was black as a fragment of night. They were very happy, these tadpoles, as they browsed with midget mouths on the brown algae of the sedge stems, or clustering merrily about a sodden insect, made a feast with many smackings, like elves at a banquet. They were so happy, in truth, that they put all danger from them, and romped in the shallows, while the Gray One drew near. And this Gray One, as the pond knows, is that terror of tadpoles, the water boatman, or oar bug, who swims on his back as briskly as any Kanaka, and who holds fast that which he seizes. Perhaps the black tadpoles were fatalists, in some formless thought of theirs, for he slew one of them each day, and yet they were merry. The Gray One came jerkily toward the herd, plying his oars . . . nearer and nearer. They paid him no least attention, for all their tails were outward as they fed. With flashing speed he cast himself among them, and his beak was fleshed.

You may well believe that all was confusion there in the pleasant sedge. The herd scattered and fled, headlong, and sundry tadpoles dove far into the lower tangle to hide away from death. And over and over above them tumbled and tossed in torment the captured brother, with the Gray One clinging to his paunch. This tadpole was huge beside the Gray One, yet the fierce boatman wore him down as a wolf worries a buffalo, and laid bare the victim's vitals the while that savage hold was never relinquished. But the striving of these two carried them hither and yon through the nursery, and even as life quitted the tadpole they rolled from the warm brink into the colder water and went wavering downward. The patient Baron struck. He struck almost lazily, despite his hunger, since there was small need for haste. The maw that would have taken Rana himself at a gulp, or a carp in its first year, engulfed the Gray One and his kill effortlessly, as a small matter. Yet he was cheered.

And, idling reflectively onward, with an eye to this and to that, he came at length to the mud pastures of the carp, where tails wave gravely from the surface, and contented gruntings may be heard by the belted kingfisher on his snag. There was a bare chance that some fat chub might linger there, feeling a greater security in that minor depth, or that thin cousin of his, the crappie . . . or something. And again he took his station where the clay slipped down to deeper water, and watched the weaving dimness of the carp, and considered his hunger, and felt a thirst for the flood, and was in all as moody a fellow as might be found in any pond. It occurred to him that he might dash in and drive the carp away as they deserved. It occurred to him that there was naught in this. He waited . . . possibly a chub.

A shadow floated through the amber stillness, describing a smooth arc. It was gone and then it came again, drifting across the pond, and, as it passed, the coolness of it brushed his snout. At the third crossing of the shadow he drew away into yet deeper water, backing slowly, until a comforting depth was over him—for shadows such as this were ominous, he knew not why. And in that moment there was a sounding splash where the carp were. The water was shot with splintered silver and ascending globes of pearl. A dark bulk was yonder. Beneath it writhed and struggled a golden fish in golden murk. Had you been there, where the sweetbrier flowers and the wild blackberries ripen, you would have seen the ruffled head of the osprey weaving from the pond, and marked the buffeting of those stout wings, whence spray was cast, as the bird rose heavily with a sleek carp in its talons. For the moment, and that only, the Baron remembered why it was that he feared the arch of a moving shadow. He was gone.

He went, when his nerves were his own again, to the place where the crawfish lives. She was at home, this wariest of amazons, who alone had escaped him, and in the grotesquerie of her countenance bliss must have been, for an infinite eye to see—since clinging to the under-plates of her tail, and burrowing among the spider-legs of her, were numerous infants of her own, fragile, translucent, pitiful and dear. In a manner of speaking she clasped them to her breast, this ugly, competent mother, until such time as they might find refuge in the sedge, and themselves grow rough and terrible. She was at home, and very near to her cave in the clay . . . and he regarded her, and she him. With such a creature as this to comfort him, the Baron felt that he might drowse. He cared not a whit for the brandished claw, that will nip a fingerling in two as though it were trash. Such claws, digestively considered, were excellent. And then, as they had played the game so often, he rushed upon her with gaping, cavernous jaws—while with a single inward stroke of her armored tail the mother crawfish flipped through the portal of her cave. Sediment arose cloudily, and sodden leaves were whirled, and in the blackness of his temper the Baron leaped high into the sunshine, his dorsal fin rigid with rage. As the pond closed over him fortune relented and was kind. For he glimpsed a bright V cleaving the pond at its surface, and knew the pliant thrust of the lean swimmer that made it. If a fish may crouch, he crouched, ere with a stroke and a swerve he launched himself.

On the northern shore of the pond called Cowfoot was but poor hunting, as any ophidian could have told you, whereas the southern bank was at this season the home of Hyla the tree frog, green as a new leaf, who had come down from the forest to be a fellow of family. You might hear him shrilling at any hour, and very sweet and clear it was, this music he made. For this reason, which seemed to him the best of all possible reasons, a questing garter snake, wearing a lone stripe of dark orange down his rounded back, took to water and swam toward Hyla's home. He dove once at whim or shadow, near the marge, then held his course for the blue clay palisades beyond.

He thought of Hyla as he swam, for his stomach had that day been comforted by but a single earthworm; and halfway over he thought of Hyla again. And if you care to be precise about it, this thought, as the water parted at his slender throat, and washed the orange stripe to brightness, was almost literally his last. All else was terror. For bronze flashed under him, and a heavy swirl marked where he had been, and he was seen no more. Midway of the pond the Baron waved meditative fins, and seemed to think long, grave, studious thoughts, which was far from the case. For this is what he was thinking: "Well!" And again, somewhat grumpily, but quite pleased with himself, "Well!"

Meantime the river, whispering, widening, with its tribute from the white, far ranges, pressed outward from its banks and through the cottonwoods—until at length it ventured a finger of chill, saffron flood into Cowfoot Lake. The trickle grew to a chuckle, and the chuckle to a frothy laughter—and as the Baron turned to his willows the taste of that invading current slipped into his astonished gills.

For an instant only he mulled it, and then —beyond question—he leaped as he had never leaped before. He saw the broken water where carp were wallowing, crowding . . . and was himself among them—striking to right and left at the largess of the freshet. This was his June returned to him.

Round and magnificent of paunch he made his way at twilight to the river, great with flood—up the log-strewn ravine, past the pale groping suckers, the prowling silver, greedy, chubs. And the river found a new lake for him, and a brave mate, after the custom of rivers, and the amber depths of the prison lake became but dim memory.

Shore Bird Extraordinary

Olin Sewall Pettingill, Jr.

PHOTOGRAPHS BY EDWARD FOX DANA
AND THE AUTHOR

FORTY-SEVEN SPECIES of shore birds inhabit North America. They are wading birds, usually with long, straight bills, long necks, long legs, and feet with four toes. Their plumage forms blending patterns of browns, grays and reds, interspersed with some black and white. One of their number is so utterly extraordinary in shape, so large and strikingly colored, that it is a personality among its class. This is the avocet.

Bird of extremes, bird of exceptions, the avocet's legs and neck are excessively long, almost to the point of being grotesque; its toes are three in number and prominently webbed; its bill curves abruptly upward. Brilliant reddish-brown colors of head and neck fade away to sharply contrasting black and white areas on body and wings.

For an abode the avocet has dual preference, either mountain-walled valleys of the far West or alkaline lakes of the great plains. In either it is ever conspicuous, always the spectacle.

Dead Dog Slough near Kenmare, North Dakota, is a typical prairie abode. Here the great rolling plains dip momentarily, leaving a shallow basin. Water gathers from spring rains and stands unreplenished, then becomes stagnant and highly alkaline. Under clear June and July skies it gradually evaporates, leaving an empty basin, white-powdered and desolate.

It is when the water has just appeared in the spring that the avocets gather here, at least a half-score of them. At first there is great activity. There are weird courtship antics when they lift their wings, lower their heads and trip along liltingly in the shallow water, ecstatically circling and pursuing one another; harmless but quarrelsome contests as each pair—the marital bond once sealed—claims a section of shoreland for private use as a nesting territory.

A shallow cup is excavated in the gravel and sparsely lined with bits of vegetation. When four or five eggs have been deposited, the monotonous routine of four weeks begins, a routine that both sexes share.

Awkwardly the tall bird straddles its nest, placing its feet so that, when the legs are folded, its body will cover the nest. With the bill the eggs are turned, thus preventing the delicate membranes of the embryo from adhering to the shell walls. Any foreign matter that may have clung to the eggs is lifted off with the bill. The nesting material is hastily rearranged. These details have promoted the lowering of the breast feathers, thus uncovering the bare areas, or brood patches, of the breast. Finally the avocet, with its body still in the same position, lowers itself carefully, bringing the brood patches to rest on the eggs and letting the breast feathers fall as a canopy over them. Once on the eggs, the bird rocks back and forth over them to assure the perfect position of the protecting feathers.

When hatching time nears, Dead Dog Slough is half its former size and the nesting area lies far distant from the water. The adults gather there to feed. Now at a communal feeding ground, rivalries have been forgotten. As they search for food they tip their bodies forward, walk along steadily, and sweep their scythe-like beaks to and fro across the muddy bottom, stirring up and catching small organisms.

For fully twenty-four hours, or more, the newly hatched, downy chicks linger in their crude cradles. From the yolk material still harbored in their bodies comes immediate strength, energy and equilibrium. Sight, hearing and other senses rapidly near an advanced stage of perfection. They are soon capable of running at great speed, of crouching at the slightest danger.

During the days that follow, the chicks are speedily transformed from ordinary-appearing shore-bird young to distinctive adulthood. The legs seemingly lengthen with each stride. The bills, notably blunt and straight at first, permit them only to dabble in the mud, shore-bird fashion. Later, as the bills project and turn upward, the sidewise sweeping begins.

Why are avocets so curiously evolved in structure and behavior? And why do they often prefer alkaline sloughs, places not only limited in diversity of food but places that perennially present the hazard of an evanescent water supply? Probably competition in the scheme of nature has forced avocets to accept places rejected by other birds and to adapt themselves accordingly.

Extraordinary shore bird, the avocet!

The sequence on the following pages depicts the avocet approaching its nest. Its approach is similar to that of other ground-nesting birds, but the size of the bird's body and its exaggerated form accentuate movements one might normally miss. The nest is straddled so that the body, when the legs are folded, will cover the nest. Then the bird lowers itself, bringing the brood patch to rest on the eggs. Finally the bird settles firmly on its eggs, rocking gently to insure perfect position.

Hello! Do You Hear Me?

E. Laurence Palmer

A FRIEND of mine has a canary with which she carries on a one-sided conversation. She insists that the canary understands what is said. I have long been convinced that the canary has not the slightest idea what I say to it, although I do not indulge in the high-pitched baby talk my friend uses. It is plain that certain phonograph records, and some radio music, will stimulate this canary to sing, while others produce no such effect. What is the story back of all this, anyway?

Most of us think that others see, hear, feel, smell and taste much as we do. It is obvious that a dog can use his nose more effectively than we can, but since he responds to our spoken commands we think he hears as we do. It is another story, but Lutz and others have shown us that insects see through a different part of the spectrum than we, and if such variations exist in the realms of smelling and seeing why should not there be similar differences in the realm of hearing? If those differences exist, some understanding of them may help us more truly to appreciate some of the things that are constantly going on about us. Such mastery might even lead us to improve some of our techniques used in carrying on communications of various types.

The psychologists have a field day when they get to discussing sounds. They tell us that there can be no sound in an empty room because there are no ears there to hear it, but a telephone diaphragm embedded in a wall on one side of the room would pick up a knock on a door on the opposite side, and this could be recorded on a phonograph disc, and when played later could be heard. This, however, implies that the room has air in it, because if there were no air, the sound of the knocking would not cross the room. It is difficult to accept the idea that no sound takes place when there is no ear to hear it. If this were true a person who has become deaf might deny that there was anything such as sound, even though his memory told him differently.

As a matter of fact, there are plenty of sounds that none of us ever hears, or ever will hear, and there are some that only a few of us can hear. Within certain limits, we can improve our powers of hearing and interpreting sounds, and the rewards are almost invariably worth the effort.

Everyone should know how the keyboard of a piano looks, and where to find middle C on that keyboard. This middle C is pitched at the same key as the "hoot" of a great horned owl. The physicist tells us that sound waves pitched at middle C would reach a given point at the rate of 256 a second. While the middle C tone is produced by striking a key in the middle of the piano keyboard, it does not represent a point between the extremes of high-pitched or low-pitched sounds capable of production by the human voice or heard by the human ear; and while a domestic pigeon may hear it, it is doubtful if my friend's canary or the English sparrow or starling in my front yard ever heard or ever will hear a middle C tone. This means that these birds would not be affected in the least by the hooting of a great horned owl because they could not possibly hear it. If the starlings were psychologists they might even deny that the owl hooted because they could not hear it do so.

One of the things that may surprise my friend who talks to her canary is that the lowest pitch at which a canary can hear a sound is the highest C a soprano can ever reach with her voice. Maybe some of my friend's baby talk hits that point but I have my doubts. And while the canary could get no information whatever from the sounds we produce in our ordinary conversation, neither can we get any information at all through our ears about some sounds that are perfectly audible to the cats, rats, bats and dogs of our neighborhood. While we ordinarily can hear no sounds higher than six octaves above middle C, bats produce and hear sounds in the eighth and ninth octaves above that point. Dogs can hear sounds an octave above our uppermost limit. Thus a whistle can be made that will call a dog but be soundless to us. Rats can hear sounds in the second octave above our uppermost limit, and it is quite possible that they can carry on communications by sounds that we can hear no better than the canary can hear our conversation. Dogs can hear sounds pitched up to 35,000 cycles per second; cats, up to 50,000; rats up to 40,000 and bats carry on their acquaintance with the world with some sounds pitched as high as 90,000 cycles per second. These last sounds are at least two octaves higher than anything we could hear when we were at our best.

At the lower end of the range of hearing, we apparently can do better than the dogs, cats and rats. Just hit the bottom key on your piano and you will hear a sound that your dog or cat cannot hear. Try sometime to see if you can make your dog or cat respond to that sound.

Of course, just being able to hear a sound is not wholly important. We happen to be at our best in enjoying sounds around middle C, but that is not the case with the dogs, cats and rats. All of them are at their best listening to sounds pitched higher than those we enjoy. A dog is more likely to be distracted by sounds of a certain pitch. Cats are not so easily disturbed. Cats are slightly more able to distinguish minor differences in pitch than are dogs, but they lose that ability sooner than do the dogs.

If we were to classify our common mammals, including ourselves, on the basis of pitch of sounds that they can hear, we would have to put ourselves at a lower level than the cats, rats, bats and dogs.

We might ask at this point why mammals make the noises they do. Undoubtedly we have listened to political debates, gossip parties, pep talks, and even some college professors, and wondered why it was necessary for them to make so much noise. Undoubtedly, it is for the purpose of communicating something to some other animal, but we know that is not always the case. Most of us like occasionally to get off somewhere where we can just yell for the sake of yelling. We like to sing our heads off in the bathroom in the morning, and those who hear us may wish us success in this effort. But few of us use sounds for the same purpose that bats use it. If we move about in the night, or with our eyes closed, we can tell something of what surrounds us by the echoes that come to us when we yell. In the old days, we used to yell down the rainbarrel to notice how differently our voices sounded; but for the most part we use our eyes instead of our ears to help us find our way around in the daytime, and we hold our hands before us to feel our way past the furniture at night. Bats, on the other hand, let out a series of high-pitched sounds as they fly about at night. Their hearing is so keen that they can pick these sounds up as they are reflected to them from objects and can fly to avoid touching even twigs and branches of trees. When bats fly in the open, they give these sounds at the rate of about twenty-five a second, but when they are flying among obstructions they increase this to fifty a second.

We must remember that not all sounds produced by mammals are produced by the vocal cords. We clap our hands, stamp our feet, grit our teeth and smack our lips to make noises. Not a few mammals produce sounds similarly. Rabbits stamp their feet, as do horses, bulls and some other mammals, but it is difficult to state definitely that they do this to warn enemies or to inform friends, or whether this communication is purely incidental. We of course excel these other mammals when it comes to using tools to make sounds, whether these tools are primitive jungle drums, hot bands, or exquisite violins.

Of course, the artists in the use of sound among mammals are the poets, the musicians and some of the literary geniuses. To them sounds are the vehicles for the expression of the higher emotions. One of these writers exquisitely defines the limit of his hearing when he says:

> "I hear a sound so fine there's nothing lives
> 'Twixt it and silence."

Poe either stretched his imagination, or was able to hear some of the finer sounds of nature, when he spoke of "the murmur that springs from growing grass." But I think that Pope best considered the role of the artist in the realm of sound when he said:

> "Music resembles poetry; in each
> Are nameless graces which no methods teach
> And which a master-hand alone can reach."

I do not care for Fuller's attempt to bring nature and modern music together by saying: "Music is nothing else but wild sounds civilized into time and tune." Rather I prefer such a viewpoint as was Carlyle's when he said: "See deep enough, and you see musically; the heart of Nature being everywhere music, if you can only reach it." Possibly this attempt to get music and happiness from nature is what unites so many of us. As one writer has said: "Music is not a science any more than poetry is. It is a sublime instinct, like genius of all kinds." Possibly this may help us understand some of the sounds of nature although it admittedly evades answering such questions as those dealing with why birds sing, why crickets chirp, why frogs croak and what do songs, chirps and croaks mean to anyone, anyway.

It might be nice to think that all bird sounds are purely expressions at the joy of living. Surely the poets would have us think this. But anyone who has listened to a barnyard fowl knows that the sounds produced are associated sometimes, at least, with an emotional state, but that there are also more practical uses. A mother hen calls her chicks to her. She gives another sound when a hawk goes by. When she is caught before being killed for supper she gives an entirely different sound, and when she is bored with life you can tell it by the sound you hear from the henyard.

It is absurd, with all these examples of different sounds associated with different states of mind in a hen, to assume that sounds produced by other birds are limited to any one purpose. It is true that probably the most vigorous of bird songs are those given by the male bird during the time of year when it has staked out and is defending a home territory against the encroachments of rival males of the same species. The intensity with which these defense songs are given varies during the breeding season, being most emphatic at the height of mating vigor. Rather than being a song to please the mate or to win her, it is probable that most songs are given for the purpose of daring other males to come and fight, or in warning them against invasion of reserved areas. With many species of birds, these songs are given from the highest perch available, but this is by no means always the case.

Just as was the case with the mammals, many of the sounds made by birds are not made with the vocal cords. The best known exception is the drumming made by woodpeckers on dead stubs or on metal roofs or even on metal cans. The drumming on the wood might be thought to be secondary and merely associated with seeking food, but this explanation does not help us understand the persistent drumming of a flicker on the metal eaves trough over our heads on an early spring morning.

It used to be thought that grouse produced their booming sound by actually beating the log on which they stand when the noise is made. Then, it was thought that the drumming was made by beating the wings against the body. Motion pictures show us that neither is the case, and the wings merely beat the air without touching body or log. The sound is produced by the vibration of the feathers, and similar sounds are produced by feather vibrations in other birds. The snipe, the woodcock and the nighthawk are among the other birds that produce sound in this way. Of course quail and pheasants rising into the air also produce a sound with their wings, but this is probably different from the more definite sound produced by the other birds mentioned.

One of the most unusual sounds produced by birds is that made by prairie chickens during their courting season, when they precede the vocal booming characteristic of them by a pattering beating of the ground with their feet. This has been reproduced splendidly in one of the records of "American Bird Songs" issued by the Comstock Publishing Company of Ithaca, New York. With the use of these phonograph records, the important sounds produced by seventy-two North American birds may be produced at will in any home or schoolroom. This offers a distinct opportunity to those interested in learning to recognize these particular sounds as they occur in nature.

Some excellent studies have been carried on to determine the hearing range of such birds as the starlings, English sparrows, canaries and domestic pigeons, but we need more of them. The techniques for determining this range have been worked out and all that is needed is the patience to follow similar procedures with other species of birds. Possibly, when this has been done, we will find that we have made many false assumptions about the reasons why birds sing, and why they produce other noises, and it is altogether probable that the world as experienced by a bird through its ears is a vastly different place from what our ears indicate. We have assumed that the prairie chicken beats the ground with its feet to produce a sound which will affect other prairie chickens, but we do not know if the prairie chicken's hearing range is such that it can even hear itself beat the ground. Certainly, it is doubtful if a canary could hear this prairie chicken sound.

Most of us associate frogs with ponds because it is from pond areas that we most frequently hear their croakings. One of the greatest joys a teacher of natural history gets is associated with showing some student a peeper in full song. Most of us can remember with considerable accuracy the first time we ever witnessed the act, and once it has been witnessed hearing the sound brings again a vision of what looks like a little bubble giving forth a tremendous sound.

The calls of frogs and toads are produced for the most part by the males, though the females are usually able to produce a sound if necessary. The spectacular choruses of sound are undoubtedly the products of males. Since each species has its own call, one can get some idea of the kinds of frogs and toads to be found in an area merely by listening to them through a season. There is no month in the year even in the northern part of the United States when some frog cannot be heard. In general, the group to which the peepers belong are among the first to be heard. They are followed by the group which includes the meadow frogs, then the toads, and finally the bullfrogs and green frogs.

Literature on the pitch of the calls of frogs and toads seems to be lacking but it seems certain that studies would show that as the season advances from the winter, the pitch of the frog choruses goes down, beginning with the high-pitched peepers and ending with the basso-profundo bullfrog.

A number of attempts have been made to learn if there is any co-ordination between the frequency with which these animals call and the temperature. Most such studies have yielded nothing of importance except to point out that the frequency is more dependent on the readiness of the individual to breed than upon the temperature of his environment. We know that when the first frogs or toads come to the breeding ground in spring the earliest arrivals are the mature males. They are followed by the immature males, and then by the mature females. The immature females bring up the end of the procession; at least this is the case in some species of frogs. It happens that this sequence compares favorably with the sequence to be observed in migrating birds.

It may be dangerous to attempt to correlate the reasons why frogs sing with the reasons why birds sing because there is a correlation between the order in which they migrate. However, it may be that our male frogs and toads are merely cussing out the other fellows of their sex rather than singing love songs to the female. Some day we may know the answer to this, but if it is known now it is not common knowledge.

While sounds are produced probably by all of the frogs and toads, their relatives the salamanders are quiet. Many salamanders have what are recognized as hearing organs on their feet but these are more likely to record vibrations in the earth than the sound waves which pass through the air. It is doubtful if these animals have any way of communicating with each other by sound.

The reptiles are for the most part quiet. As exceptions we have the hissing of such snakes as the hog-nosed snakes, the rattle produced by the shaking of the tail of rattlesnakes, and a murmuring sound that some turtles have been known to make at breeding time. The turtle sound has been described as a little like that produced by a tea kettle when the water in it is boiling gently.

When we remember what we have found out about sounds produced and heard by the bats and how the hearing range of dogs and cats and rats is higher than our own, it is foolish to say that turtles and snakes do not make and hear sounds that we cannot possibly hear. We might readily assume that the bats must depend on hearing to some extent because of the elaborate development of their ears. No such development is present in the snakes and turtles. The bats must, when they are in flight, depend upon sounds traveling through the air, while the snakes and turtles remain for the most part in contact with the earth or with water. Sound vibrations pass more readily through earth and water than through the air, so ears might not be so necessary with the animals that remain independent of sounds carried through the air.

Hold a pencil lightly between the lips. Scratch the free end with your fingernail. You will probably hear nothing. Now close your teeth on the pencil. Again scratch it with the fingernail. This time you should get a distinct sound. In the latter case, the sound is carried through the pencil to your teeth and to the bones of your head to your ears. This use of bony structures to carry sound is probably highly important in such cold-blooded animals as the fish. Sound waves passing through water to fishes are undoubtedly slightly significant to a fish. All this provides a fascinating field for research for the inquiring mind.

With many invertebrate animals, it is difficult to determine to what things they are sensitive. Particularly is this so with those animals that live close to water and the soil. With these, how can we be sure that the animal hears a sound as we understand it, or feels the vibrations in the earth or water that may accompany the sound waves? Possibly this very difficulty is what has led our psychologists to define sound. When they say "sound," they mean "sensations due to stimulation of the auditory nerves and auditory centers of the brain, usually by vibrations transmitted in a material medium, commonly air, affecting the organ of hearing especially through the tympanic membrane, or sometimes by internal disturbances affecting the nerves or nerve centers directly." If an animal does not have a tympanic membrane and special auditory centers in the brain he is just out of luck so far as sounds are concerned.

However, there are plenty of invertebrate animals that do respond to sound waves, and some that deliberately produce them with significant effects. We can hear crickets chirp and katydids repeat their calls from the treetops. We can bring tuning forks near spiders or play violins near them to see what they will do. These animals definitely respond to certain sounds in certain ways.

Dr. Frank Lutz of the American Museum of Natural History was one man who did not believe that the crickets should be allowed any privacy in their conversations. Accordingly, he experimented widely with them. He had photographs made of their songs on a movie film. He put individuals together and kept them apart under varying conditions in varying combinations of sex, age and health. Out of his experiments came the conclusion that in general the chirping of male crickets is a matter of defiance of other males rather than an invitation for a date with a member of the opposite sex. By this time, this suggestion should sound familiar because it is obviously similar to what happens with the birds.

One of the most delightful accounts of insect music is to be found in the Smithsonian Publication Number 2775, by R. E. Snodgrass. In this bulletin on "Insect Musicians, Their Music and Their Instruments," we find excellent sketches and discussions of the instruments used by common insects in making sounds. We see the location of the "ears" on the legs of many grasshoppers and the location of these ears on other species on the sides of the abdomen.

The photographic records of the songs of some insects show us that the cricket-on-the-hearth chirps at a pitch of E just above the highest key on the piano keyboard. The snowy tree cricket on the other hand chirps in the last octave represented on the piano keyboard and up to D just above the range covered by the piano. This is something you can check in part on your piano. More interesting yet will be your attempt to determine the temperature by the frequency with which snowy tree crickets call. If you will add 37 to the number of calls given in 15 seconds you will be surprisingly close to having the same number as would be indicated on a thermometer placed about where the animal is making its sounds.

It may not be easy to follow the suggestion that you find where an insect is chirping. Again our ingenious Dr. Lutz comes to our assistance. He suggested that one use a doctor's stethoscope with the terminals provided with little funnels. If these are held some distance apart and directed in the general direction of the insect sound and are so adjusted that the sound comes in equally strong over each, the insect will be found at the point towards which each funnel is pointing. This same result can be approximated by asking a number of people to point to where the insect is singing. The pooled judgment will be relatively near to the desired place.

It should be obvious from what has been written that people who are interested in the sounds of nature usually specialize on definite groups of animals. The psychologists generally confine their studies to the mammals. Ornithologists like Brand, Allen, and Kellogg have stuck to the birds, and Lutz, the entomologist, stuck to his insects. F. L. Wells of the Harvard Medical School developed a considerable amount of information about how spiders respond to sounds. He worked mostly with the common garden spider and noticed that certain stimulating sound waves make spiders shuttle from one side of the web to another; others induce the spider to spread its legs; others, to seize something and still others to drop from the web to the ground. If you have a tuning fork or a violin, you may enjoy experimenting on your own to see what responses the spiders in your neighborhood make to the sounds you produce for them. You will find the results interesting.

Of course, any discussion of insect sounds should remind us of the significance of different sounds produced by bees and their kin. It takes little training to appreciate how a swarm of bees sounds when it is angered by something. And when it comes to the disturbance flies and mosquitoes can make in buzzing about our heads, we realize that it is fortunate that at least some of the insects that can harm us must announce their visit by a loud buzzing of the wings.

We have some knowledge about bats and cats and rats and ourselves, but there must be much that goes on in the realm of sound in that area of high pitch which is above what can be significant to a sensitive human ear. We need more careful and more simple homely experiments in this field than we have had. Possibly some people will be stimulated by this article to learn if their canaries really do understand "baby talk"; if their dogs can hear the sound produced by striking the lowest key on the piano keyboard; and what note on a violin makes a spider drop from its web. If you do not believe trying these things is fun, then try just one of them as a starter.

Glimpses of Flying Squirrels

Ernest P. Walker

PHOTOGRAPHS BY THE AUTHOR

TWO TYPES of flying squirrels are known to science as *Glaucomys volans* and *G. sabrinus*. These two species, whose ranges overlap slightly in a few places, inhabit most of timbered North America. In many sections they are plentiful, although few people ever see one. These beautiful, delicate little gliders are active only by night, have their homes and sleep during the daytime in old woodpecker holes, old bird nests, hollow limbs, or any other shelter they can find, preferably high up in a tree. Since they are nocturnal, quiet and shy, they are seldom seen in the wild except when someone cuts down a tree with a hollow in it where several may have been living, or when they take up abode in a bird house. Scarcity of natural shelters sometimes forces the little animals to seek homes in attics of houses, and occasionally one will get into human living quarters and be unable to find its way out. Sometimes they are seen at bird feeding shelves at night.

They are little creatures, the length of the head and body ranging from five to eight inches, and the tail is slightly shorter. The weight of the small eastern species, *G. volans*, is two to three ounces.

The gliding membrane is an extension of the skin of the body. It extends to the wrists and ankles. The tail is flat in cross section, because of the long, slightly stiff hairs on the sides that stand well out from the vertebrae, while the upper and lower sides have short hairs that lie close to the bone. The fur is soft and silky and always perfectly groomed, if the little creatures are in good health.

When active, flying squirrels are marvels of grace, beauty and speed. The word "flying" is a misnomer, for they do not fly, but glide. To start a glide they dash to a point higher than the one to which they wish to go, then leap toward their objective. Extending their front legs forward and outward, and their hind legs backward and outward, they are under way as efficient gliders. They lose some altitude and land at a lower point than the takeoff. Thus they could well be called gliding squirrels.

If obtained when young, flying squirrels tame so readily that they become fascinating pets, for they are gentle and enjoy human companionship. In a person's pocket, inside a shirt, or a woman's blouse, are preferred places to cuddle and sleep.

At one time or another I have raised about a dozen baby flying squirrels. It is not difficult if one uses care and a good baby milk formula. However, a nursing white rat is an ideal foster mother for the little ones. She can devote her entire time to the project. The little ones nurse about sixty days.

Whether babies or adults, flying squirrels are the most gentle, friendly and beautiful little creatures one could wish for. However, they are delicate, small, and extremely quick, so they are not entirely satisfactory as pets for children.

Acorns, beechnuts, hazel nuts and pecans are important foods for them, but they eat any nuts they can open. They also like grain, seeds, buds and the bark of twigs, small amounts of fruits and berries, and many different kinds of insects. They are especially fond of grasshoppers, cicadas, katydids, butterflies and moths. The worms out of ears of corn are delicacies, as are the grubs that develop in acorns.

Should flying squirrels fall into your possession and you do not liberate them, try to give them the special care, including the exercise, such charming creatures deserve.

Top: *"Beautiful" certainly has her hands full with a walnut and appears to be puzzling as to just what she is going to do with it.*

Above: *"Beautiful" launches on a glide toward the author.*

Blackburnians of the Pines

Louise de Kiriline

ALL OF A SUDDEN spring came. There was that special feeling in the air, that tender caress of the south wind upon my cheek, that peculiar fragrance of myriad unopened buds. The birches stood decked with pendulous blooms, and their tiny crinkled leaves pushed impatiently out of their sticky coverings. With a crown of pale green, the quaking aspen looked like a young innocent attired in her first party dress. Even the austere evergreens unbent before this special occasion and sent forth a heady perfume of sun-baked, glistening resin. The stage was set.

A song heralds the first arrival, a song that has not been heard for many months but that now, in its fresh first rendering, seems lovelier than ever. Gorgeous in his multicolored spring dress, an animated warbler appears, the first seen, on this day, of these enchanting sprites of the woods that belong to the Americas alone. He moves through the trees, hopping along the branches, a flash of color playing hide and seek with the watcher in the dappled sunlight. Often he flutters like a suspended butterfly at the end of a twig, busily picking tiny insects with his slender bill. At set intervals he stops, raises his head towards the blue heavens and gives forth his sentence with wide-open bill, possessed by such an ardor that his body quivers violently from crown to tip of tail. And in that inspired sound and gesture all nature's truth and essence are encompassed.

Then uncountable warblers surge through my woods in a gigantic wave of color and movement. Song fills the air. Endless variations of color patterns flit past my field of vision with exasperating rapidity. Fleeting glimpses of yellow breasts, with streaks or without, of wings plain or with bars, a bay line along a flank, a chestnut cheek patch, a blue hood, often afford the single chance of recognition, sometimes with the conclusiveness of a certainty, but often vaguely lacking the additional marking that would have settled the matter.

Throughout North America, from south to north, these scenes are repeated each spring. But to most bird watchers, many of the warblers are transients, only to pass quickly, to be heard and seen briefly, and then to be gone. Finally, perhaps hundreds of miles north of the International Border, they reach the vast lands of lakes, rivers and forests, where their breeding grounds begin.

There is one among the warblers whose name seems to fit it singularly well—Blackburnian, although in fact it is called after a bird enthusiast named Blackburn. This feathered elf in black and white, with throat aflame and dashes of orange on crown and cheeks, prefers the northern coniferous forest, and goes there to nest either in the mountain ranges at higher altitudes or in the north. Perhaps, therefore, the striking plumage of the adults, which differs little between the sexes, and does not change much with the seasons, is what most bird watchers in the southeastern part of the hemisphere know best about this warbler.

In the "Loghouse Territory," my study area so named from the house we live in, 250 miles almost due north of Toronto in Canada, the Blackburnian warbler may be seen during four months of the year. A few of them stay there, seldom longer than sixty days, during their nesting season.

When he appears in the spring, in full song, this warbler is one of a large group of birds whose arrival dates fall within the second and third weeks of May. From the top of the tallest tree come his high notes announcing his presence, mounting the scale with emphasis and deliberation until lost entirely in the uppermost register, "zree-zree-zree-zree-zree-zree-eee-eeee." One may ask, how many of these thread-fine Blackburnian notes do we actually miss? Judging by the comparative infrequency with which he utters his songs—I have counted two and one-half to six in a minute—it might well be that none of us have ever heard the actual finale of this bird's song, which may be far beyond the capacity of the human ear.

Around our house is a fine locality for a Blackburnian territory. It contains everything that this warbler seems to prize most —tall well-feathered evergreen interspersed sparingly with young and full-grown aspens and white birches, and slopes with dense growth that harbors rich supplies of small moths and other insects included in his favorite menus. It also has water. But this is evidently no obligatory condition, although a fine asset in midsummer, when clouds of May flies arise from the lake to dance out their brief existences and then to cling helplessly to every twig and leaf. Then all a warbler has to do is to pick and eat. For many years the Blackburnian tradition has been maintained upon this land, and the destinies of a pair and their offspring, developed and fulfilled each season; but not in an unbroken line, since both the male and the female have changed identity in the interval.

In spite of the fact that there is no lack of suitable habitat in this locality, the Blackburnian warblers do not settle close to one another. Usually two, never more than three pairs have occupied sites within the sixteen-acre Loghouse Territory. The living-space required by each pair is not much more than two or two and one-half acres, but to settle border to border appears well-nigh out of the question, and a buffer-zone of "no bird's land" seems a necessity. Whether the reason for this is a sparse population of the species in general or downright intolerance, remains to be determined. The fiery belligerence of Blackburnian males about their territory, and their frequent entanglements with unsettled males with obvious intents of annexation, make the question even more puzzling.

One such encounter lasted a whole afternoon. Accompanied by high-pitched squealing, in whirlwind pursuits alternated by pauses in challenging attitudes on respective twigs, two males vied with one another for the possession of land, vegetation and partner. In a striking manner they showed off their orange-colored spots, dashes and bibs by ruffling these fiery feathers. They quivered their wings and spread their flashy black and white tails. In the course of the battle, neighboring myrtle, magnolia and mourning warblers, as well as a red-eyed vireo, also were involved in the fracas, and this caused the Blackburnians to become highly excited and to lose their heads completely. But, all of a sudden, the whole affair dissolved with the disappearance of the intruder. Hostilities were dropped forthwith and everybody returned to his previous occupation.

The female arrives, on an average, eleven days later than the male. But this interval varies considerably and depends on such factors as the weather and the number of females that actually pass through the region. In one instance it was twenty-three days, the male arriving at a record early date, May 8, and the female at a record late date, June 1. It would seem that these circumstances combined adversely on this occasion.

The female Blackburnian is a beautiful little bird, demurely dressed in a subdued version of the male's brilliancy. In her, his bright orange patches are paler, and the vivid contrast of his black and white markings softened. It is of note, too, that all the females I have known personally exhibited dispositions quite in keeping with this modesty of attire. They are birds that go about their business in a detached and airy way, efficient and adept, but seldom tempted to frivolities. In my experience, all the tempestuousness in the Blackburnian belonged to the males.

I am even under the impression that the female's acceptance of the male's invitation to stay is less of her doing than his. True, she may have directed her flight to the place whence she heard his song, but he meets her with such persuasive demonstrations of wings and tail and his whole body, that she is hardly left a choice. And having convinced her, he fusses over her, guards and pursues her with a zeal that, not only would she indeed have difficulty in escaping before the nest attaches her to the spot, but he, temporarily, forgets to sing.

Soon after this, the female begins looking for a nest site. For the most part I have found her settled in the tops of the stalwart white pines around our house. One nest was situated far out on a branch, forty feet from the ground; another was wedged into a three-pronged upright crotch at a height of fifty-five feet, in a rather bare spot close to a sticky bunch of opened cones. But a third one, which was the second nest of the pair, I found almost invisibly hidden in the bushiest part of a horizontal branch of a white spruce, not more than twenty-six feet from the ground. At two of these nests, a young poplar beside the nesting tree served the birds as a stop-station before they entered the nest site. But in the case of the nest in the crotch, the female habitually "spiraled" up the trunk of the pine, appearing and disappearing, until she neared the top and then hopped sideways along the branch to the nest, to the onlooker a most confusing approach until he learned her method.

It is surprising to note the extent spider webs are used in the nest-building of this warbler. The nest in the spruce was literally suspended from its moorings in twigs and leaves by this adhesive material, like the cradle that hangs instead of stands. The female found the webs on twigs of bushes and trees. She took a piece in her bill and pulled; if it stuck she applied her weight by falling backwards and hanging onto it, fluttering until it gave way. Sometimes she carried it in small, whitish balls in her bill, or else in loose strands trailing behind her. The existence of these invisibilities was revealed only by the bird's movements and impediments as she dragged the fine stuff home over branchlets and twigs.

During the nest-building, the male spends his time in close attendance upon the female. He sings; he escorts her to and fro; he watches her. He may go to the nest and sit down in it for a few seconds, as if to learn what a good nest ought to feel like. But this is all the help he gives her with the actual building. Perhaps it is just as well. The nest in the spruce took three days to complete; but on the third day both birds were not very attentive in comparison with the almost frantic fervor with which they applied themselves, each in his own way, during the first day.

Incubation is a time of rest for both birds, for the female on the nest and for the male in the territory. He sings a great deal, feeds, wanders, fights if occasion presents itself. Sometimes he comes to the vicinity of the nest and, with a song, signals to the female to come off; sometimes he accompanies her upon her return. Once in a while, he approaches his sitting mate and feeds her a morsel, which she accepts, her head thrown back and her wings lightly aquiver. She alone incubates the eggs. She turns them quite often, using feet and bill. Her usual time on the nest is twenty-two minutes, and five minutes are generally enough for her to feed and rest, sometimes a little more or less.

After twelve to thirteen days the young hatch. Now dawns the period when the male makes his greatest contribution to the raising of his family. At least this is what happened at the crotch nest from which I gained most of my information. Already on hatching day the male feeds twice as often

as the female. But as the young grew older and needed less brooding this difference evened off and the father fed them a little more than one and one-half times as often as the mother.

Events at this nest took a dramatic course and I happened to be present at the crucial instant. On the day the young were four days old, a pigeon hawk swept out of the sky, pinned the female to the nesting branch, and the next second dashed away with her dangling from the talons. I shall always regret the loss of this little bird in a personal way, and I shall never know whether she, with her greater versatility in the care of the young, knowing both how to feed and to brood them, would have been able alone to raise her family had the male been taken in her stead. But, on the other hand, the death of the mother bird brought the male's protective instinct into action.

She was killed in the morning in the absence of the male. But he soon became aware that something was amiss. When he came to the nest he looked about him, hopped and flitted around, as if searching for his mate. Often, previously, he had come while she was brooding, and as he fed the young she perched on the rim and thereafter settled down to brood again. Moreover, less than half an hour after the tragedy, the young, now fed only by one parent, became hungrier, and their insistent gaping stimulated the male to more frequent feeding. In the time I watched, during the twenty four hours in which he succeeded in keeping them alive by himself, he stepped up his feedings to an average of once every fifteen minutes. In this way he maintained fairly well the previous feeding rate of both parents. But he did not know that the brood needed warmth as well as food. This part of the program belonged to the female and it was not laid down in his behavior pattern. And for this reason, all his efforts were in vain.

That disaster overtook all three of my nests must not be taken as an indication of an exceedingly low rate of nesting success for this warbler. It was only that the nests I happened to find were not favored by fortune. But if six Blackburnian warblers come to nest in our neighborhood, I have good evidence that at least eight or nine leave the area when they begin moving southward in late summer, even in years of highest unsuccess. For so long as the Blackburnian habitats remain undisturbed and adequate for the bird's needs, I firmly believe that the racial powers of perpetuation of the species are equal to the drain of any normal rate of mortality. This seems true in spite of the fact that a second unsuccessful nesting attempt ending in July is not followed by another re-nesting.

The male of the crotch nest began to sing again after his last young died, once more to announce himself as an eligible mate. For two weeks he sang with great vigor and persistency, even into the late evenings. And then he was no longer there. But the next spring he returned to the pines overshadowing our Loghouse. For how could it be any other individual that took up the same territory and sang the very same kind of songs!

Just Maggie

Marjorie Shanafelt

MAGPIES HAVE never been known to pass over our city until last fall when several flocks flew over. Calls came in again and again from interested people who wished to know what the striking black and white birds were. More than that, we soon found that some of those who inquired had been out with guns and had brought down these fine living targets. One flock was entirely annihilated. Of another flock there was but one left, and that one wounded. She was brought to Professor B——'s house by a small boy and the Professor brought her to the Museum in an old waste paper basket with a piece of cheesecloth tied down over the top.

When I unlocked the office door I found a great black and white bird solemnly stalking over the table, hopping upon chairs, and tapping at everything with her long thick bill. It hadn't taken long for her to tear a hole in the cheesecloth after the Professor had departed for an early class. The bird was friendly from the start. One wing trailed along at a grotesque angle but she had strong legs and hopped from one thing to another until she had tried nearly every perch the place afforded. I went out and bought her some steak, which she devoured ravenously, taking it directly from my hands.

Since there was nothing to be done about the wing if nature did not heal it, it was necessary to give the bird a refuge for the time being, so on a good-sized table we erected a fine roomy cage made of galvanized iron wire. There were perches inside and when it was all completed Maggie had a home about four and one-half by four by four feet. We put considerable sand inside and a big pan of water. It had to be a big one for Maggie required a great deal of fresh water. She would screech for fresh water and when it came would take about three swallows, letting it trickle slowly down her throat, after which she turned her back on the pan and kicked it full of sand. She wanted to hide everything she could get hold of, and since the cage offered few opportunities for burying her keepsakes, she worried over the problem a great deal. She punched things in the little cracks about the perches, and stuck them down between the wooden frame of the cage and the wire meshes. She dug holes by the hundred in the sand. Sometimes she would dig up an

extra precious article again and again, hiding it in every corner of the cage. Visitors to the Museum were always giving her shiny things just to see what she would do with them. Every time the sand was changed we found a collection of pennies, nickels, dimes and even quarters that more than paid for the meat we bought for her.

Maggie's cage sat in the lobby, near a wire door leading into the workroom. When the sounds of hammering, drilling, and conversation began to come from the workroom she was happy. She would jump around her cage, kick the sand into clouds, dig up and rebury her treasures, and finally subside on a perch whence she sang with great gusto even if little real knowledge of harmony. She learned to imitate our phrases. If she was in a friendly mood she struck her perch sharply with her black bill, after which she would begin to gurgle and finally spill out a tirade of throaty sounds that dwindled away into charming little soft cooing notes. Although she always looked well groomed, only once was she caught taking a bath.

Maggie consumed one pound of boiling beef a week. She would accept pieces of meat as long as she could hold them, for instead of swallowing the bits, she stored them in her throat, and regurgitated them later, eating at her leisure. She preferred, however, to be given a piece big enough to enable her to stand upon it and whack and tear it with her bill. Sometimes she got a piece of liver for dinner but she didn't like it, for it got her feet all messy. She soon found a remedy for this. When the liver was presented to her, she threw it down upon the sand. Seizing it by one corner she would drag it around. With some difficulty she would next manage to turn it over and drag it around again. This covered both sides with sand after which she would take it onto a perch and devour it. She liked nuts but ate no fresh vegetable. Fruit she ate sparingly, although cherries charmed her because of the pits, which she rolled around and around in her mouth.

One day we put a live mouse in the cage. She spied it before the door was shut and with a sudden movement, too quick to analyze, descended upon the mouse, killing it with one stroke of her bill. She spent nearly an hour killing it over and over again before she ate it, skin, meat, and bones. For days she would look eagerly all around the cage hoping for another mouse, but never again did we catch a live mouse. It seemed as though all mice had taken warning and moved to some other building, following the fate of their brother.

Maggie came to us on a September day. She stayed all winter. Her wing was healed, although it was a little out of line. February, March, April and May passed. The windows were open and our hearts ached for Maggie. We decided to get her into the open and see if the wing could carry her north to her companions. There was a great deal of squawking on the part of Maggie at being carried out to the edge of town. We put her down on real ground again, amongst grass and field daisies. She was plainly delighted and stalked about majestically but sad to say, she could not fly. We waited a long time thinking that it might be just disuse that kept her from winging away, but the wing was hopelessly injured. Then we knew that we must take her back to the safety of her cage, for to leave her there meant an early death at the jaws of some dog or the sharp claws of some lean neighborhood cat.

She kept warily just at the end of our fingers. We pursued her, faster and faster. She ran here, there. She grew tired, her bill opened and she gasped for breath. "Poor Maggie," we said but kept right after her. "Now I have her," cried the Professor and put his hand down hard. "Yaa!" screamed Maggie and with a great effort bounded away, leaving all but one feather of her lustrous tail in the Professor's hand. But at last we got her, too tired to utter another scream, and carried her back to the smallness of her wire cage. The weeks passed, Maggie seemed perfectly contented, and was quite busy growing a new tail. In four weeks she had not only grown a beautiful one, but several new wing feathers.

One day a little boy came to see us. He wanted Maggie. He had a big chicken yard with a little house in it, and he had had a magpie before, so after thinking the matter over we told him that Maggie might pay him a visit and see how she liked the proposed quarters. We went out to see her once or twice and found her very happy. The little boy said she had managed to break out of jail several times but at length the danger of this was remedied and she was secure. There was a pine tree in the chicken yard and Maggie could hop from branch to branch of this. She would sit on a limb and sing and gurgle her thanks for the out-of-doors palace that was hers, entertaining the children who came and chattered to her, calling her "Pretty Maggie."

For days as we came into the lobby or passed through into the workroom we missed her gurgling notes, her soft happy little notes, and the sight of her glossy feathers, but knowing she is happy we have left her to live out her life in the shade of the pine tree and remember her as one of our orphans whose little tragedy found a most fortunate termination among friends who cherish her and who can give her a suitable home.

A Genius in Feathers

Alan Devoe

HENRY WARD BEECHER once said that if human beings wore wings and feathers, very few of them would be clever enough to be crows. He might have added that few would be humorous, mischievous or unpredictable enough. The common crow, *Corvus brachyrhynchos*, whether in the wild state or kept as a pet, is a genius in feathers and an endlessly astonishing bird.

There was the one owned by a lady in Stuart, Ohio, that was so dainty that he insisted on washing worms before he would eat them. There was the Staten Island crow that not only could pick pockets, but, when he found a pocket empty, would cry, "Go to hell!" and fly away in a huff.

To be sure, not all crows can talk. Their individual ability varies greatly in this respect, and probably no crow can talk better if its tongue is split; but certain ones taken young have been known to learn a hundred words, and half as many complete phrases, and there are even records of wild crows picking up and raucously using such human expressions as "Giddyap!" and "Whoa!" and "Hey!" which they hear farmers shout in the fields.

When a crow does speak human language, he often gives the impression that he knows the exact meaning of what he is saying. A moonshiner, who had kept a pet crow as a lookout for revenuers, was taken to the jail in Harris County, Georgia. The crow was taken too. The human prisoner gave no trouble, but the bird proved something of a problem. He yelled, "I want water!" when the supply in the cell began to dwindle, and whenever an attractive female visitor passed through the jail corridor he craned his neck between the cell bars, ogled the lady and muttered ribaldly, "Oh-boy-oh-boy-oh-BOY!"

The common crow, with his three closely related varieties, the Florida crow, the southern crow and the western crow, is found practically all over our country east of the Rocky Mountains, as well as in sections in the Northwest and along our western coast down to southern California.

In building their nests, as in everything else, crows prove that they are individualists. Most often the nest, a bulky structure of coarse sticks, twigs, grasses and tree bark, lined with soft rootlets or fur or moss, is in an evergreen, and is about thirty feet from the ground. In rare instances it may be on the ground. They often decorate a nest by inserting in it a shiny pebble or glittering piece of glass.

As a rule there are four or five eggs, pale bluish-green, mottled with brown and black. I once watched the nesting-history of a crow family whose brood consisted of just one egg. In Wolfville, Nova Scotia, an astonished ornithologist found a nest loaded with ten eggs.

As crows are always more or less clannish, there are usually a number of nests within a small area, and the occupants exercise their sly mischievousness by incessantly stealing each other's nesting materials. When one of the nesters flies off to feed for a while, one of his dark neighbors rushes to the unprotected abode, adroitly removes from it the choicest bits of moss and rootlets, and secretes them in his own nest. Then, when the thief is absent from his nest for a while, the recently burglarized bird flies over and regains all the stolen goods, plus half a dozen other choice bits. This pilfering is probably a friendly joke, for actually crows are devoted to one another and are bound by a sense of unity that leads them to show each other extraordinary courtesy and understanding.

I have often watched how, when an injured crow emits caws of distress, his fellows rush to him from the surrounding countryside, lament over him as though agonized by his misfortune, and try to feed him restoratives. Edward Howe Forbush, the famous ornithologist, tells a story of a crippled crow that fell into the Merrimac River off Newburyport, Massachusetts, cawed desperately for help, and was rescued by fellow flock-members who worked in relays to keep him afloat and gradually to drag him ashore.

Being individualistic and unconventional, crows in the nesting season frequently become involved in sex mixups, and the eternal triangle is common among them. When this happens, fights rarely result; the trio settles down to an unorthodox design for living. It is not uncommon to see two males feeding the same brood of fledglings, with no disputes about the question of fatherhood, and I have seen two females alternately brooding a nestful of eggs while accepting the attentions of one strutting male who was their mutual husband.

Before crow babies hatch, mother and father usually go through a rehearsal of coming events. The female in the nest flutters her wings, coos, and pretends to be a baby; the male brings her tidbits and sings to her a peculiar, low sweet song. In a triangle situation involving two males, both perch on the nest-rim and sing a harmonious cradle-song duet.

The young stay in the nest about three weeks, consuming their weight in food every day, and by the time they are ready to leave they look almost like their parents except that their coats have less luster. For several days they practice flight maneuvers and wing drills before the critical elders of the flock. The oldsters show them the lay of the land and teach them the rules of the community of fifty or sixty crows nesting in the neighborhood.

Despite the individualism of its members, a flock is as disciplined as an army. It posts sentinels in a high tree to keep watch while the others feed. It has special flight maneuvers; low, fast and scattering for the mornings; high, slow and single-file for the evenings; forty-five miles per hour in absolute silence when the sentry signals that a man with a gun is coming. When traditional enemies such as owls or foxes are sighted, it is a rule that all flock-members must raise a terrific rumpus. Only when the young have been rigorously trained in these observances are they ready for adulthood.

The youngsters take advantage of their long apprenticeship to swindle as much free food as possible out of their parents. Although perfectly able by now to forage for themselves, they pester their elders with loud and piteous petitionings to be fed.

Sometimes the wilier of the young apparently feign illness in order to sponge on their parents. Crows begin to be geniuses at an early age.

Life for crows, as for all other creatures, consists principally of getting enough to eat and coping with enemies. Getting food affords an uproarious exercise, a never-ending antical game of sly jokes and preposterous stratagems.

Crows can and do eat almost anything; a wasp, a toad, or even poison ivy. They eat so many other things that a list of them takes three pages of fine type in a Department of Agriculture report. Certain items are special favorites, and crows' inventions for getting them are endless.

Hunting for mice, for instance, is tedious, so a crow sometimes rides on the back of a pig that is foraging in the field; when the rooting porker turns up a field mouse the wily bird gobbles the mouse and flaps off with a mirthful cackle. To get shellfish, which he loves but which his beak is not strong enough to open, a crow picks up a clam or oyster, flies high in the air, and drops the bivalve on a rock.

If a crow spies a fox carrying prey, he sets up a tumult that fetches all his brethren in the neighborhood; they then swoop down and pester the fox until he gives up his prize. Crows seek out a watermelon patch, puncture the rinds, and drink their fill of the sweet juice.

All crows have the gift of mimicry, but certain outstanding geniuses among them have so perfected the art that they can imitate the squawk of a hen, the whine of a dog, or the crow of a rooster. I have watched a crow, artfully concealed in a chicken yard, clucking and cackling and crowing to lure a hen from her chicks. When this failed, the crow strolled forth from concealment and walked maddeningly up and down in front of the hen until she made a rush at him, whereupon he skipped deftly aside, cawed stridently twice, and summoned two hidden crow-cronies who darted down and seized two of the chicks.

There is no limit to the hunting tricks of *Corvus*, and very little limit to his appetite and digestion. A pet crow belonging to a Long Island naturalist once consumed a pint of house paint and survived.

Aside from man, crows have few dangerous enemies. An owl sometimes raids a crow roost at night and kills a sleeping bird. Whenever crows locate an owl in daylight they mob him and thrash him to the accompaniment of a hubbub of foul imprecations. They gang up similarly on hawks, raccoons, skunks, cats and any other creatures that they know might harm their eggs or young.

Of humans, the wise and wily bird can afford to be almost contemptuous. Sentinels can spot a gun-barrel half a mile away, and never confuse it with a fish-pole or a walking-stick.

Crows have a vocabulary, some naturalists believe (and I am one of them), of at least twenty-five caw-words for keeping each other posted on doings in the neighborhood. All crows can hear so well that they detect the snap of a twig in the woods more acutely than any other wild creature except a deer. State and local governments have offered bounties on crows for years, but ornithologists wryly agree that there are more crows in the country today than there were when the Pilgrims landed.

Without serious threat from enemies or starvation, crows are free to spend much of their time in games and practical jokes. One favorite and rowdy game is Waking the Sleepers. On hot noondays they love to fly silently over the countryside, sneaking up on a slumbering rabbit and rapping him sharply on the skull or settling silently on the backs of drowsy cattle and then setting up a sudden uproar that terrifies the cows.

Another sport is Hide and Seek. A young crow leaves the flock unobtrusively, hides in a hollow tree, and loudly sounds the distress caw. The flock rushes to the spot, fails to find him, and flaps away again. The distress caw is again sounded. Back comes the flock, hunts vainly again, and again goes away. This may be repeated a dozen times, after which the young crow pops out of concealment and guffaws. The flock, far from being annoyed, bursts into a hawing and cawing of general merriment.

Crows amuse themselves by roaming the countryside looking for white pebbles, shells and similar bright objects, which they hide in caches to gloat over, and which they also use in their crowish version of a ball game. I watched this game last summer in a birch wood, which provided a perfect grandstand seat. There were seven crows playing. One, holding a white snail shell in his beak, would launch out from one of the small birch trees. The other six would fly after him, swooping down on him and buffeting the shell-bearer to make him drop his prize. When he did, the fallen shell would be snatched from the ground by another of the players, who would then launch forth, only to be set upon by his playmates in a repetition of the earlier performance.

Crows often stage concerts. An expert mimic and singer performs his repertory while the others of the flock perch in a rough circle around him and caw their applause. The most extraordinary rites of the flock, however, are the "trials" they conduct. When a crow has committed an offense against the laws of crowdom, the flock gathers together in judgment. The offender perches on a branch at some distance from the rest of the assemblage, while the other crows hold a caucus, parleying sometimes for hours. Then the discussion suddenly ceases and there is a moment of silence, after which the flock either rises in unison and flaps away about its business or swoops down in a mass dive upon the offender, pecks his eyes out, and buffets him to death.

In autumn the small summer flocks of crows gradually merge together into larger flocks, and presently they make their way to their great winter roosts. These roosts are sometimes 1500 miles south of the summer feeding grounds. A Johns Hopkins scientist calculated that the crow population of a vast roost not far from Baltimore was 230,000. A roost near Arlington National Cemetery once housed 150,000 crows; another at Peru, Nebraska, contained 100,000. These great roosts are used for centuries; records show that some of them have been occupied by wintering crows since the white man first arrived in this country.

The crow's cycle of life lasts (unless a shotgun interferes) for about twenty-five years. Except for guns or poison, almost the only thing that kills a crow is roup, a disease that causes inflammation of the mucous membranes, and blindness.

Crows' influence on agriculture is about evenly divided between harm and good. About 72 per cent of a crow's diet is of vegetables, fruits and nuts, about half the vegetable category being corn. The remaining 28 per cent is of insects, rodents, and a few odds and ends such as eggs and fledglings of birds, chicks, carrion, and reptiles.

If a tar or red lead repellent is used on seed-corn, crows leave it alone, and their rodent and insect diet makes them an asset on the farm. Sometimes, however, the crows come trooping back to the same cornfield when the ears are ripening, and peck small holes in the husks. They do not eat much, but water gets in and rots the ears.

Many are the tales told of the amazing doings of pet crows. One owned by William Crowder, the well-known naturalist, developed the perilous habit of playing with kitchen matches. Having to be away from home and not wanting the house burned down in his absence, Crowder hid the kitchen matches and left a box of safety matches in their place. On his return he found his pet throwing the safety matches out of the window one by one, and as he hurled them he leered at Crowder and cried, "Ha! Ha!"

An eminent crow named Pete that lived in the South in the 1830s was one of the most famous characters that the bluegrass country ever produced. Pete was responsible for the introduction of starting bells at race tracks. He was in the habit of frequenting the Georgetown race track, and on the day of a big race, just as the horses were being lined up, Pete created pandemonium by yelling, "Go!"

The knowingness of a crow is not the thought-born "intelligence" of a man. It is a thing of wild guiles and natural ingenuities, instinctive cunnings and an innate prankish glee. Its unexpected workings make its dusky possessor a perpetual entertainment and the source of constant surprise to all who observe.

A Question of Taste

Arthur Newton Pack

RANGER BUCHANAN had found a lick. This was no mere man-placed block of rock salt, but a great landslide scar where winter storms had sent tons of earth tumbling headlong down the gorge of Coal Creek and uncovered a soft powdery rock which had not been evident before. Was there some faint scent, or had some stray elk or deer discovered it merely by chance? Now every horned creature in the region seemed to know that here was a health-giving substance—a moderately alkaline mixture of iron and aluminum salts, so the chemist told us after analyzing our samples. But what did the animals know of chemical names? A month ago Buchanan had found it while on the lookout for poachers on the nation's preserve. He had reported to his chief, who knew we wanted to study elk; and here we were.

The American elk, or wapiti, is the most beautiful and stately of all the deer tribe. He is not really an elk, for the name belongs to the elk of Europe, an animal closely related to our moose. Some of the Indian tribes called him wapiti, and we might well let it go at that, believing that it is a good name. At any rate, when I first saw one of these great, tall, antlered bulls looking at me as I crept to the edge of the lick, my heart certainly went wapity-wapity-wap. I remembered that once—once upon a time—these handsome fellows had ranged from the Atlantic slope to the Rocky Mountains and beyond to the very Pacific; but now there are relatively few left and most of those were here in the Rocky Mountain woods. While the elk are content to stay in the mountains during the summer, the deep winter snows drive them down to the valleys where men make fences out of piled antlers.

We had traveled by train to the little flag station of Red Eagle on the southern boundary of Glacier National Park, to stand upon the diminutive platform and watch the transcontinental steam away. Then, shouldering our camera packs along the short trail to the middle fork of the Flathead, we ferried the swift crystal current in a rowboat and joined our pack train beyond at the point agreed upon several days before. Back in the saddle again after ten months of people and cities! A trail winding through the spruce forest, and at the end one of Vic's suppers, bed rolls and, most assuredly, the stars overhead!

Boots and saddles again while the morning dew still silvered the grass. No talking this time. Elk tracks cut the trail, here, there, everywhere, crossing and recrossing our path. Then at a blazed tree we dismounted, unlimbered our cameras and followed the marks of innumerable cloven hoofs toward the creek.

Crash! "Look! Two elk running through the brush!"

"Worse luck—we have startled the animals before we can reach the opening where we can photograph. There must have been outposts or sentinels between the lick and the trail."

"Listen—that curious high whistle is an elk calf calling."

Stumbling noisily, as humans do for all their efforts at silence, we emerged abruptly upon a great eroded slide of claylike material, which fell away from the brink in steep descent to Coal Creek, a hundred feet below. A band of about fifty elk had been pawing and licking the soft soil for the sake of the alkali or mineral contained in it; but, as the animals above stampeded, the whole herd broke away and charged downhill into a belt of trees along the stream. A few moments later we saw two bands, each herded by a large bull elk, strung out in single file as they climbed the opposite bank. Had we lost our chance for pictures? Patience would tell. Quietly we lay in the brush and after a few moments a lone cow and calf appeared from the thicket below and climbed the bank to delve in the mineral clay. Bill Finley sneaked down behind a log and got a few feet of film before the mother elk and her offspring became nervous and trotted away. We saw no more elk, but to the surprise of everyone a Rocky Mountain goat nanny and her kid appeared on the opposite slide, perhaps a thousand feet away across the stream. The mountain peaks were some miles distant, and she must have traversed a considerable area of forest between this natural lick and her ordinary home. It is rare to see a goat at so low a level in the summertime. The nanny and her kid worked back and forth across the slope, licking the soil from time to time. They were still there when we left to return to camp.

After breakfast the next morning we again rode up the trail. As we cautiously approached the edge of the lick a band of

ten animals could be seen about two hundred feet away. The cows, with their calves, quickly took flight and trotted down the well-marked trail toward the creek; but now a splendid bull seemed to materialize from the overhanging woods and walk slowly along the steep clay slope. I had put on the seventeen-inch telephoto lens and was only concerned lest the power should be too great for the nearness of the animal. The camera buzzed softly, and the big bull, who was really a remarkably fine specimen, seemed to lose his first fear of the silent human figures on the bank above him. Knowing that he could easily see us, we thought it best not to try to hide, but to appear busy about our own affairs, being careful only to make no sudden movement. This plan worked so well that after a while

I could even wind the camera without making him unduly nervous. The big wapiti stayed approximately in one spot, and there was very little action for the movies, until a feeling of nervousness suddenly possessed him and he, too, trotted swiftly down the worn path. Thereafter nothing happened. We simply waited and watched the mountain goat nanny and her kid, which we had observed the day before. They fed all across the opposite slide about a hundred feet down from the top; but, as noon approached, the old nanny also made her way up into the timber; and with the aid of the glasses we could see her lie down just within the shadow, the kid with her.

I spent an hour cleaning and repairing lenses, which had loosened up in some way from the horse transportation. The nanny and kid came down the opposite side of the lick to the very edge of the creek and appeared about to cross toward us. However, at the last moment she seemed to scent danger and worked around back up the hill. About three-thirty a smaller bull elk, but nevertheless a fine, full-grown animal, came up toward the lick from the brush along the creek. He sauntered up to the very top of the slide and gave me a number of good chances with the big telephoto lens before, like the others, he grew nervous and trotted away down the trail toward the crossing.

It was then that Bill Finley had a real inspiration—a brain wave we called it then; but none the less, next morning found our party of four divided. With repeated cautions to the others not to approach the upper side of the lick until a prescribed hour, two of us crept down to the creek and worked along the bank until the signs indicated that this was the main animal crossing. It was not hard to find, for the elk trail had been cut deep with the pounding of countless sharp hoofs, and the brush along the sides was worn away.

"Now one of us ought to hide up here in the bushes while the other crosses over to the opposite bank," whispered Bill. "Whichever direction they come, we'll shoot 'em from both sides. Shall I cross, or will you?"

Crack! Swish! Thump! Nearer and nearer came the sound. It meant just one thing—wapiti! They were coming on the run; coming directly down the hillside on top of us.

"Quick, get into the bushes behind that tree! There's no time to cross over or anything. Get going!"

Somehow we found ourselves on our knees far enough above the trail to avoid being trampled. We were barely in time, for at that instant three cow elk rushed down the slope, taking in effortless leaps logs and obstructions around which we had struggled painfully. Straight toward us, past at a distance of only a few feet, and then out, over and into the water, which flew into shining particles of spray. A calf clung closely to its mother. For an instant the vanguard paused in midstream, only to leap forward as with another crash a great, antlered bull bounded clear over log and bank and landed close behind them. Quickly the whole band plunged through the shallow water, wheeled to the right, and swung into a long, distance-covering trot. A few seconds later they were lost among the trees and only the rushing stream disturbed the stillness.

"I got 'em, Bill. Did you? We must have misjudged the time it took us to get here, for those animals were certainly running from something in the lick, probably from our own party."

Bill merely held up his hand and motioned, for there were more sounds above us; and immediately another band of wapiti came tearing by. We needed no telephoto lenses. There hadn't been time to fix them, anyhow. Once more the water churned into silver beneath three more cows and a slightly smaller bull—once more the glorious thrill, the buzzing of motion picture cameras—once more, silence.

Finley crossed the creek and set up his camera in a blind beyond. Hours passed. The wapiti had been frightened and were suspicious. One lone cow appeared upstream for a few moments and then hastily trotted back. She was the last. Indeed, although we left the lick strictly alone for a day or so and then returned cautiously, we never had another chance. The message had gone out that the mineral lick was being used by humans; and as far as the wapiti were concerned, we were welcome to eat all we wanted of the alkaline iron and aluminum salts—but certainly without their company.

We fished successfully and hoped in vain; the elk were too suspicious. But a mule deer doe made our acquaintance and came each morning and afternoon to our camp. Vic, the cook, put out salt for her in several places, but she did not seem to care for it. Mary, for we soon felt intimate enough to name her, had a predilection for camp fire ashes. No doubt it was the lye in the ash residue which satisfied her craving for something alkaline in a region of sweet water. At any rate, she came and licked and came again, until some inquisitive human who wanted to see whether Mary liked candy placed a wintergreen Life Saver on her favorite licking spot. Mary came trotting up, now convinced that even Vic's wood chopping nearby meant no harm. She stuck out her tongue, licked her lips, bent her head, and her tongue brushed the round white disc of wintergreen. Like a shot, all Mary's wiry muscles responded. She leaped into the air, wheeling at the same time, and bounded away with that curious, stiff-legged, jack-in-the-box motion of the mule deer kind. We did not see her again.

From the viewpoint of science we had not, perhaps, contributed greatly to the sum total of man's knowledge, even though we had observed at first hand the ways in which elk and deer obtain the minerals which their systems crave. Yet I think that there is a moral in the Life-Saver story, and that is that tastes are not all alike. Thank goodness!

Rocks that Left Home

Paul Mason Tilden

THE ADVANCE of the last great ice sheet over much of the northern portion of North America—the Wisconsin advance of the Pleistocene Ice Age—did more than alter the face of the land. It was subtly to touch and affect the lives, the habits and the history of the people who were to come to occupy its abandoned territory, some fifteen or twenty thousand years later.

The glacial ice determined, of course, the kind of life that would be lived on the land it uncovered. New rivers were formed. Glacial bogs and ponds were left strewed about in haphazard fashion. Old lakes were deepened, or perhaps eliminated entirely. The ice even dictated what portions of land the farmer-to-come could economically plant, and what portions he should allow to remain in pasture and woodland.

The line of demarcation between glaciated and unglaciated land in the United States undulates westerly from the eastern tip of Long Island far out into the Pacific Northwest, paralleling roughly the courses of the modern Ohio and Missouri river valleys. Few persons born and brought up north of this line are conscious of the difference between themselves and their brothers to the south. But let them cross the line, and they suffer from a queer nostalgia. There is something missing. They seldom know what that something is; but the moraines, the kames, the drumlins and the erratic boulders are not there, and the land somehow seems very different.

The glacial ice has entered into the daily life, the legend and history, and even the simple problems of creating homes, not only of our prehistoric Indians but of inhabitants down to the present day. It has created events and stories impossible in unglaciated lands. The Great Stone Face, immortalized by Nathaniel Hawthorne, is merely a case of the plucking of a mountainside by flowing ice. And you may recall the story of the young New Englander who joined the Continental Army in order to escape the back-breaking drudgery of laying up stone walls?

Riven from the mountainsides and carried either within or on the back of the great ice field were innumerable boulders of many shapes and sizes. Some of these were of majestic proportions. They encumbered the lands. Some of them traveled long distances, like the jasper boulders that originated north of Lake Superior and were dropped just south of what is now the Ohio River.

Man has a way of utilizing whatever nature has placed at hand; and the glacial boulders are no exception.

The Franconia Notch of New Hampshire's White Mountains is not a pleasant place in which to be caught in a full-scale blizzard, even in modern days. Despite the fine highway and the "blue angels"—below-zero patrol cars—a breakdown can still lead to discomfort, if nothing worse.

A Mr. Boise, traveling north through the Notch in the early eighteen hundreds, had neither a good highway nor a safety patrol to comfort him. He was on horseback riding over a road that was hardly more than a trail hacked through the wilderness. His destination was the tiny mountain village of Franconia, some miles to the northwest. In the Notch he was overtaken by a midwinter blizzard. With the temperature below zero and the snow driving horizontally through the ancient forest of the narrow valley floor, Boise must have concluded that the moment for an important decision had arrived.

Just off the road to his right, a great boulder loomed through the veil of snow. Boise urged his horse to it. Dismounting, he proceeded to kill and skin the animal. He then wrapped himself in the folds of the warm hide, and wedged himself under the deep overhang of the boulder. The next day a search party discovered him there, still alive, and extracted the hardy traveler from his armor of solidly frozen horsehide.

This friendly boulder is still commemorated as Boise Rock, in the Franconia Notch State Reservation. The unromantic geologist would tell you that Boise Rock is a glacial erratic. A bigger than average specimen, surely, but still just one of many millions scattered throughout the glaciated northern third of the nation.

Centuries before the arrival of the white man on the shores of the New World, a compact group of large erratics kept a close watch on the quarrying operations of the American Plains Indians at "the place of the red pipe-stone"—now Pipestone National Monument—near the city of Pipestone, Minnesota. From this curious soft red stone, later named catlinite, the important Indian ceremonial pipe was fashioned.

Incidentally, George Catlin, the traveler-painter for whom the pipestone was named, visited the quarries in 1836 and sent a sample fragment to a Boston mineralogist for analysis. The Boston mineralogist pronounced it a new mineral, although we now know that catlinite is not a mineral at all but is similar in composition to an indurated clay. Our modern geologists are somewhat puzzled, however, as to just how the catlinite at Pipestone was formed as a thin seam in a bed of massive quartzite, like a slice of luncheon meat in a huge sandwich.

While Indian legend concerning the pipestone quarry and its surroundings varies in detail from tribe to tribe, it is pretty much in agreement on one point; that the guardian spirits of the place made their abode beneath the group of glacial boulders. Before the brave could quarry and carry away his precious bits of pipestone, humble supplication and offerings of tobacco to the spirits were necessary.

One would naturally expect to find the greatest abundance of erratics in places where the ice sheet had plenty of upthrust bedrock to pluck away. In the New England States, erratics occur in great swarms at many places; and now and then we come on an individual, sitting in woodland or old pasture, that appears to have had a segment bitten from it. Freezing water, of course, will get into cracks and fractures of a boulder and wedge out pieces. But freezing water has never been known to leave a line of drill marks on the broken edge of the rock. Earlier settlers of New England lacked such conveniences as quarries, so when a man needed a good solid door-step, or some underpinning for a new barn, he

took a stone drill and sledge to the nearest suitable erratic and hewed out what he wanted.

Now and then a giant is found among the lesser fry, like a whale in a school of minnows. A hundred and thirty years ago, a flourishing lawyer in the village of Lancaster, New Hampshire, decided to build a stone house. Every slab of granite that went into the house was cut from a single glacial boulder found at Maidstone, Vermont, a few miles up the Connecticut River.

Just east of the pleasant hamlet of Bristol, Vermont, where the highway strikes through a break in the precipitous western front of the Green Mountain range, there is a great glacial erratic on which is engraved the Lord's Prayer. Reasonably enough, it is known as the Lord's Prayer Rock. But there is no visible explanation for this piece of handiwork, and curious tourists who stop for a closer look are naturally perplexed.

As a rather sensitive youngster growing up in Bristol, Joseph Greene was all too familiar with the blasphemy of the teamsters who whipped their horses up the long grade of the highway east of town. Possibly the teamsters of Bristol were more vivid of language than their brothers elsewhere. Whether or not that is so, Joseph Greene carried the memory of the bad language with him, even after he had become a successful physician in Buffalo. So, during one of his visits to his childhood home of Bristol, he ordered that the Lord's Prayer be engraved on the boulder by the side of the highway that had so offended him.

There is a glacial erratic in the town of Nottingham, New Hampshire, that would tip a rather larger-than-ordinary set of scales at about six thousand tons. It acquired its name in a rather unorthodox manner. It appears that a mentally disturbed man by the name of Churchill, being detained in the neighborhood of Nottingham, escaped his keepers and made off through the woods. A pursuit party was organized, and the demented man was finally discovered perched atop this great glacial fortress. Considering the near-vertical sides of the boulder, Churchill had performed a climbing feat of no mean proportions. The question arosc as to how bcst bring him down, keeping an eye on minimum casualties. After several fruitless attempts by the party to scale the boulder, someone suggested that a tree be felled across its top to act as a bridge. This was done, and the occupant of the summit was taken safely into custody. Churchill Rock had thus been christened.

At about the same time, Benjamin Prescott, Governor of New Hampshire, heard stories about glacial boulders of fabulous size in neighboring States. Feeling that the honor of the Granite State was impaired by such reports, the Governor personally led an expedition into the field to search for an erratic that might qualify as the Biggest Boulder Ever Discovered. The results of his investigation were not apparently wholly satisfactory. However, some years after the passing of Governor Prescott, a real find was made in the township of Madison—a glacial boulder that is believed to be the largest discovered to the present time. It is a single block of granite measuring eighty-three feet long, thirty-seven wide, and twenty-three high, with an estimated weight of something more than seven and a half thousand tons. No collector's item, that!

Glacial erratics used as historical or commemorative markers are a familiar sight in the public parks of the north. Where the ice sheet was most accommodating, the boulders were dropped in the right places, ready to be inscribed, or smoothed for a bronze tablet. The less favored park managements are constrained to scurry around and bring one in, which is easily done in most glaciated areas.

Perhaps the most famous of the commemorative erratics sits astride the line drawn up by the American minutemen April 17, 1775, on what is now Lexington Green in the village of Lexington, Massachusetts. On this boulder are engraved the fateful words of Captain Parker: *"Stand Your Ground—Don't Fire Unless Fired Upon—But If They Mean To Have a War —Let it Begin Here."*

High up on one of the sloping granite shoulders of the South Bubble in Acadia National Park perches a great round boulder. If you should climb up to this rock—as many visitors do every year—you can easily see that the boulder did not originate from the bedrock of the mountain. From the valley below, there appears to be no good reason for it to stay there. As you look, you almost expect to see it start plunging down the bare upper brow of the South Bubble. Actually, there is little chance of such a happening, although possibly an earthquake of the first magnitude might turn the trick.

To thousands of visitors from unglaciated parts of our country this boulder, silhouetted darkly against the skyline, is a first experience with the substance of the phenomenon we call the great continental ice sheet. Even those who have been brought up among the glacial relics of the north sometimes leave Acadia with the impression that this child of the ice is waiting for something—possibly the return of its parent. Who can tell?

Tail Tales

Edwin Way Teale

MANY YEARS AGO, I wrote a syndicated editorial that I called "The Pig's Tail."

A cat, I pointed out wisely, has a tail that *is* a tail. It helps her maintain her balance when she walks along a back-fence. It is furry enough to wrap around her feet and keep them warm in winter. It is long enough to form a kind of lightning rod and warn of danger from the rear.

Other animals also have tails of some utility. The long hairs of a horse's tail provide it with an efficient fly-swatter. A dog's tail is a barometer of emotion. A woodpecker's tail is a brace and a prop when it clings to the bark of a treetrunk. But what does a pig's tail do?

Nothing, I concluded. It is not long enough to curl around its feet and keep them warm. It is not strong enough to form a prop, or hairy enough for a flyswatter. It is a mere spinal raveling—a blemish on an otherwise streamlined body.

That is what I thought. But not for long! No sooner did the editorial appear than my mailbox overflowed with letters. Farmers took their pens in hand to set me straight. Butchers laid down their cleavers to heckle me. Pig-raisers took delight in ribbing an ignoramus. There appeared to be some sort of a fraternity of Friends of the American Porker at work. The barrage continued for weeks.

Did I not know, the letters asked, that the curl in a pig's tail shows its physical and emotional condition? Did I not know that a limp-tailed pig is a sorry sight? Did I not know that a porker with its tail tightly curled is something to gladden the heart of the farmer? Furthermore, had I not heard that, in some circles, pigs' tails are considered a great delicacy and bring a fancy price?

The final stroke, however, came from a man of seventy-five, a retired farmer living in Champaign, Illinois. If, he inquired blandly, I were trying to catch a pig in a barnyard, would I not appreciate the convenience of having a handle at the rear? Just how would I hold a pig if it did not have a tail?

From that day forward, I have been a changed man. No more have I referred to anything in nature as entirely useless. Things may seem pointless. They may appear devoid of utility. But that is just because we do not know enough. Once we comprehend their possibilities, we usually discover they have many uses—as many as the tail of a pig.

There is, for instance, the matter of other tails in the animal kingdom. The uses to which they are put are amazingly varied. They form tools, and weapons, and means of locomotion. They are used for everything from breathing mechanisms to catapults, and from plows to pantries.

Everyone is familiar with the tiny, red-eyed *Drosophila* fruit fly that swarms around bunches of overripe bananas. Most people know the important part it has played in the study of genetics because of the rapidity with which generation follows generation. But few people are aware of the wonderful way in which the children of some of these flies, the wingless larvae, travel through the air by using their tails as springboards. Bending their bodies like bows, they grasp their tails in their mouths. Then, as they suddenly let go, they are tossed aloft. Catapulting through the air in this manner is their strange form of locomotion.

One whole group of primitive insects, the springtails, have a somewhat similar method of moving about. A locking mechanism beneath their bodies holds the end of their bristle-tails when they are curved forward. Whenever the insect wishes to move, it simply releases the locking mechanism. The tail straightens out, and its owner is hurled forward in a leap through the air. Some springtails appear on the surface of snow during mild spells in midwinter. At times, their numbers are so vast they look like patches of dust blowing about. These insects are commonly known as snow fleas. Other springtails hop about on the surface film of water.

Under water, tails play an important part in the everyday life of aquatic creatures. They are the powerful propellers of the fish, driving them about or holding them against swift currents. In the sun-warmed shallow water along the muddy edges of ponds, tadpoles swim with tails they later lose, tails that suggest detachable outboard motors. The alligator uses its long lizard-tail, tapering and armored, for a propeller in water and a weapon on land. Pushed forward by its sinuous drive, it can swim like an otter, while one sidewise lash of the heavy tail on land can knock a man off his feet as though he had been hit by a club wielded by a powerful giant.

Among the underwater vegetation of ponds and streams, the nymphs of dragonflies creep about on six spindly legs. They move slowly. But when a dragonfly nymph wishes to make speed, it can become almost literally an underwater rocket. After drawing water into its body, it expels it forcibly from the end of its tail. This jet propulsion drives it forward in sudden spurts of speed.

Another aquatic nymph has similar ability. This is the immature May fly. Still another distinction is held by this insect. Long appendages, frequently feather-shaped, extend back from the end of its tail. They are external gills. As the creature moves about, they are constantly bathed in water from which they extract oxygen. The nymph of the May fly thus breathes through its tail. In the manner of a fish, it obtains its oxygen from the water.

Another odd creature, living a submerged existence during its early days, also breathes through its tail, but it breathes air. This is the so-called rat-tailed maggot. Ever since the days of the eighteenth-century scientist, Réaumur, who gave the creature its name, it has been of interest to entomologists. The offspring of the drone fly, *Eristalis tenax,* the rat-tailed maggot feeds on decaying matter in shallow water. Every summer I find several of these curious creatures in the water collected in a small knothole in an apple tree near my home. The adult flies lay their eggs on the water in small white rafts. The hatching larvae sink to the bottom. As they have no gills and must breathe air, nature has provided them with the prototype of the submarine diver's air hose.

Their tails are drawn out into a long tube, which can be lengthened or shortened like a telescope. The tip is held above the surface film by radiating hairs which keep it from sinking down into the water. Thus the immature flies spend their days and nights on the bottom of the Lilliputian lake within the knothole cavern of my orchard tree, all the while breathing through their hollow tails air from a far different realm beyond the surface film. When their larval days are over, they enter this world as winged adults.

The surface film of water, transparent and amazingly thin, is the roof of the world for many creatures that dwell in ponds and lakes and streams. Although it is so insubstantial we can neither feel nor see it, it is a solid support to mosquito larvae. From it, like the proverbial monkey, the wigglers hang by their tails. The surface film is connected with still another odd employment for a tail. Female damsel flies sometimes descend beneath the water to lay their eggs in submerged vegetation. Because they might have difficulty breaking through the surface film again, the male damsel fly acts as a kind of living locomotive pulling ahead of the female. The tip of its tail is equipped with a pair of claspers, which, like the coupling on a train, connect it with the damsel fly behind.

When a squirrel leaps from branch to branch in a treetop, or a falling cat twists so it lands on its feet, its tail plays an important part in the procedure. It aids the animal greatly in maintaining its balance. In a different way, the long tail of the kangaroo—besides providing a kind of chair on which it can sit when at rest—acts as a balancer when it is making tremendous leaps through the air, standing erect and using its hind legs alone. A slow-motion version of an animal using its tail to maintain its balance is provided by the king crab, that primitive dweller in the sea that is shaped like a shallow dishpan with a slender spikelike tail projecting to the rear. The tail is a pry with which the crab rights itself when it is upset. Without its assistance, the horseshoe crab might never again regain its feet once it was overturned on the shore.

The tail of this sea-dweller is a lever. The tails of other creatures resemble plows and shovels and hammers. When an immature ant lion digs a pit in the dry sand in which to catch its victims, its half-inch, seedlike body begins moving around in a small circle. The ant lion always walks backward. The tail of its flattened body, tilted down, cuts into the sand like a plowshare. As the quartz-grains slide up along its back, it gives convulsive jerks of its head to throw the sand to one side. Moving in a narrowing circle, and using its tail for a plow and its head for a shovel, it produces its conical pit.

The tails of several animals aid in the identification of tracks left in snow, mud or sand. Thus the dainty deer mouse usually leaves visible evidence of its slender tail. The muskrat registers its tail tracks beside its watery home; here the turtle also, dragging its smooth plastron, often leaves its mark.

More aggressive is the part played by the tail of the porcupine. The stroke of its tail driving home quills and the stroke of a hammer driving in nails have much in common. Far different employment is found for the smooth bare tail of the sleepy-eyed opossum. When taking her children for a ride on her back, the mother opossum curves her tail forward so all the riders can wind their tails around hers and, thus, like inverted subway strap-hangers, cling safely.

To anyone who has had cxpcricncc in the woods, the sight of a skunk with its tail cocked at a certain angle is a warning not to be disregarded. Tail signals of other kinds are likewise familiar. On forest ponds the beaver brings its wide, flat tail down on the surface of the water with a slap that echoes far through the woods. It is a warning signal that sends all the other members of the colony diving into the safety of the pond. However, of all tails that provide warning sounds, the most famous is undoubtedly that of the rattlesnake. The high whir of the horny rattles at the tip of its tail is a look-out signal understood by every creature of the wild.

Although the mouth of the western gila monster, like that of the rattlesnake, contains poison, its tail serves a far different purpose. It is a kind of living pantry. In it the lizard stores up food in the form of fat for a time of need. In the case of the scorpion, it is the tail and not the head that is poisonous. This tail ends in a needle-sharp tip that is jabbed into a victim to inject the venom. Not far different is the tip of the tail of the honeybee and wasp. Their stings, like hypodermic needles, inject a milder venom into the body of a victim. The tail of the parasitic ichneumon fly, a relative of the wasp, has an even more sinister application. It ends in an ovipositor, or egg-placer, which operates something like an old-fashioned corn planter to deposit eggs in the tissues of caterpillars. These parasitic eggs hatch into larvae that devour their host. Another more pleasant application of a tail in relation to eggs is found among the crayfish. Here the eggs, or crayfish "berries," are fastened by a sticky secretion to the underside of the tail. They are carried about and protected in this manner until they hatch. Lobsters have a similar practice.

In numerous ways, tails are lifesavers. The mole, tunneling in the darkness of its underground burrow, depends upon its extremely sensitive little tail, thrust out behind it like a lightning rod, to warn it of danger from the rear. The Luna moth, fluttering about in the dusk of summer evenings, trails its long ribbon-tails behind it. They are thought to form a sort of matador's cape, attracting the attention of enemies so they direct their attack farther away from the vulnerable body of the moth.

A few years ago, a noted New England ornithologist told me of something he had seen with a friend in Florida. On a field trip, one day, they came upon a water snake in the process of swallowing a smaller garter snake. The victim had twisted its tail around until it was actually tied in a knot, which would have prevented the attacker from completing its meal. When the two men disturbed the water snake, it let go its victim. Immediately the garter snake untied the knots in its tail and wriggled away apparently little the worse for its experience. This seemed such a tall tale that the ornithologist told me he had never published anything about it for fear of being called a nature faker. But he had asked his friend to write him his recollection of the event some time later, and it tallied in every respect with his own.

I told this tall tail tale, one day, to my friend, Dr. Charles M. Bogert, head of the herpetology department at the American Museum of Natural History. To my surprise he said he did not doubt it at all. Then he told me another even more remarkable instance of a reptile using its tail to save its life. With it, I will end this record of the odd and manifold ways in which various creatures put their tails to special uses.

In the West, there is a lizard that sometimes employs an astonishing ruse to avoid being swallowed by a snake. The lizard loops its body around the limb of a tree and grasps its tail in its mouth. In this position, it presents the appearance of a doughnut. There is no loose end at which the snake can begin the process of swallowing. After futile attempts to find a starting point, the outwitted serpent may crawl away down the tree. Its intended victim lets go of its life-saving tail and scrambles away, alive and relatively unharmed.

Flowers Tell the Easter Story

M. H. Berry

PHOTOGRAPHS BY THE AUTHOR

"BEHOLD, He has risen," the angel said. "His countenance was like lightning, and his raiment white as snow: And for fear of him the keepers did shake."

Through the centuries fact and legend have become intermingled with the story of the Crucifixion. Animals, flowers, and even the elements have become woven into its story. But in the spring, at Easter, it is especially fitting that flowers should help tell of it, for they too, in a different way, are resurrected.

Man, through the ages, has marveled at this wonderful awakening of the wild things, and has naturally associated the advent of spring with the resurrection of the Lord. Thus, in fact and legend, the flowers tell the Easter story.

Left: *According to legend, the flowers of the redbud tree were white, but upon the night that Judas betrayed Christ, the flowers changed to crimson, and when the body of Judas hung from its boughs, the branches drooped and drops of blood from the flowers stained the ground.*

Right: *The Legend of the Easter lily belongs to Mary, the mother of Jesus. St. Thomas refused to believe in the resurrection of the Virgin Mary and had her tomb opened, which he found full of white lilies. Then he looked up and saw the Virgin ascending into heaven. She dropped a snow-white lily at his feet—an Easter lily—symbolic of the purity of the Virgin Mary and the flawless life of Jesus.*

Above: *As the Savior was carrying His Cross, most of the plants along the way laid their bodies prostrate so that His feet might be spared the rocks in the path. The trumpet flower was an exception; as the Lord passed he was cruelly tripped on its branches. From that day the trumpet flower became a dependent vine with the blush of shame upon its petals and the mark of the Cross on its pith, and it is appropriately called the "cross vine."*

Left: *As far back as the fourteenth century, Jehan de Mandeville wrote, "Then was our Lord yled into a gardyn, and there the Jewes scourged hym, and maden hym a crowne of the branches of the White Thorne, whiche grew in the same gardyn, and setten yt vppon hys hed."*

Above: When Jesus said, "Father, into thy hands I commend my spirit," he gave up the ghost. The darkness that had prevailed gave way to sunshine. The shadow of the Cross fell upon a violet, which drooped its head in deep sorrow and a purple color spread over its petals as it mourned.

Left: In this single flower is found the entire story of the Passion. The fringed border is the crown of thorns. The column in the middle spreads into a cross. Above the cross are the nails that pierced His hands and feet. The lance-shaped leaves represent the lance that pierced His side, and beneath them are brown spots symbolic of the thirty pieces of silver. Along the stem are tendrils representing the cords that bound Him.

Upstream with the Alewives

Edith M. Patch

PERHAPS IF THE alewife had been differently named, poets would have sung of its beauty and made epics of its travels. Better than a poem, however, is the experience of lifting one of these fishes from the water and holding it to the light for a moment before returning it to continue on its strange journey. It is worth a memory to hold in the hand a spirit of spring: a living mosaic with jewels flatly pressed and overlapping, blue-black gems near the back, then amethysts brilliant and deep, then gleaming hundreds of opals fading to pearls.

When the fish slips into water again, its colors are lost. There is little more to be seen than its dull dark-blue back so near the surface of the water that the dorsal fin is exposed like a small black sail unfurled.

Nearby are thousands of similar sails, a fleet of small black fins voyaging from ocean depths upstream to the ponds. For spring has called the alewives. Who knows how? Let a physiologist fathom their reactions if he can. It is not for a mere naturalist to guess how the alewives feel when they steer their fleets toward fresh water where their little black sails, in annual millions, pass up the Atlantic streams.

The scent of arbutus is still in the air when they come, the elder buds, in purple cones, are nearly ready to burst into cream white bloom, and the maple blossoms are hanging red; but I doubt that the scent or color of flowers reaches the alewives in the sea. The frogs are in full chorus, the toads are trilling, the bobolinks are jubilant with Northland joys, the meadow larks are calling "Spring is here"; but I doubt that song of batrachian or of bird quickens the alewives in their ocean depths.

Yet, somehow, spring touches them intimately, impelling, and the alewives can no more resist their impulse to migrate to fresh water than the bobolinks can refrain from their northward flight. The birds that come four thousand miles for a nesting site have, I think, an easier journey than the fishes; for however smooth their way may be during their ocean voyage, the alewives that venture into a certain Maine brook head into a hazardous course when they enter fresh water with its unknown dangers.

Pausing one day in mid-May at the mouth of Patten's Pond Stream, I glanced down upon a fleet of little black sails.

Countless thousands of alewives were waving their dorsal fins above the surface of the water in Surry Bay just where it was rippled by the rapids of the stream. The fishes were held until the rise of the tide. As they waited there, not deliberately of course, but blindly, they seemed a parable. How often we wait, as unwittingly as they, for the turn in some inscrutable tide.

The fate of that fleet suddenly gripped my imagination with its pathos, its exhilaration. The refrain of a passing meadow lark reminded me that pathos was a false note, sung out of key by a foolish human dread of the dangers that were ahead. So I choked that back and resolved to follow the fortunes of the alewives from sea to pond joyously as a spring adventure.

The water in the bay was calm and shining under the morning sun. The birches on the near shore still showed that grace of line and tracery against the vivid sky that is theirs before the buds burst bounds and hide the twigs behind their shimmering green. Across the bay, pine and cedar and fir dotted the slope with dark shades that accentuated the delicacy of spring tints. From shore to shore stretched a white line of waiting gulls.

The tide was low and the water gushed out of the mouth of the stream over rocks that were too high for the fishes to climb. The leaders of the eager migrants pushed up into the fresh water as far as possible before they paused, edging into easier eddies at the right of the main stream.

The adventure of following the alewives, it seemed, was for the present somewhat whimsically an affair of inaction. Well, if the fish could wait and the gulls could wait, I could.

The slow tide came in. The eager alewives begain to mount the rapids. The gulls circled up and pounced down. The birds were not lovely to watch while they fed upon the flapping fish they dragged to the shore. Their curdling screams may have voiced a mad joy at the sight of food, or they may have expressed frantic warnings to their fellows to give way to desperate comrades. It was their right to feast. They had waited the turn of the tide and there was so many thousands of fishes. But their weird racket cut through my logic to my heart and I went down to the edge of the rocks. The gulls lifted a wail of anger and disappointment but I refused to give heed. After all, my self-appointed adventure was not with the gulls but with the fish, and while I stood guard near the entrance of the stream the alewives mounted the initial rapids unmolested.

When the swift and swirling water threw one of them out of balance the fish would often fight up and over a rock sidewise, perhaps getting a purchase with its fins and the saw-edge of its belly against the irregularities in the surface of the rock. That was a comparatively slow process during which its silver side shone through the shallow water. The normal way for one to mount, however, was to shoot straight up the current, back up and belly down. This was done in a flash, the back showing under the water a "blue streak" as it went. An alewife does not leap clear of the water to jump the rapids as a salmon or trout does but takes its chances, head into the current.

Again and again the migrants were tossed back by the water. Again and again they made undaunted efforts. Even those—and they were very many—whose backs and sides had been torn open by the gulls kept steadfastly to their purpose. Courage and almost inconceivable patience are the terms one naturally applies to their performance. Yet as I watched I wondered whether either virtue, as humanly considered, had anything to do with an alewife's endeavor. Was it not, rather, desire that led them up the stream—whelming desire possessing the fish physically and, as much as may be, mentally? Watching them, I hoped so. Courage and patience seemed too inadequate, too pathetic a vista through which to view them. It needed something more fundamental, more relentless, more unwavering and less sad to explain a struggle like this. There must be, to guide them, desire, sufficient in itself, its gratification its own reward. I could not believe that nature forced such an annual issue without inherent compensation. And, though the alewife must mount the stream or die in the attempt, there was no reason why I should mix human psychology with its journey. It must be that each movement of its splendid body was made in physical enjoyment of even the struggle. And once up the rapids the quiet water above was a comforting place for resting.

The alewives gathered in such placid stretches after their initial triumph, their numbers increasing until their black dorsal fins showed a fleet filling the quiet water. After a respite they swam on and through a second series of rapids a few rods up stream.

They rested again near Surry Bridge and thousands of the fishes went no farther on their journey. A fate more potent, if less spectacular than the gulls met them here. Mankind took a large economic toll. I liked to note that, while his livelihood was linked with his catch of alewives, the captain who directed their affairs at the bridge looked kindly at such of the fish as were permitted to pass on. He moved lodged bits of wood to give them easier passage. He shifted stones to widen a resting pool. When tormenting youngsters were inclined to disturb the fish he prevented them, saying "Don't do it, boys. They have a hard enough time as it is."

Indeed, the whole course looked to a bystander like an obstacle race; although I surmise that had the alewives voices they would have gone upstream singing. It helped me, somehow, to listen to the bobolinks that had concluded their migration as I watched these other voyagers still with a long, long way to go.

Not long as miles are measured, for it is about three miles from Surry Bay to Patten's Pond. But long in hours when the weather is cold, for it took the fishes a week to climb the half mile between Surry Bridge and Six-foot Falls.

An old willow, leafless still, stood beside the rapids a little way beyond the bridge. How many springs had its bare branches reached over the migrant parents as they went up toward the ponds, and how many summers had its leaves shaded the migrant young as they came down toward the sea? The tree looked so large and lasting. An alewife looked so small and fleeting. Yet the life of the willow was a mere hour in the stretch of years during which alewives had been coming and going on their annual way.

It was, indeed, a place for solitude. A group of leafless birches stood at the brook's brim, their trunks tall and slender and white against the dark neighboring evergreens and their reflections shimmering in the water.

The dark fins of many alewives showed in quiet places and at the falls the fishes were nosing into the rapids. Their attempts, rebuffs, repeated efforts, ultimate successes, stirred my imagination and admiration as they had at the initial rapids at the mouth of the stream. I found myself again praising their courage and patient endeavor. And again, as the fish sped up into the strong tumbling water, I was reminded that not courage but something more steadfast led these migrants irresistibly on their way. Each fish, as it conquered the rapids, seemed glad of body.

It was, this season, a fortnight's journey for the fasting alewives from the sea to the mill pond, a distance of about two miles as men reckon it. The mill, with its cellar of gushing torrents and bewildering detours, held many handicaps and not a few tragedies; but most of the fishes fought through and around and then up a sluiceway into the Mill Pond, the first in a chain of three lakes.

Once in placid water, would the fish stay? Was not one pool as good as another? Evidently not, to journeying alewives. They must be moving again, after a rest. Perhaps the sound of water roaring at the dam challenged them to yet another victory. Perhaps the feel of the incoming current lured them to even better waters for their errand. At any rate on to the dam they swam and there again made difficult passage. They could not know that they now had their ultimate triumph over the wayward stream, and that the last serious obstacle in their fresh water race was behind them. But I knew it and felt strangely relieved.

While I stood looking across the water of the Lower Pond, my eyes resting on a pleasant island and then beyond to the strong hills, a glad sound, not soon to be forgotten, poured into the June day. Above me in the branches of some old birches more than twenty purple finches, rich of hue and melodious of voice, were in full chorus, filling the air with their song of June.

The songless fishes in the water below—had they some quiver of springtime joy? I liked to think they had while they were on their now quiet trail which led to one more pond, the third.

In the woods not far from the shore of that Upper Pond was a brown bent stem of a last year's bracken fern. Under the fern there was a brown nest lined with the dry spills of white pine. In the nest were the green-blue eggs which betokened that a pair of hermit thrushes had reached their migration's end.

The migrations of the finny wanderers had also come to an end; and in due time their eggs would be entrusted to that watery cradle which is the annual goal of alewives, passing upstream from sea to pond.

The Wit of a Red Squirrel

William L. and Irene Finley

YEARS AGO before we built our home, we had a little cabin on the lower part of our ten acres by the river. We used this for a summer camp and for occasional outings the rest of the year. One day in midwinter when I went out to work around the place, I put my lunch on the table and at the side of it I laid three apples. The morning was spent cleaning up some brush, but at noon when I entered the cabin, I noticed the apples were gone, while the rest of the lunch was untouched. I thought someone had played a joke on me and was hiding nearby. I looked all around and waited, but no one appeared.

The disappearance of the apples puzzled me. They were not in the cabin, not even in the stove, the woodbox or under the sink. As I was down on my knees looking under the cupboard, my eye happened to catch a tiny bit of peeling in the corner. It looked like a clue. If someone had eaten my apples, the cores and even the seeds were gone. I went outside, examined the ground, and climbed to the roof. Of course I knew a pair of red or pine squirrels lived in the big Douglas fir, but I hadn't heard or seen them during the morning. Besides, I saw no way a squirrel could get the apples out of a closed cabin.

The more I thought of the matter, the more I felt the pair of squirrels might know the whereabouts of the missing fruits. I climbed up the steep wooded hill toward the fir. Looking across to a maple tree, I saw one of the apples in a crotch twenty feet from the ground. Another was in the crotch of the next tree higher up. On the branch of the fir, with his tail curled over his back, sat Mr. Douglas Squirrel enjoying the third apple.

Going back into the cabin, I said to myself: "If the little fellow will tell me how he did it, I will gladly give him four times as many apples." Looking over the situation, I discovered a round hole that looked about the size of the apple up in the corner just below the shingles. One fruit looked to be a good-sized load for a squirrel. I decided he had sunk his teeth into each apple and climbed up the side of the wall. The tiny bit of peeling I had discovered in the corner showed he had had difficulty at least with one apple. He had surely earned the fruit; the joke was on me.

The red squirrel of the east, often called

Chickaree, and the red, pine or Douglas squirrel of the Pacific Coast, with their near relatives, live in most of the wooded country of America north of Mexico. Wherever there are forests of pine, fir, spruce or hemlock, from the seashore to timberline on a snow-capped peak, and beyond the trail's end in the forest, you may find the red squirrel with a jerking tail at one end and a chatterbox at the other. He flashes from branch to branch with an outburst of energy. His playground is the trunk of a tree. Dashing up, he circles, then swings around the rough bark, stands on his head and jumps into almost impossible positions.

On the Pacific Coast, Chickaree is a sleight-of-hand artist in the matter of his clothes. He changes with the climate. In the humid, heavily wooded region bordering the Pacific, he wears a coat that is rich, dark brown, but underneath it changes to a beautiful orange tone. A day's travel from there to the eastern slope of the Cascades, and his dress changes to grayish above and tan instead of orange below. Another day's travel to the east, and the little fellow is paler gray with white under parts, more like the Chickaree of the Atlantic.

John Muir called the Douglas squirrel "Phillillooeet," an Indian name. Pronounce it rapidly with the first syllable heavily accented, and it is not unlike the call of the squirrel when he is excited. The typical note is his explosive, musical whistle —clear and emphatic. He sings this for his own pleasure and amusement. Sometimes it has a pleading tone. His rapid trilling song is often drawn out with longer or shorter cadences. At times he gives a peculiar note that is very birdlike in character, quite enough to deceive one into thinking he is about to meet a strange feathered friend.

"He is the mockingbird of squirrels," sums up John Muir, "pouring forth mixed chatter and song like a perennial fountain: barking like a dog, screaming like a hawk, chirping like a blackbird or a sparrow; while in bluff, audacious noisiness he is a very jay."

When we come to study Chickaree's habits, shall we ever know his real influence in planting seeds and the distribution of our forest trees? Nearly every fall when the hazelnuts are ripe, we watch him gathering his store on our side hill. He never travels any distance on the ground but always follows his aerial runways across the bridges of the limbs. One day, when he was busy, I sneaked around through the trees to the bottom of the hill. He was making regular trips about fifty yards up to some hazel bushes. I marked the spot where he was storing nuts in a hole in the ground. When I thought he had finished, I sneaked over and, clearing away the covering of dry leaves, I dug out twenty-three nuts. Before I could replace them and get away, the squirrel had discovered me. He was as mad as an old hen when her chicks are bothered. He sputtered and chattered until I went away; then he ran down, uncovered the store, and one by one got the nuts out in a hurry. He was so excited he would grab one and run off a short distance, shove it hurriedly under the leaves and grass, and go back for another. Thus he soon had the nuts scattered in a dozen different places. I was satisfied he would never find them all again, yet the squirrel family stood to win in either case. Those that he did find later on he could eat when he needed them, and those he failed to find would grow up into more bushes for a future harvest.

The cones of the Douglas fir ripen in August, and by September they begin to open. This is Chickaree's busiest season. Out to the tip of a limb a hundred feet from the ground he runs, snips off the cones with his scissorslike teeth, springs quickly back and jumps to another branch, the very model of industry. With his quick, jerky disposition, he is never slow. His task looks dangerous, yet he never seems to miss his hold. At the end of the long, swaying branches, he is just as sure-footed as I am walking on the ground a hundred feet below.

But this is not saying he may not meet with an accident. For years, our pine squirrels have used a regular trail through the treetops from one side of our ten acres to the other. They know the exact branches to take along the maple lanes and the by-paths of the dogwoods, oaks and firs. They travel with speed and guide their steps with almost unerring accuracy. But once I saw an accident. A Douglas squirrel was up about thirty feet and jumped from the limb of a fir to a maple. He lost his footing and landed in the bushes below with all feet spread like a flying squirrel. He was mad through and through at his foolish slip and scampered up the fir trunk in a jiffy, spitting out words which, if interpreted in our language, might not be suitable to print.

In building a home, Chickaree may select a variety of places. He generally has a nest quite high up on the limbs of one of our firs or in the hollows of the alders and maples. His house is a warm structure of twigs lined with bark and other soft material. He does not sleep away the winter as the chipmunk does, so he must store up for a rainy day. He carries off fir and pine cones and always some of our walnuts, sometimes accumulating them at the base of a tree, under the shelter of a log, or hiding them in crevices and crannies of the ground. He has a remarkable way of locating these stores when they are needed, even when they are under cover of the snow. Like his store of hazelnuts, if they are not found, his cache serves the purpose of reforestation.

But the red squirrel is not the only sprite of our woods. He is one of three varieties of tree squirrels that are found living near our home. The big squirrel we call the silver-gray has much the same habits of storing his food and nesting in the trees, but he is twice the size of his red cousin. The flying squirrel with his large eyes, like the owl, is a creature of the night. He differs from the red squirrel by the extension of his skin, which spreads out like a cape along his sides between his front and hind legs. When he leaps from one tree to another, he glides on a downward, sloping course like a small parachute. He springs into the air with considerable force, but the distance he can "fly" depends upon the elevation from which he starts. By this unique method of traveling from the top of one tree to the base of another, he can bridge the gaps in a way that no other squirrel can. Strangely enough, however, with all his remarkable equipment, the flying squirrel cannot make as good time through the forest trees as the red squirrel. The airplane method of gliding down and then climbing up makes a longer course.

All the tree squirrels are expert climbers and have somewhat the same habits of homemaking and storing up provisions for a rainy day.

We once made a little box, roofed over and sheltered from the weather, as a winter feeding place for the squirrels, and supplied with nuts, wheat and corn. When the Chickaree discovered it, they raced around twitching their tails and pouring out a torrent of excited comment. Then they set to work to carry away everything in the box, hiding the food in crannies in the trees and holes in the ground. Although the store would not be half as safe from the elements as it was in the box, it was scattered and hidden from other woods folks who might want a bite. The pine squirrel is not inclined to look after the interests of other people. He is as faulty as some humans. Indeed, his sharp tongue, quick wit and inquisitive nature have led him into some bad habits.

In April, a pair of robins had built a nest about twenty feet up on one of the limbs of the white fir that stood just below our house, and the mother robin had been sitting on four eggs. One day I noticed she was off the nest. She did not return during the morning, and in the afternoon she was still away from home. Something had happened. I climbed the tree to a point from which I could look into the grassy cup. The eggs were gone.

The robins built another nest in the same tree just seven feet from the ground where two small bushy limbs had sprouted from the trunk and made an ideal nest spot. Then one day they began calling in such an excited manner that I knew they were in trouble. I rushed down the hill and, coming around the tree in sight of the nest, I saw to my amazement my friend, Mr. Red Squirrel, whom we had long called Piney, on the edge of the nest lunching on a robin's egg he held in his paws.

I reached for something to throw. There was nothing at hand but a little stick. I hurled it with all my might. The little wretch dropped the shell and scampered up the tall fir.

"I'll fix you for this," and I clambered up, swung my leg over the lowest limb and started after him toward the top. At least I would teach him not to rob birds' nests. This tree was tall and in the open, so he could not get away. I would get him in the very top and with a big shake catapult him clear out into the garden. It would give him a scare that would teach him to keep out of the tree.

I had reached the topmost branches where the trunk was slender. He saw he was cornered. He watched me from the very tip. Just as I hooked my leg around the tree to give the top a big flip, he sprung lightly out into the air, and sailing downward, caught the end of a bushy branch about eight feet below me. Before I could descend, he had run down the trunk and was chattering as if he thought it was a good joke.

I was exasperated. There were three eggs left in the nest. Perhaps I had scared him enough to keep away. I would keep close watch on the remaining eggs. Two days later they were gone.

We had fed and watched and enjoyed the pine squirrels for years here on the hillside. Piney was so attractive; but now we were losing faith in him. Here was a little fellow with long, gnawing teeth whom nature had raised to eat nuts and seeds; yet how had he become so depraved as to steal eggs and even young birds? Did he have weasel blood in his veins? If he was bent on murder, I should have to get rid of him.

It is a queer world, this out-of-doors in which we live. Not far away is a neighbor who insists that all robins should be killed because they eat his cherries and strawberries. Another wants a bounty on moles that are such a pest in his garden and lawn. Another neighbor advocates the killing of hawks, owls and cats. Another feels that insect pests will in time take everything. A letter from a man in Pennsylvania states that there ought to be a campaign started to exterminate the red squirrels in order to save the birds. I am on the point of killing those that make their home on my place.

If we begin a campaign of extermination, just where is it to end? If we put ourselves up as judges, we must look at things from all angles. We are told that all forms of life fit into their places like the stars in the solar system. The lives of all the animals about us are worked out on a plan of checks and balances. If we eliminate some species that appear detrimental, we may destroy nature's equilibrium and are likely to have greater difficulties than before. If we could destroy all the red squirrels, as some advocate, who would take the place of these little foresters in all parts of our country?

Here is Pillillooeet: he chatters and barks through our treetops. In spite of his faults, we love him. When we go down by our spring, he begins to scold as if he owned the place. The ivy and the grapevines have grown thick in the alders and cedars for many years, and there are matted places and old holes where he lived long before we came. We have decided that he may always have dominion over these.

Uncle Sam's Bird

Donald Culross Peattie

THE United States of America has a king. He shows himself in every state in the Union, and is seldom seen outside this country except in the dominion of our friendly neighbor, Canada. He is king of the air, undisputed ruler of the sky, the American or white-headed eagle.

As a proud monarch should have, he has regal features—a snowy head, an aquiline nose, a piercing eye. In fact, he bears a distinct resemblance to Uncle Sam himself. The eagle was officially placed on the Great Seal of the United States by act of Congress on June 20, 1782, while Uncle Sam, as an impersonation with familiar features, began to show his face in newspaper cartoons more than thirty years later. So it is true in this case that people grow to look like their pets!

Congress chose well when it picked this species for the national emblem, rejecting the golden eagle, which was originally proposed by the designer of the seal. This darker bird, although also found in the United States—rarely west of the Rockies—for centuries has been a heraldic symbol in such undemocratic states as Czarist Russia, the Austrian Empire, Napoleonic France, the Prussian Empire, the Roman Empire, and, indeed, of tyrannies and dictatorships running back to Assyria.

Handsome it may be; as a harrier of young stock the golden eagle has a thousand marks against it for every one that can be charged to the American eagle, whose favorite diet is fish. Honest old Ben Franklin, who wanted to make the strutting and stupid turkey gobbler our national bird, charged the American eagle with being a coward, a bully and a verminous thief. He did not know, apparently, that this bird of our choice is more attached to its home, is more faithful to its mate, and spends more care in the education of its young than almost any other in our skies.

Eagles mate for life. This is claimed for many birds, but usually falsely. The eagle pair do stick to each other, in breeding season and out, until death does them part. Only then will the bereaved one disappear from its accustomed haunts to roam the skies—now so often empty of eagles—till somewhere it finds a new mate and leads it home. Courtship begins earlier in the year (or later, if you prefer to call November that) than that of any other of our birds. And it lasts longer, continuing until June. In their eyrie, usually at the top of a very tall tree not far from water, the couple live in fierce and ardent devotion. There seems reason to think that the mating act is repeated, at dawn and sunset every day, until the eggs are laid and even after—as if the union were not for reproduction only. One ornithologist tells of the wild cry that rings out from the mating birds, over the tops of the trees steeped in shadow and awed silence.

No other bird is so deeply attached to his home. The eagle never leaves his bailiwick, except to seek a mate, or when forced to migrate from failure of food supply. Most birds desert the nest at the end of one season; it is to them not a home but a cradle. But the eagle each year builds a new nest on top of the old one. And an eagle may live as long as an average man—perhaps longer. So the nest grows and grows in

grandeur, and serves not only as a cradle but as a permanent home for the parents, summer and winter. One nest in a tree that blew down near Lake Erie was found to weigh nearly two tons, and represented several decades of occupancy. Another, found on a rock off the California coast, contained several wagon-loads of sticks and leaves. Coarse branches sometimes six feet long formed the breastworks of this bird castle. Within, it was lined with soft grasses, lichens, moss and feathers. And the view from such a wilderness mansion is usually the grandest in the countryside.

The female eagle lays two or three white eggs. The egg of a hummingbird is bigger! —that is, in proportion to the bird that lays it. Not three inches long, an eagle egg is smaller than the Canada honker's and only half the size of a whistling swan's. From such a small beginning grows the king of the air.

Both parents take turns at incubating, which lasts for about thirty-five days. Without stirring, one bird will sit as long as seventy-two patient hours. When weary it will signal the mate with a chittering sound. Then the change of guard will be made swiftly and quietly. If an eagle must leave the nest unguarded, the sagacious creature will rough over the top of the nest with dead leaves to make it look deserted.

The eaglets, being born so small, have a long infancy. And the life they are going to lead is so much more complex than that of most birds that their education is long. At first the chicks get food popped in their mouths, but when they should begin to feed themselves, the parents tear up a fish before the youngsters' eyes to show them how to do it. Presently they bring a whole fish and stand back while the little fellows learn to dissect it themselves.

Eaglets in their nursery play with sticks, just as children play with toys, and learn to grasp objects with their talons. Before they can fly, they must first get rid of their gray down, and develop and preen their new, strong flight plumage. They are taught to exercise every day. Their parents show them how to jump up and down on the ample platform of the eyrie, flapping their wings. They do this by the hour, squealing and stamping the while, like children in a game. All this is preparatory to flying, and to fly as an eagle flies is something that, it seems, is learned only by weeks of practice.

At last the young eagles make a first terrified flutter beyond the edge of the nest. Usually they tumble back again as fast as they can, scared but apparently proud and excited. If they are too slow about trying again, the parents discipline them by withholding food. Shriek with hunger as they may, the youngsters are not fed, but tantalizing morsels are dangled just beyond their grasp. When at last an eaglet completes his first solo flight, he gets a reward of food.

Like girls and boys approaching maturity, young eagles, once they can fly, spend less and less time around home, until, toward the end of their first year, they go off to seek their own fortunes in the world. They do not mate until, in the fourth or fifth season, they begin to wear the snowy crest and white tail of the adult, but long before that they are on their own as masters of all they survey. Their tremendous wing spread of seven or eight feet is matched by the internal strength of their great pinions. The longest primary feathers are twenty inches long. The wing tips are slotted, that is, the eagle can spread the primary feathers apart like fingers.

This slotted wing tip is a feature of all birds that can soar, glide and even rise without flapping the wings. It seems to act as an anti-stalling device, much like the slotted wing of the airplane invented by Handley Page. He found that a slotted wing increased the maximum lifting power by 250 per cent at an angle of forty-two degrees. Ages before, the eagle knew how to bend his wing upward and forward at the tip, with the result that the air is deflected over the wing top, leaving the main shank of the wing free to function several degrees beyond the stalling angle.

With such equipment the eagle is the absolute master of flight. Airmen have found him flying at 9750 feet above the earth. His marvelous eyes have been known to detect a fish three miles from the spot where he was soaring and capture it in one long slanting dive. It is this power that makes him the dread of the fish hawk or osprey, whom the king of the air frequently forces to drop his fish, the eagle recovering it with marvelous dexterity as it falls.

His fishing skill has also earned him the hatred of fishermen who will not share their luck. In Alaska, where reckless commercial exploitation of the salmon runs brought the canning industry to an all-time low, a bounty of fifty cents was the price put on the head of the national bird. Stringent laws regulating the take brought the industry back until it produced 8,000,000 cases a year. But the bounty, on the 20,000 breeding pairs of eagles officially estimated to remain in Alaska, was raised to a dollar anyway.

The eagle has many dangerous enemies —all of them human. Since Congress gave it the kiss of death in 1782 by publicizing it as the national bird without giving it legal protection, the eagle has had to fly through a barrage of lead and raise its young in the midst of its ill-wishers. For a century eagle eggs were at a premium with the class of collectors who rightly call themselves "fanciers." And unnumbered thousands of dusty, moulting, stuffed eagles still adorn the top shelves of drug stores, barber shops, and country offices. Every farmer who misses a hen thinks, if there is an eagle nest about, that he may pay it a punitive visit. Added to injury is libel—a charge so criminal that if it were true it would justify the vicious attacks on every eagle pair. But there is no truth in the hoary newspaper story of the eagle who snatches the baby from the cradle. No American eagle has ever been known to make an unprovoked attack upon any human child. For twenty-five years the National Audubon Society has patiently followed up each one of these accusations, and every case melts away to fable.

Only during the 1940s did Congress get around to passing legislation to protect the symbol of our proud freedom. It is now unlawful to kill, or shoot at, or capture Uncle Sam's bird, or to take eagle eggs or molest the nest. The enforcement of this law is no stronger than the vigilance of game wardens and the attitude of country judges.

So, if you ever find an eagle's nest, rush right home and tell—nobody. News of it will spread from your best friends to the eagle's worst enemies. Every hunter who thinks he must kill whatever fair and shining mark dares stir, every curiosity-seeking robber, will learn of it. When you come to the nest again there may be no eagle. Then you can take a silver dollar out of your pocket, or a quarter if you are feeling cheap, and apologize to the brave emblem. But the American sky over your home will be lower than it was.

In spite of all that Americans have done to exterminate their grandest bird, it is still not uncommon in certain localities, and it is most abundant in Alaska and Florida, around the Great Lakes, along the Mississippi river system, and along the coasts of the two oceans. Wherever you saw it, you never forget your first American eagle.

He may be sitting in motionless, unblinking majesty upon the highest limb of the tallest tree in all the countryside, keeping guard over mate and nest, over wood and water. Or you may first have seen him taking a power dive from the skies, uttering his war cry as he swoops to pounce upon the shapes that stir beneath the waters. Or perhaps you have watched, as I have, a flock of eagles soaring, circling, rising up around one another until they become specks against the blue. Then it is not the dark spread of wings that vanishes last, but the flash of the proud crest, like the twinkle of snow on distant mountains.

The Mountain Heronry

Edward A. Preble

ON A JULY EVENING many years ago I sat on the little bridge that still spans the outlet of Archer's Pond. The sun had already set beyond the New Hampshire hill whose rugged brow—The Ledge—surmounting the steep, tree-clad slope, seemed almost to overhang the lakelet. Ages ago a glacier had overspread that broad-topped hill, pushed over the margin of the mighty rock that formed its backbone, and sent its slow-creeping flood of ice down the steep incline with a force so stupendous that its front gouged a deep furrow in the vale below. When the ice had ceased its advance and slowly melted beneath the increasing warmth, a long ridge of sand and gravel, ground from the massive rock and pushed forward, made a dam that held the long narrow lakelet back against the steep-sided mount. What was the original depth of that ice-born tarn no man knows, for the oozy mud that nearly fills its bed has never been plumbed.

The purple shadows were lengthening and the details of the forested slope and the surface of the pond grew each minute more obscure. Even the starry flowers of the lilies scattered among the broad floating leaves were fading from my sight. From about the lakelet there rose on the still night air those sounds that are so much a part of a New England pond that they seem its own voices. A bullfrog a little way down the shore started a deep-throated chant that was borne to the ears of the farm people a mile up the valley. Occasionally a bream or perch snatched some morsel floating among the lily-pads and, attracted by the faint splash, one could just see a circle of tiny wavelets ripple the glassy surface. A louder splash near the opposite shore told that a pickerel, nosing its way along the shallow margin, had seized a fish or a frog. Over all surged the low hum of myriad dancing water insects, humble parts of the varied chain of life.

As I watched the night creeping over land and water, and listened to its voices, a huge bird suddenly became visible in the darkening sky. The long neck, so set in a double fold that the bird's head seemed to rest on its shoulders, and the legs that trailed straight out behind like a rudder, marked it as a great blue heron. Its broad wings were flapping deliberately, but with a power that carried it swiftly on its way.

Almost as I caught sight of the bird, it set its wings and sailed gradually down to the pond, so skillfully shaping its course that, seemingly without effort, it skimmed closely over the surface for several hundred yards, and alighted silently in the shallow water of a wooded bay. Evidently it had just come from some nesting place in the mountains for a night's fishing.

Thus the two of us, boy and heron, had paid this evening visit to Archer's Pond for the same elemental purpose. We were closer akin than either of us knew. The bird had come in obedience to the call that predominates among the primal instincts of living creatures, the urge to prolong its own life, and to provide for the young that would perpetuate its species. Much of the same feeling, although I did not sense it, was responsible for my own presence there, for one of man's earliest pursuits was fishing, and within most of us there still persists a germ of this primal heritage.

If the heron was aware that a potential enemy was watching him, he gave no sign. My own fishing was neglected, and I watched his every move as he stealthily waded the shallows, and gathered in what the pond provided, fish and frog and insect.

When the gloom had grown so dense that the alert form was no longer visible, I shouldered my fish pole and slowly made my way homeward, enjoying the coolness and glamor of the summer night, and leaving the heron to pursue its fishing alone. But the memory of that great bird, fishing at dusk by the lovely pond, stayed with me, and I longed to find its nesting place, and learn more of its life. It had come from the general direction of the hogback to the northwest, but I felt sure that no herons were nesting in those nearby hills. So I asked Grandpa William, whose mountain lore seldom failed me, where the bird's home could be.

"Oh—them blue cranes," said the old man: "Why, they build in the tall beeches on top of Thurley's Mountain, the other side of Dan Hole Pond. Anyway, they used to, and they love to stick to the same place. If you think you can stand the trip, we might go up there some day."

The sight of a "blue crane" rising heavily from the margin of a shallow pond, or from among the willows beside a meandering trout brook, was not a rare experience to one who so persistently haunted the wilderness as I did, but the sight of a nest was an unfulfilled ambition. I could imagine no trip too hard or too long if at its end I should see the nests of these great birds. A tramp over the hills to Dan Hole Pond and the mountain beyond called for no special preparation, and early one morning we set out.

To the old man each mountain road or trail was as well known as though it were a highway. We followed an old wood road that led through "The Gulch," a deep ravine from whose cavernous depths came one of our best trout brooks. What words can picture the beauty of a summer morning in the mountains of New England! Hermit thrushes, vireos and warblers voiced their hymns of praise from the woods; from the towering roots of a century-old pine stump in the fence, in a hollow of which his tender young were sprouting their flight feathers, a bluebird warbled his love-notes; here and there a yellowthroat scolded from the moist thickets. As we passed through the gulch we caught a glimpse of a huge porcupine as he scuttled to his sheltered cave. In the depths of this valley the junco loved to nest, and her mottled young were trying their new-fledged wings. A black-throated blue warbler sang from a maple bough his *zee-zee-zee*, such a strain as an insect might claim, if one did not see the real artist. And so we crossed the first ridge, and came to the banks of the stream that carries to the Saco the clear water of the Dan Hole Ponds.

Years before the first pioneer farmer blazed his way up the valley to these lovely lakes, tradition tells us, a trapper from down-country, Dan Hole by name, came here each winter with a pack of trading goods, and trapped and bartered with the vanishing Pequakets. His methods and manners were fair and the Indians liked him. Then the fisher and marten abounded; each spring he hid his traps in a dry cave and took his pack of fur back to the settlements. Dan Hole and his Indian friends, and the white settlers who followed him, are long since in their graves, but the trapper's name is still perpetuated in these lovely twin ponds.

The higher mountain slopes that border the basin in which nestle the lakes of Dan Hole were then yielding to the saw their virgin cover, and a busy little community found support there. Through this we passed and entered the logging road down which had been dragged the great trunks of spruce and pine. Above this trail hung the supple, drooping boughs of striped maple and broad-leaved viburnum. In the woods on either side the white star-flowers of dalibarda, the lovely pink-veined blossoms of the dainty wood sorrel, and the erect spires of the wintergreen or pyrola were mingled on carpets of yielding moss with the glossy leaves of the trailing arbutus, whose sweet bells had long since fallen and given place to seeds. As we climbed, the spruces were more frequent, and here and there an olive-backed thrush, a bird unknown to the lowlands, poured out his simple song, while in the more open spots the hermit thrushes and white throated sparrows—for they, too, love the heights—sang for their mates.

But where were the herons we had come so far to see? Well, they were near the top of the mountain, and we should reach them in good time. And I was content, for who would not be while following a summer trail to the summit of a New England hill?

Finally, from a group of tall beeches a little to the right of our path came a series of hoarse squawks, and a number of great birds flapped heavily from the treetops, and there, sure enough, were the nests—great masses of dry sticks lodged in the boughs of the beeches, some in forks, but mostly far out on the slender limbs. They were all around us, sometimes five or six in a tree, sometimes alone.

In May, when the leaves of apple green were unrolling from their swollen brown-scaled buds, the birds had come, and had patched up the old nests that had been the nurseries of many generations of awkward young herons. With the veterans had come young birds, to essay their first nesting, and add new homes to the colony. Then, in June, the month of egg-laying and brooding, each mother had sat patiently on the big blue eggs until the young broke their way out to a world of swaying treetops.

It was July already, the month of long flights to fishing grounds, for the nearest points where food for the young was surely obtainable lay in the valley nearly two miles away, and some of the herons, like the one I had seen at Archer's Pond, would have to take an air-line flight of five miles before they could settle to their fishing. But soon the young could leave the nests and start fishing for themselves, and the whole colony would leave their mountain-top and move southward, seeking the broad swamps of great river-systems where fishes, frogs and salamanders had populated the warmer waters with the fruit of their spawn.

How I wish that the rest of the story might be different—for the nests were empty! Newly-felled trees, shattered nests, and festering bodies of slaughtered birds told plainly a bloody tale. A few days before, a gang of sawmill hands, intent on a holiday, had marked from the valley below the place where the great birds, laden from their fishing, had settled on the mountain top. Up climbed the horde, laden with guns and axes, and plied their murderous task until the last of the young birds, and all the old ones, whose anxiety for their helpless young had drawn them within range, had been killed. Probably resentment toward the birds, because they ate the small pickerel of Little Dan Hole, contributed to the motives that urged this devastating raid. Fifty years have flown by since that day, but a few of the men who formed that thoughtless crew still remember the trip of slaughter and wonder why they took part in that murderous foray.

Many changes have come to Dan Hole since those days. The virgin forest that once supported a populous community has vanished, but Thurley's Mountain still clothes itself with verdure, and as one traces the old road down which logs were once hauled, the olive-backs and the hermits still greet him as of old. With the passing of the intensive industries that peopled the region summer and winter, some of the larger wild creatures have come back. The bears revel in the raspberry patches that mark the more recent of the cuttings, and the timid deer, unknown here in our boyhood days, leaves his pointed track in the sandy shallows of the trout brook.

Pickerel still hunt the shallow margin of Little Dan Hole, and trout are planted there, and form an attraction. Perhaps, if the heron colony were there now, its members might be recognized as valuable agents in maintaining a better balance between pickerel and trout, for the pickerel is considered an enemy of the more favored species. Herons eat many other enemies of the better fishes—the predaceous larval forms of water beetles and bugs and dragonflies that prey on young fishes. Other fishes eaten by herons are the destroyers of the spawn of trout and other game species. But the herons never again nested on Thurley Mountain.

All in all a more kindly sentiment toward even those wild creatures that eat what we covet is growing among our people. To kill a heron without specific permission is unlawful, yet many people do not know this, and only an occasional lone bird now fishes the shallow margins of Dan Hole or Archer's Pond.

A Wasatch Grizzly

Dallas Lore Sharp

WHEN FRANK CLARK'S sheep allotment on the Cache National Forest was changed to the headwaters of the Right Hand Fork of Logan River in 1911, he came early upon a set of bear tracks that for size seemed to cover the whole allotment. Clark had trapped and shot many brown and black bears as a sheep man, but he had never crossed a trail the like of this before.

The new allotment extended from the Right Hand Fork of Logan River east and south to Saddle Creek Divide and over to Trail Hollow on the west. As soon as Clark had brought in his sheep, the forest ranger visited him, and told him of an immense bear, a grizzly, that seemed to occupy this exact territory—had for years—leaving him with the distinct impression that nobody in that section very much relished the idea of bagging this particular bear.

The ranger's story and the sight of the tracks left Clark of a mind not to go out of his way to meet the grizzly if they could share the allotment in a neighborly way together. And that seemed to be the grizzly's mind too, for if Clark kept out of the bear's way, the bear kept out of Clark's, each respecting the other.

It was not until the next year, 1912, that anyone in the Clark outfit caught a sight of the big grizzly, and from then on, not again until 1922. Clark thus described the first occasion to Dr. Hill:

"Sam Kemp and me was herdin' on the knoll across from Dog's Springs. It was about four in the afternoon. Sam carried a number 405 Express rifle. He was sittin' on the knoll, which we called Ephraim's Knoll, when a bear as big as a horse and lots longer came out of the brush and crossed over the curve about twenty-five yards away. The bear stopped and looked at me and Sam a minute, and then went on up the hill. Sam was a dead shot, and I said, 'Why don't you get him, Sam, ain't we killin' all the bears we can on the range?' And Sam he said, 'I don't want that bear.' He was ready that he should go just as soon as he would go. And the bear went on out of sight in the brush."

A brief and casual meeting this, but both parties got hold of the essential points of the situation, and it was not necessary for them to meet again. They divided the range between them, mutually sharing it, crossing and recrossing each other's trails, but avoiding one another's presence with a delicacy and skill entirely unusual between bears and men. The impression got generally abroad that the big grizzly was a gentleman, attending strictly to his own business, and asking only that others do the same.

Of course he killed sheep, but only his rightful share of the range. When the sheep would come out on the range about the middle of June the herders would look for the grizzly's tracks, and if one man didn't find them another would, and there would be a killing. When Clark came across the tracks "goin' up the trail" he would go over and tell Joe Peterson to look out for the big bear. About the third night later Peterson would lose a bunch of sheep. Then the bear would go away for a time or start back over the Divide, and Peterson would warn Clark. On about the third night later Clark could expect a killing among his flocks. Usually it was the forest ranger who plotted the curves of the bear's movements and kept the herders informed.

The extraordinary thing about the situation was the acceptance on the part of the herders of this levy on their flocks as part of nature's scheme and entirely within the grizzly's rights. The sheep thrived. It was a rich country here about the headwaters of the Logan. And hadn't it been allotted to the bear before it had been allotted to the sheep? Or as Clark put it: "This much I've got to say for that grizzly: he never killed more than he wanted—not until the last two years when he had got old. He was the most gentlemanly bear I ever saw, and now that he's gone I'm sorry, I am. And I've a mind to put up a monument over his grave to say that here was a bear that lived like a man and died like a man."

Clark was not a sentimentalist. Sheep-raising on the wild western ranges is not an occupation to breed any special softness. Lions and lambs may sometime lie peacefully down together, but sheep and bears cannot do it yet in Utah. The herders killed every bear that raided their flocks, and would have killed the huge grizzly had he forced the issue. Instead, he kept wisely to his own hidden ways, gave no unnecessary offense, asked only to live and let live, and so did much in that section to mend "the broken social union" between man and nature.

The conflict between man and the larger wild beasts, his equals, and more than equals, in strength, is inevitable. One or the other must rule, and there is no question as to which one of the two dominion belongs. The warfare is immemorial, and still goes on; but it has long since become a one-sided fight, and a fight without quarter or mercy. Down to the present moment the victory sought has not been peace but extermination, the social consciousness of man not far enough evolved to include all of nature's beings, the wild ones as well as the human.

All life is one. Society includes good and bad germs, good and bad men, good and bad beasts, good and bad birds and plants, as we see them self-interestedly; but seen socially, all plants and birds and beasts and men and germs are somehow good.

The vague, uneasy consciousness of this great truth was coming like a slow, dull dawn to the country about the headwaters of the Logan. The big wise grizzly was quietly socializing Clark and the herders, and sending them to school. Of course they would have killed him, and they did kill him, as they had to, or move away, but not before he had taught them tolerance; that men and bears can live together on the same allotment, sharing, even, a few of their sheep.

And I must say that what happened finally was the grizzly's fault. But he was old, and after all he was just a bear.

If the grizzly had been the only bear upon the range his extraordinary size and unobtrusive ways, even with his occasional raids, would have exempted him from the constant hunting that went on. But the country about the Right Fork of the Logan was overstocked with black bears, panthers, and other predators, so that the government kept a professional trapper there to help the sheep men protect their flocks. Clark, Peterson, Ward and Nebeker shared the country about the head of the Logan, and all four of them made war with guns, traps and poison on the "varmints," but from 1911 to 1922 no one got the drop on the grizzly, or so much as a sight of him. And no one seemed very sorry about it.

"He was too slick for me," Clark would say with a smile. "He would dodge my trail, shy my traps and spring them with sticks, and do a lot of other things to show me that there was room on the range for both of us without crowding. And as for traps—well, he didn't set any for me! That bear would make a Christian ashamed of himself."

Thus it went on for about nine years. Then the bear, growing old, and possibly morose from years alone and from ceaseless sense of danger, began to kill for the lust of killing. One night he got into Clark's flocks and killed twenty-two, then went over to Peterson's and got nineteen more. There was no mistaking the marauder, shocking as the revelation was, for the immense footprints told a convincing story.

This was the beginning of a degenerate and bitter end. Something had to be done, and done quickly, for there is no cure but death for this sort of thing. The best-trained and gentlest dog in the world, once he has turned killer, must himself be killed. The great bear rapidly went from bad to worse. Yet in spite of every effort to take him the wily old brute eluded every gun, and even the keen eyes of his pursuers. He couldn't cover his mighty tracks, but although nearly as big as a horse he had a trick of fading from his hunters as if he carried magic fern seed in his shaggy pocket.

During the late fall and winter of that year nothing was heard of the grizzly, for he suddenly ceased his depredations. The sheep men concluded that the old fellow had "gone home." But when Clark came on the range in 1922 he ran almost at once upon the giant tracks. Only one bear in the Wasatch Mountains could leave that terrific trail.

"Early in July," says Clark, "I thinks to myself, I'll ride up to Ephraim's Wallow, for that's what we called the little seep spring up on the knoll across from Dog Springs where Sam Kemp and me first seen this critter. He had a habit of comin' there to waller in the mud.

"So up I goes and sure as you live the brute had been there. He had squashed out a hole in the mud about as big as a wagon box, and his fresh tracks was all about the place. So I rode back to camp and got our twenty-five-pound bear trap and clamps. You know this trap is so strong that you can't set it without clamps. It has three or four teeth on each jaw, and the bear that gets in that trap stays there.

"Well, I got a fourteen-foot log chain and fastened that on the trap, and set the trap right in the middle of the wallow, carefully covered. We had caught lots of black bear in that wallow, and I had a log about ten foot long which I usually fastened the chain to. So I pulled up this log, wrapped the chain around it a couple of times and wired it there good and solid.

"A couple of days after I rode up there again. Ephraim had been there, but he was gone now. Before he left he picked up that ten foot log of mine in his arms and carried it over and laid it down by the side of the trail. Then he goes over and sees the trap's unsprung and careful-like, picks it up in his paws and puts it unsprung beside the log.

"But he don't go back into that old muddy wallow. Oh, no! He goes around to yon side of the spring and digs him a brand new wallow! Wasn't he some bear, now? It hain't right to kill so human a critter.

"Well, it had to be done, I reckon. So I left the log where he had left it. Then I extended the chain and carried the trap around to the new wallow, and careful-like buried it in the soft mud, covering with sticks and dirt every sign of the heavy chain. 'Now,' I says, 'Ephraim, I'm going to get you.'

"My camp that summer was located down at the mouth of Long Hollow where this little seep spring was which the big grizzly visited. A small stream came down it past the camp, which was about a mile below the spring.

"On the very night that I had reset the trap, about twelve or one o'clock, I should guess, I was wakened by a terrible roarin' way up the canyon. Then I heard the horses begin snortin'. We had eighteen head of saddle horses hobbled in that little flat at the mouth of Long Hollow, and as the roarin' got nearer and louder the horses began to mill about on the flat till I was sure of a stampede. Then I grabbed my 25-35 and started up the canyon to face the music there rather than be mixed up with it in camp.

"It was a bear, of course, but I didn't think of the big grizzly. Yet I never heard a wild sound the like of this before. It shook me in my boots. It started kind of low, like an old bull's bellow, and wound up with a roar like a herd of lions. And comin' down the narrow canyon at me in the dark made me all goose flesh, and pretty near horse flesh too; for I was about ready to stampede.

"There's something hereditary, I suppose, the way our nerves rear up and pull their

picket pins and gallop off from the dark. But mix wild beasts in with the dark, and steep, close walls, and I go loco in spite of any 25-35, though there ain't a better gun made to be a fit companion on the range.

"The sound seemed to come down to me from a clump of willows about three hundred yards up the draw. That's why it never occurred to me to think of the big grizzly, for the trap was fully a mile up the canyon and no bear could get away down here with that trap. All I knew was that something was in its last agonies, or in such a fury comin' down the canyon as to take my tent and the horses on down the mountain with it.

"As I stumbled up the trail in the dark I heard him groan in the willows, or thought I did. But I guess he heard me comin', for I went right past the willows, within five feet of them, and never a sound or a stir. I didn't push in amongst them to be sure, not in the dark. When I got well above I turned around and stopped. Whatever it was must be in that thick willow patch. And I sat down to watch.

"I had hardly got my gun across my knees when the whole canyon began to thunder with the roar. I had had enough, and I was altogether too close to them willows. I just needed to hear that sound from where I sat to start me up the canyon on the jump. I spotted a burnt pine stub about fifty feet up on the wall of the draw, and didn't lose no time getting up to it either. I sat there shiverin' till morning ready to climb that pine if I had to.

"By and by everything got quiet. When it came daylight I went down near the willows and threw some stones in to see if I could start anything, but there was nothing there.

"Just then, down toward my tent, I heard a low groan, and creeping along I could just see the shape of something movin'. It was furry. A bear I was sure, and I fired. The bullet grazed the shoulder of the critter, and up rose the form of old Ephraim, the great grizzly!

"He stood head and shoulders above the bushes. He had the bear trap on his left paw, and he had wrapped the whole chain about his caught arm. His mouth was open. His lips were spread back. His white teeth glistened. Up he rose and looked at me, and instead of rushin' down the canyon, came right over the bushes at me.

"I was froze stiff. I couldn't run. I couldn't shoot. I never saw a more terrible sight. He didn't come like a bear. He come like a man, a great hairy giant of a man, his left paw with the awful trap raised high as his head to strike me down. But I had to shoot. The ball knocked him down. He was up and comin' on. I shot again. Again the ball knocked him down, and he stayed down till I got some four feet higher up the wall, when on he came. I stopped him once more. But nothing could stop him. Half a ton of awful fury he came, as if death itself were driving him. I emptied the last shell into him, dropped the gun and ran for my life, the great brute almost breathing upon me.

"Then I heard my dog at the bear's side, and the great beast turned to strike him. But the lead had done its work. He rose high up and looked without any fear or malice at me, just like a Christian, then crumpled and spilled into a lifeless heap.

"I couldn't move for a whole minute. My knees wouldn't hold my weight. Besides I felt just like I had done murder. There's something terrible human about a bear. When I got down to the camp there wasn't one of the eighteen hobbled horses there. But I saw my gray mare over in the sage with her hobble caught in the bushes, and takin' her I rode over to Peterson's and got his herder, Joe Brown, to come back with me. We could hardly get the horses up to the bear. When we finally got him lassoed the two horses together couldn't drag him off the trail. I had pulled many a steer from the saddle horn, but we couldn't budge that bear.

"We rode up to the seep spring for the

clamps in order to get the trap off of his foot, and all the way down found that he had come along on his hind legs, never once dropping to all fours. About four rods below his wallow we came upon the log. It had got caught in some aspens. He had broken down the small trees and chewed up others to get free. But he couldn't get free. Then he chewed the heavy log in three places nearly through, until finally it broke and the chain slipped off. I never want to trap another grizzly.

"He was the length of a five-foot shovel and two double spans from the tip of his tail to a point midway between his ears, or about nine feet long, as we reckoned him. I uncovered a lot of dry willows and piled them on him, and set them afire.

"And I'm sorry he's gone. That bear belonged to the range. And I wasn't so afraid of him alive as I am now he's dead. And he *was* like a man! The way he faced that rifle and kept coming straight on and on! We are all of us much the same I guess, men and bears. And it is a pity we can't get on better together."

A Box Turtle Lays Her Eggs

Lewis V. Kost

PHOTOGRAPHS © BY THE AUTHOR

THE SITE chosen by an eastern box turtle for her nest was not the wisest, but it afforded an opportunity for prying eyes and camera lens to record her nesting activities and thus won for her special protection. The site was on the edge of a lawn by a driveway. What went on during the digging, filling and covering of the nest is recorded here in pictures, part of a larger series.

Between the time that the mother turtle started to dig her nest and the time when, eggs laid and carefully covered, she walked away never to reappear, three hours and fourteen minutes elapsed. During that period the box turtle worked with precision and without any lost motion. The digging of the nest was done in skillful and efficient fashion. Yet during the whole process she never took a look over her shoulder to see how she was progressing. And she walked away without a backward glance, certain that all was well. Her concern for her young was ended then.

A tiny fence was placed around the now expertly camouflaged nest, which was watched carefully from day to day. Eighty-nine days elapsed before anything happened. Then a hole was discovered, through which showed the back of a baby turtle. The following morning the first turtle emerged, and four hours later four baby turtles had hatched. One egg was sterile and another contained a fully developed young box turtle, which, for some undetermined reason, had died in the egg.

The young turtles were immediately active and eager for food. They took readily to water. Their shells were quite pliable at that age, and a drab, earthen color that would provide them protection in the wild. Two of the youngsters were kept as pets and flourished on a diet of earthworms, fresh tomato, grapes and other fruits.

Above, left: *In digging the nest the box turtle used each rear leg alternately, methodically pushing each clawful of soil into a pile that was deposited behind the opening.*

Above, right: *After 1 hour and 34 minutes devoted to digging the nest, the turtle laid her first egg.*

Right: *The second egg emerges. The eggs were laid at approximately 4-minute intervals. One rear foot was held in the nest opening as each of the eggs was laid.*

1
2
3
4
5
6
7

1. Six eggs filled the nest. Pure white, about 1¼ inches long and ⅝ inch in diameter, they had a leathery covering and an appearance of semitransparency. Specks on the last egg deposited are bits of soil that adhered to the wet shell of the egg.

2. For 3 hours and 14 minutes the box turtle's forepart held this position. Its legs were driven into the ground like stakes, serving as bearing points, anchor and fulcrum. Since the turtle worked by touch, this position of the forefeet seemed to be important in aiding the clocklike precision and accuracy of the mother box turtle in her egg-laying.

3. The eggs laid, the mother turtle raked the grass on each side of her body, bringing bits of dried vegetation over the nestful of eggs. Then the earth was scratched in, spread about and patted and kneaded over the nest opening.

4. In tamping the soil to close the nest safely and securely the turtle used the "knuckles" of her feet. She moved her body from side to side and up and down, as though in a dance, the procedure tamping the earth over the six eggs in the nest.

5. When the nest was finally closed to the satisfaction of the turtle, it was perfectly camouflaged. For this reason, and lest something befall the nest, it was protected by the erection of a small, twine fence, and was designated as a bit of hallowed ground.

6. Eighty-nine days after the turtle had laid her eggs, an opening appeared in the ground at the nest site.

7. The ridge of the carapace of a young turtle was visible through the opening. At 8:20 A.M. on the nineteenth day after the eggs were laid a baby turtle took its first look at the world.

8. The newly hatched baby box turtle placed on the edge of a ¾-inch board to show its size.

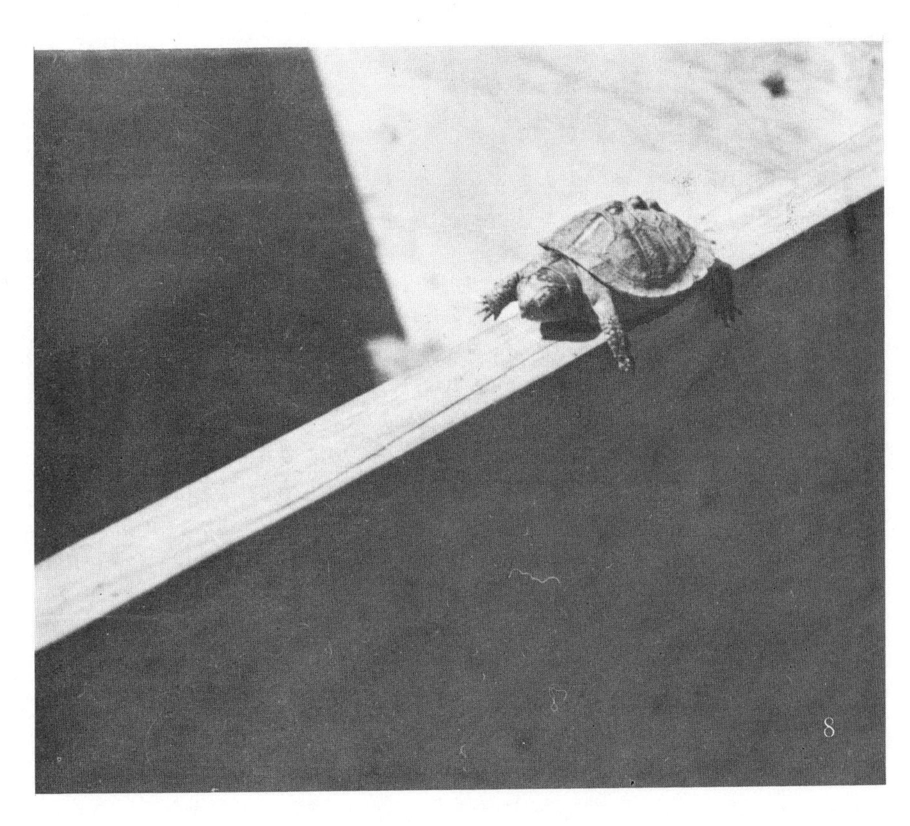
8

Andy, a Mischief-Loving Crane

George L. Bird

YOU WOULD HARDLY LOOK for a sense of humor in a crane, and much less expect a crane to be arrested, sentenced, and imprisoned for being a public nuisance. And undoubtedly you would attach the title of Ananias to anyone who told about the crane going on a hunger strike because of his imprisonment. Yet it's true.

Andy was a sandhill crane of great dignity. He frequently visited my home in northern Florida until his pranks sent him into exile to the remote estate of Royal Dixon, the naturalist.

At the time of his arrival from his birthplace in the Everglades, he was a youngster of a few tender months still dressed in down and pinfeathers. Before he was able to satisfy his enormous appetite unaided, he learned to depend upon and cherish his charming mistress, who lived by a lake near my own home.

One day his mistress left the state on a visit. Andy thereupon called on a retired minister living nearby. Whether he went to improve his morals or to while away the lonely hours is not clear, but it helped to land him in jail.

The minister was setting out onions in long straight rows. Andy followed him closely and entirely unobserved, pulling up the onions one by one. When the minister straightened at the end of the row, it would have been difficult to tell whose dignity was the greater. But it was the man's composure that first succumbed, and Andy escaped only by taking wing.

The onion sets were replanted, but the next morning they had again been pulled up. No one saw Andy do it, but the blame centered on him.

After that the incident that led up to his disgrace was not long delayed. Across the lake were kept a few chickens that from time to time roamed down to the lake shore and fed there. From Andy's point of view they were poaching on his own private hunting grounds.

One evening he was seen giving them a careful scrutiny. The next morning the entire flock was found dead. Each one of the chickens had been killed in the same way, apparently by a very sharp round-pointed instrument.

It couldn't be shown that Andy killed the poachers, but circumstantial evidence and his growing bad reputation proved too strong. He was now arrested and imprisoned. But the city fathers reckoned without Andy.

The crane promptly went on a hunger strike. He refused to eat and drink. Since there is no known way of force-feeding a crane, Andy grew thinner each day. In three days he was but skin and bones, and his emaciated body soon matched his elongated legs and neck.

The city marshal notified the city fathers. An emergency meeting was called. The debate grew hot, but it could end in only one way.

Andy was released, and he stalked away without a backward glance, taking his offended dignity and his victory with him.

Yet at home he was a docile and an amusing pet with a broad sense of humor and a bagful of tricks, both playful and otherwise. He thoroughly enjoyed three roly-poly pointer pups that frolicked with him. Although he was only a little more than two months old when he came, he soon learned his name. His grayish-blue body gradually changed to a slate blue in maturity, although there was no time when he did not seem all legs and neck.

When he arrived, he weighed about four and a half pounds and stood just twenty-five inches, which is about right according to insurance charts in crane circles.

Of his own choice he never touched fish; instead, he pursued crickets and grasshoppers, or the water beetles and the tiny sand beetles that make the beautiful molelike tunnels in the bed of the white sand-bottomed lakes. Tiny frogs and mole crickets were dainties that he eagerly hunted.

Strangers were often afraid of his bill, which was fully five inches long, needle-pointed, and manipulated by a long and extremely muscular neck. I saw him thrust it into the sand nearly to the eyes countless times in probing for a mole cricket or a burrowing beetle.

It is not strange that stray dogs and cats shunned his neighborhood. No animal seeing him come with head down, mouth open, and wings widespread hesitated long. This trait had its good points, though his greatest usefulness came through his appetite, which kept the insects thinned out to a minimum.

Although I never saw him battle a snake, his methods were described to me several times. They must have been instinctive, because he never had the chance to observe his relatives. He pounced upon it with both feet, kicking out right and left. He followed that with a lightning thrust of his head, catching the reptile back of the head and crushing its neck, at the same time flinging it away with a snap of his long neck. He repeated this until no life was left.

As has been indicated, Andy had more than one trick in his bag. But there was one of his stunts that had a flavor of its own and which was probably the strongest link in the chain of circumstances that hastened his exile.

His nearest neighbor lived only a few rods away. For some unknown reason—which may have been perfectly understandable to a crane—he took a dislike to the housewife. From week to week it was his pleasure to wait until Monday morning when the washing had been hung out and members of the family had disappeared within the house. Then, appearing from concealment, he swiftly walked to the prop that upheld the clothes, pulled it loose with his powerful bill, and left the flapping garments to flutter to the ground about him. After which, he would again disappear into the woods.

This was bound to lead to trouble sooner or later, but try as his guardian did, she never succeeded in breaking him of this habit. He had another amusing and annoying trick, however, that was not quite so malicious as soiling the Monday wash.

Seeing a lady hiker ambling along he would plant himself in front of the woman and attack the bright buckles on her shoes. Retreat was the only recourse, and retreat it would be. This happened many times to pedestrians of that sex. Once having put them to rout, Andy followed up his advantage, stalking after his enemies for blocks to see that they did not attempt a return.

Although he had many delightful traits and displayed affection for his master and mistress, he could not be saved in the end. Despite the fact that he learned to recognize the family car while it was blocks away and often came running to greet it, despite the crazy dance he performed for his owners alone by hopping into the air repeatedly as he flapped his seven-foot wings, his jokes could not be overlooked.

Antipathy against him grew because his neighbors did not recognize that he was a man-about-town and should, therefore, be treated with the consideration due a bird of distinction. For instance, his social calls were always conducted with great dignity—although less can be said for his human friends.

Once he came unbidden to a fashionable neighbor's afternoon tea. Being young and comparatively inexperienced, he had not learned that "all is not gold that glitters." He tried to collect whatever buttons and buckles were loose. And it is said that he sampled the tea and cakes—but that may be mere slander. Anyway, the party broke up at that point.

Most women didn't appreciate him because he was too ungainly to be cuddled in their laps and he resented baby talk. Men tolerated him because he destroyed insects and was a good watchdog. He loved little children and played peacefully with them by the hour. But parents remembered the old saying about "birds of a feather," and forbade their offspring to associate with him.

So he was banished to the home of a naturalist a few miles away where his dignity and his sense of humor were better understood and where his wise nature was studied for the benefit of future generations.

Ookpikjuak the Lonely

A. Marguerite Baumgartner

THE TUNDRAS were carpeted with a mat of snowy *Dryas* when Ookpikjuak first opened his fierce yellow eyes upon the world. The last snows in the hollows had melted under the early July sun, but far out on the blue waters of Hudson Bay a line of ice still shimmered against the horizon.

Ookpikjuak had been the first of the little owls to peck his way through the dirty white shell beneath the soft breast of Old Snowy. Now there were seven of them in the shallow depression in the reindeer moss that covered the knoll. They were about two days apart, ranging in size from the tiny white chick that tumbled helplessly among the broken shells, shreds of fur, feathers, and castings that lined their nest, to Ookpikjuak, clad in a heavy coat of long gray down that already showed the tiny quills of his winter plumage about the glaring eyes and powerful beak.

They were alone much of the time now, for the local supply of lemmings and small birds had long since been exhausted and the parents were foraging in ever-widening circles. Mosquitoes and small flies buzzed their irritating chorus above the tender owlets. The summer sun, eighteen hours a day, beat mercilessly upon the bare nest, and Ookpikjuak gazed with dull longing at the little pool at the foot of the knoll, fringed with arctic rhododendron and tall sedges that cast wavering shadows across the green water. Resentfully he pecked at a small sister who was chewing hungrily at his toes. Stretching his long neck he peered across the wind-swept barrens for a glimpse of white, but neither parent was in sight.

Then, beyond the pool, appeared a form that made the little owl's blood race in his veins. Loping lazily across the marshy flats was an arctic fox, nose to the wind and headed straight for the owls' knoll. He paused at the pool to sip the tepid water, then leaped gracefully across and sauntered up the lichen-covered slope.

Ookpikjuak stiffened for the assault and met the fox with a mighty hissing and snapping of his tiny beak, but in spite of his bravado the little owl shrank back against the smaller brothers and sisters, who only stared sullenly at the intruder. For a brief instant the fox paused, gathering his lithe muscles for the spring. In that moment of grace Ookpikjuak tumbled awkwardly out of the nest and scrambled frantically, half hopping, half rolling down the knoll. The fox leaped, and with the deadly accuracy of a killer his jaws closed rapidly upon one helpless form after another. Simultaneously a white bolt from the skies descended upon the fox, yellow eyes shooting fire, diving and swooping, ripping into the heavy hair with powerful beak and sharp talons. The fox made one last spring, then, with a limp gray owlet dangling from his jaws, ran for the rocky shore line, pursued venomously by Old Snowy until she lost him in the tumbled mass of granite.

The marauder's visit had been brief but lethal. Five crumpled forms lay lifeless in the bottom of the nest; Ookpikjuak alone had escaped by the bare margin of two days' seniority. Peeping dismally, he now stumbled back to the nest, where his mother humped desolately over the ruins of her home. He was hungry as he had never been before, but the lemming she had brought from the far meadow had been lost as she dived upon the fox.

But now his father, the White One, appeared, carrying in his talons a small plover. Lemmings were scarce this year, for the cycle of their abundance had not yet reached its peak, but there were always shore birds in the marshy sloughs below the knoll, and longspurs and snow buntings on the windy ridges. Ookpikjuak eyed his father with admiration. A good hunter was the White One, who had provided well for his mate and their large family in spite of the scarcity of rodents. And a handsomer owl never coursed over the tundras of Keewatin. He was not so large as the female, but more beautiful, for the glossy white plumage was barely flecked with blackish, while hers was heavily barred and often blood-stained on the breast from the endless meat supply shredded for her young.

Now there was but one left, and little Ookpikjuak grew fat and strong on the rich diet of young birds that were beginning to run everywhere about the marshy meadows and across the crisp reindeer moss of the sun-baked tundras. Ducklings there were in the innumerable little lakes of the lowlands, a choice variety of downy young plovers and sandpipers, and the plump chicks of the ptarmigan, grouse of the Northland. Often Ookpikjuak wandered down the knoll to the pool and nestled in the little fringe of shade of the stunted rhododendrons that overhung its banks.

Through the long lonely days he sat quietly, adding layer upon layer of fat over his strengthening muscles, while the quills of adolescence lengthened and burst. Circles of white feathers formed spectacles around the great yellow eyes, and an epaulet of white appeared on the bend of each wing, followed at last by a mantle of barred brown and white that concealed the gray down of babyhood.

By the time the rains of August had overflowed the pools, and changed the crackling gray of the reindeer moss to a spongy carpet, Ookpikjuak was ready to try his wings. Flapping wildly, he now stumbled up the knoll toward the White One when he brought food, or hopped with widespread pinions to greet Old Snowy as she soared homeward across the grassy meadows.

It was on a wild, gray morning when the wind was rolling tumultuous breakers against the rocky shore, and myriad black flies and mosquitoes were silent in the sodden grass, that Ookpikjuak reached his majority. He had clambered to the top of the knoll and stood a full two feet tall, leaning against the wind while his keen eyes

scoured the distant lakes and meadows for a spot of white. Now she was coming closer, the Old Snowy, but as he stretched in eager anticipation she passed by him and circled with strong, steady wing beat until she was again passing the impatient young owl. As she flapped over him Ookpikjuak hopped angrily after the half-grown duck that dangled from her talons, and found himself soaring on outstretched wings into the wind. A great surge of power swept through Ookpikjuak. Raising and lowering his wings rhythmically, he followed Old Snowy down the knoll and came to rest beside her, panting and exuberant.

And now Ookpikjuak followed his parents on their eternal hunting trips, the three together, companionable and carefree. Daily they ranged farther, and the young owl learned the lessons of survival. For a time they still dropped food for him, although it no longer had to be torn into small bits. Eagerly he followed them as they coursed on silent wing over the grassy lowlands and the quiet blue water of the little lakes. In time he learned to differentiate between the browns and golds of the dry grasses and the browns and golds of a young ptarmigan. He learned how to maneuver his heavy body from a measured horizontal flight into the abrupt vertical plunge upon a swimming duck. He learned to watch for the runways of the lemming through the crowberry and reindeer moss of the uplands, and to detect the rustle of its nondescript brown form as it scuttled from hummock to hummock. Rarely as they were seen, they were worth watching for, for the owls had a definite preference for mammal food when they could find it.

And then came a day when the tundras were quiet. Young birds were full grown and more wary, and for several weeks there had been so much movement that the owls could no longer find their prey in the customary haunts. Shore birds and ducks, longspurs and snow buntings had left the countryside in great hordes, for the air was crisp and winter was creeping down from the North. Even the ptarmigan, which should have remained in abundance, had ominously disappeared, following the lemmings in their periodic cycle of scarcity.

As they flew slowly over the deserted lakes Ookpikjuak noticed that Old Snowy was drifting off toward the rocky shore line, and as the hours passed and she did not return he realized that their days of companionship were over. He would not see her again, his mother, but she had done well by him and he no longer had need of her.

And now Ookpikjuak must learn a new trick, or starve on the almost deserted barrens. After one last, unsuccessful foray, the young owl followed the White One to the rocky shore. Here, at high tide, the water lapped the boulders and made deep pools where the small fish came in to feed. With every appearance of lazy indifference the White One stretched out upon the rock at the water's edge, supine and comfortable. But his head was turned toward the water and his great eyes were alert. Ookpikjuak perched on a neighboring rock and watched his father intently. Without comprehending, he had long since learned that the White One's ways were wise ones, and that he had much to learn from them. Motionless they waited; then at last a small splash and a glint of bright fin in the autumn sunlight flashed in the little pool. Quicker than eye could follow, the White One had scooped out a small trout and dragged it back from the water's edge in his viselike talons.

Fish for dinner! Ookpikjuak, then, must also learn to angle, and he promptly chose a suitable-looking boulder and spread himself out as he had seen his father do. The wait was not long, but his muscles were untrained. When a fish broke water Ookpikjuak's foot splashed awkwardly and came out empty. With a flounce of annoyance, the young owl sailed back to the meadows for game he could understand. Dejectedly he ranged over the deserted lakes and marshes. A thin film of ice had already spread over the quiet waters and the tundras and grasslands were dead. As the hunger that gnawed his stomach crept out into his aching muscles Ookpikjuak returned to the shore and picked the scattered bones that the White One had left. They were tasty, these creatures of the Great Water. Resolutely he tried again. Another eluded him, and another, but at last the young owl hooked a small grayling and flapped it out on the rock before it could tear itself loose. Ravenously he ripped it open and gulped down great slabs of the white flesh. The next fish came more easily, for the children of the wild must learn their lessons quickly or starve. Now again Ookpikjuak was adding on the layers of rich fat over his heavy body that would keep him warm and strong through the long winter.

Then came the week of the great storms, when a roaring northeast wind lashed the Bay into an avalanche of black water and dashing spray that froze as it fell, leaving an ever-increasing coat of ice over the rocky shore. A line of eider ducks scudded southward, passing the two owls far out over the turbulent bay. To Ookpikjuak they were but a streak of black shadows against the overhanging clouds, but in the mind of the White One they stirred a vague remembrance. Once before there had been icy storms, and an empty belly, and a line of ducks silhouetted against a murky sky. With the next dash of spray the White One rose off his rocky perch and sailed majestically down wind. Ookpikjuak followed, not knowing where, and but dimly sensing why.

For many days the two owls followed the irregular coastline to the southward, but everywhere it was the same. Occasionally they found a matting of white feathers and bleached bones of a ptarmigan, more rarely a belated flock of ducks or plovers. For the most part they fished wherever they could find open water and moved onward toward better hunting grounds. From time to time they passed other snowy owls along the long trail, but the hunting was too precarious to encourage sociability, and the White One always shied away from his own kind.

One morning the sun rose directly ahead of them, for they had reached the bend where the shore of Hudson Bay circles around to the east. While Ookpikjauk blinked in wonder, the White One veered as if guided by an internal compass toward green horizon to the southward. And now, day and night, they traveled over a carpet of trees, trees such as the young snowy owl had never seen, stiff green spruces and lacy tamaracks, for uncounted hundreds of miles, a shadowy sea of green, broken occasionally by alder-fringed lakes and serpentine rivers. About the water the two owls fared well enough, but the woods were deep and forbidding to these dwellers of the windswept tundras, and they moved on restlessly, stopping only for food.

They came at last to a vast stretch of sunny sand, rising in long winding hills and deep valleys as far as their eyes could see. Beyond the sand to the westward lay the placid blue waters of Lake Michigan, rimmed with a broad fringe of rough ice that caught the last rays of the evening sun. There were little rafts of ducks floating here and there at the periphery of the shore ice. There were mouse and rabbit tracks everywhere in the snow that had drifted in the valleys. Here was food at last, here was space in abundance, and illimitable water and sunlight and wind that breathed the spirit of home to the weary owls.

They spent the night on a little mound overlooking the dunes, and were astir as the dawn tinged the irregular pattern of the ice fringe along the lake. The ducks were milling sleepily in their compact little rafts, stretching and splashing their wings and cackling among themselves in unsuspecting contentment. The two owls attacked together; two balls of snow on swift, unerring wings, they plunged into the midst of the terrified, bewildered waterfowl. Together they turned toward the shore and flew laboriously, laden with the most sumptuous meal they had seen in many weeks.

Near the shore was a pile of driftwood interwoven with bundles of dry grass, the only promontory on the entire beach. Unfamiliar with the devices of man, these dwellers of the arctic solitudes approached it without misgivings. A sharp report shattered the still morning air and a terrible pain throbbed through the left leg of Ookpikjuak. The duck fell from his grasp as the limp talons relaxed. With eyes glazed by fear and agony he saw the White One in a crumpled heap upon the sand, and a two-legged creature in a baggy, brown canvas coat running from the pile of driftwood. Another shot echoed against the dunes and Ookpikjuak flapped heavily to the far hills.

"Missed him!" shouted the man to his companion in the duck blind. "But by cracky, look here, Pete. How's this for a day's bag? Two ducks and an owl with one shot!"

He turned the White One over with a boot tip, while a squat little man, beswaddled in elaborate hunting togs, waddled up behind him. "Say, Hank, he's really a beauty! Pure white, almost. I believe I'll have him mounted; I've always wanted an owl for our store window."

"Too bad we missed the other one," observed Hank. "Duck thieves! I tell you, Pete, these owls are a murdering lot. And now our whole durn raft of ducks is gone. Guess our hunting is over for today. Let's get back to that pan of ham and eggs."

Smacking their lips over their prospective feast, the men picked up the White One and Ookpikjuak's breakfast, leaving a thin trail of blood across the drifting sand.

Through the lonely day Ookpikjuak crouched in the grass of the farthermost valley, his leg lying stiff and useless beneath him. For a time he was too sick to care about the loss of the duck, but as the hours dragged over the dunes the old gnawing returned at the pit of his stomach. At dusk he finally pushed himself unsteadily from the ground and flapped in wavering misery down the valley.

Near the border of the woods his keen ears detected a slight rustle, and soon he could discern the shadowy form of a little screech owl humped over the body of a deer mouse. Half-crazed by hunger and pain, Ookpikjuak swooped down upon her and the smaller owl slipped back into the shelter of the trees, leaving her prey behind her. Ravenously Ookpikjuak tore at the mouse, tottering wildly as he tried to use his one leg for both prop and anchor, flapping his great wings in an effort to balance himself. Revived now by the food in his aching body, Ookpikjuak drifted on down the valley and was able to capture a few mice for himself.

And so the winter passed. The leg healed slowly, but the dunes were a rich hunting ground and the crippled owl managed to eke out a meager existence in spite of his handicap. Out in the lake the ducks came and went, but Ookpikjuak never again ventured from the shelter of the hills. The memory of the White One, handsome, fearless father and companion, lying motionless in the sand, remained an indelible picture.

As the days grew longer and the sun beat warmly again upon the lonely owl, a vague restlessness stirred in the heart of Ookpikjuak.

In the woods behind the dunes the oaks were turning yellow-green and the flies had begun to hum incessantly in the dune grass. As the glowing fire of the sun sank into Lake Michigan the last red rays were reflected in the gleaming bodies of a flock of sandpipers. Circling high over the dunes they disappeared to the north. Sandpipers! As if in answer to a signal Ookpikjuak rose from his sandy hummock and turned his face, too, to the north. Over and beyond the dunes, over the carpet of trees that stretch for hundreds of miles across Canada's southern provinces, up the barren coast of Hudson Bay to the tundras of Keewatin.

Where the white tents of the Eskimos' summer encampment huddles companionably about the neat, re-trimmed buildings of the Post, Ookpikjuak veered suspiciously far inland. But he soon circled back to the shore, for the frozen bay and the wind-swept ridges were part and parcel of his lonely being.

Why one little stretch of hummocky tundra and a chain of scattered lakes should look any more desirable than another is a matter that only a bird can understand. Yet Ookpikjuak knew, and settled upon a rocky promontory with a deep booming croak, "*kroh-go-go-gok*," that proclaimed to all who might hear that this land was his, for home and hunting ground. Across the barrens there were answering booms, and he could see an occasional white form coursing over the distant meadows, but his territory remained unchallenged.

Whence She came he never knew, but one bright morning he found her sitting demurely on his favorite hummock, watching him with quiet, yellow eyes. To the lonely Ookpikjuak her soft white plumage with the delicate tracery of brown was more beautiful than anything he had ever beheld. Flying to a nearby boulder, Ookpikjuak lifted his head to the sunny skies, filled his throat with the crisp spring air until it was ready to burst for joy, and welcomed her with a series of solemn bows and low, resonant booms. Gravely She bowed in reply. Ecstatic, he jerked his tail upward until it almost brushed his back, bowing violently, hooting his deep boom of joy, bowing and booming, bowing and booming.

It was She who decided to build their nest upon the grassy hummock where they had met. It was She who scraped out the shallow depression and added the soft bits of reindeer moss and feathers that made the scant lining. Ardently he brought her every lemming he could find, and a rich assortment of the shore birds that were flooding the marshy meadows with new life. With feverish devotion he kept her sleek and fat while She brooded the five white, oval eggs. In time life's eternal cycle began anew, and there were five downy chicks peeping for food.

But the sun that had warmed the lonely heart of Ookpikjuak was hidden all too soon. Thunderheads were forming over the ice floes of Hudson Bay, and day after day a cold rain pelted the tender young birds of tundra and marshes. On the wind-swept hummock the shallow nest of the owls filled with water and one by one the owlets chilled and died. Ookpikjuak eyed them in silent anguish, but She was inconsolable. For two days She sat desolately upon the lifeless bodies. Then with a low hoot She sailed across the distant meadows and did not return.

And so the summer passed, as lonely as before. Again the birds moved southward, and again Ookpikjuak drifted down the barren coast and over the forests to the sand dunes of Michigan. Again he returned with the spring, drawn by an instinct stronger than hunger or fear, to the grassy knoll that had brought only misery.

What invisible magnet pulls a bird back from a thousand miles of woods and lakes and meadows to that infinitesimal plot that he recognizes as home? She, too, returned, his lovely mate, and again Ookpikjuak wooed her and hunted for her while She warmed the white eggs beneath her downy breast.

But the lives of the wild folk are full of peril, and Ookpikjuak was not destined to feed her young. Before the eggs were three days old a party of Eskimo boys wandered up the coast from the settlement. They carried small pails and their eyes were keen, for they, too, were hunting for food. As they topped the rise Ookpikjuak sprang into the air and circled conspicuously high over their heads, hooting a deep angry "*kroh-go-go-gok.*" Then he soared far down the distant meadow, eyeing them balefully over his shoulder. But the Eskimo boys were not misled by his ruse, for they had hunted the greater part of their young lives, and he who does not learn the ways of the birds and beasts goes hungry in the North. Scattering out across the tundra, they tramped in orderly circuits, taking their bearings by the willow twigs around the pools and the irregularities of the rocks that are signposts of the Barren Lands.

Suddenly She, too, was in the air, darting menacingly at one of the boys, circling his head with an angry rush of wings and furious snapping of her vicious beak. The boy promptly stood in his tracks. With a last abrupt dive on folded wings until her sharp talons grazed his cap, She veered toward the meadow to play her last trump. Flopping into a snowbank in the shadow of the ridge, She waddled awkwardly in irregular circles, dragging her wings and bellying in the snow, hobbling forward, flapping and falling, whining and barking feebly. With a great surge of wings Ookpikjuak joined her on the snowbank. But again the young Eskimos were unimpressed. The four boys worked in toward the lad who had flushed her, and soon one of them was waving his hat from the top of the nesting knoll.

She saw him first, and was over his head like a thunderbolt. But meat was scarce at the settlement and the bow was ready. A twang of his sealskin bowstring and the beautiful bird lay quivering at his feet. With a croak of despair Ookpikjuak sailed across the marshes and lakes to the farthermost ridge.

Thus another summer came and went, lonely, as always. That year the lemmings were plentiful and Ookpikjuak had no need to leave the Northland with the coming of the snows. And so he hunted over his solitary domain through the long months of winter, resting by night in the lee of a snow-drift, coursing the frozen marshes by day.

When spring came again to the tundras the Dark Lady drifted into his territory, a young bird of last summer's brood, heavily barred with brown. Ookpikjuak accepted her casually, for the race must be perpetuated, but the light had gone out of his heart when She fell at the feet of the Eskimo boys.

And so the years have rolled by, good years and lean in their turn. Some seasons the owls have reared their young successfully, in others the rains and their incessant enemies have taken heavy toll. The Dark Lady has been replaced in turn by several others, for even the wary may meet with disaster, but Ookpikjuak, the Lonely, has become more shy and solitary with the years. The Eskimo boys have invaded his domain many times, but they can never approach him within a hundred yards. And if you should tramp, some crisp June morning, up the barren coast of Hudson Bay, you might see him, a white dot sitting watchfully on the highest promontory of the rocky shore. Up close, you could not mistake him, for his eyes are as fierce and yellow as in his nestling days, although he is almost pure white now, the handsomest owl that ever coursed over the tundras of Keewatin.

The Chronicle of Obadiah

K. F. Bascom

OBADIAH'S PARENTS were plain, dumpy, unassuming people with plenty of gray in their hair. His father farmed a little and did something in the contracting line—excavating, I believe—and his mother was said to be not too proud to help now and then as needed. In front of their home stretched one of those pleasant, sloping cow pastures along French Creek, with a row of trees looking down from the brow of the hill and at the bottom the water rippling over its flat shale bed on its way from one quiet pool to another. A rail fence wandered down to the water's edge, and a great oak and a gnarled cherry tree stood halfway down the slope as if they had started toward the creek and could not decide to go forward or back. There were a few broad stumps in this pasture—stumps of pines that had been saplings when a lean, lank Virginia boy, not unknown to chroniclers as the Father of His Country, paddled and poled a canoe up this creek, bearing messages to the French. The full-grown pines had long since crashed to earth amid the shouting of the axmen and had gone down the creek in the spring to the thriving village of Pittsburgh.

A quiet life the family led until one fine May morning. Such affairs had happened often enough in western Pennsylvania in the early days, but in those stark dramas the villains had worn little else than the red skins in which they were born. This morning one of the overalled gang hid behind a stump and sniped the old man as he started somewhat stiffly for his day's work, and a few minutes later the gang broke into the house and shot the old lady neatly between the eyes. At this point it should be added that it alters the story a good deal from the human standpoint, if not from all others, to make it known that this was merely a family of woodchucks.

There were four little fellows thus orphaned—little chucks with brown, beady eyes and wiry gray hair, shading to almost white beneath but tinged with reddish-brown back of the front legs. The dog got two. The others were saved for the time being and, since I was the professor of zoology in the local college, they came at last into my possession. Putting orphan woodchucks into the hands of a zoologist, and a bachelor to boot, was a scurvy trick on the part of the furry equivalents of the Fates who may be presumed to preside over the destinies of the wild brethren. I had no knowledge, theoretical or practical, of pediatrics, but warm milk by way of a medicine dropper seemed logical. The starved, shivering, stiff little creatures swallowed feebly three or four times and would have no more of it.

A feminine bystander watched with some interest the amateurish attempt at feeding and christened the orphans forthwith. "This one is Obadiah and this one is Jonah." She gave no reasons for this choice except that the orphans looked as if those might be their names. As to marks of distinction, the livelier one was Obadiah. A bed of cotton and excelsior in a dry aquarium received the casually christened orphans.

Morning showed the choice of names to have been not wholly inappropriate. Jonah had not left his bed but lay there, brown eyes open and still bright, the stiff and pitiful effigy of a little woodchuck. Obadiah, goaded by curiosity or by pangs of hunger, had climbed from his bed and started adventuring, beginning the performance in good earnest with a sheer plunge from the table. He squeaked protestingly from behind a desk and seemed to swear when prodded into the open with a meter stick.

Refreshed and warmed through after his night's rest, and hungry as well, Obadiah drank copiously of warm milk from the medicine dropper, slept an hour, and then chattered indignantly for attention. He had fallen from the table into the wastebasket, had climbed to its rim, and was there balanced precariously in grave danger.

I regret to state that Obadiah required certain delicate attentions of a personal nature before being entirely fitted for human society. To put the matter plainly, he harbored upon his person a considerable society, most of them ticks ranging from the small shrunken ones miscellaneously distributed in company with sundry large and active fleas to swollen patriarchs between his toes, gorged with blood and clinging for dear life. After the largest ticks had been picked off and Obadiah had received a few dustings with insect powder, which he resented, he was thenceforth free from fauna.

Obadiah soon reconciled himself entirely to drinking from the medicine dropper and fed as nonchalantly and copiously as from nature's font, even standing up on his hind legs and grasping the dropper quite as an old toper might hold a bottle. In such manipulations the four toes of his front foot acted as fingers, while the little black pad he wore instead of a thumb was used in place of that organ. He drank milk at each of his four meals a day until his little belly was as tight as a drum and the hairs which before so snugly covered it separated and let the stretched skin of his round paunch shine nakedly through.

Once he had regained his strength and had learned of the world outside of his glass bedroom, contentment left him, but much as I sympathized with his wanderlust, even the foster-parent of a woodchuck must labor, and so I laid a screen over the aquarium, weighted it and turned a deaf ear to his squeakings, chatterings and scratchings. At mealtime he showed a well-skinned nose. As his guardian had leisure to supervise such adventures, Obadiah toured the lawn before the building, testing carefully everything he found. The first solid food which he seemed to relish was the yellow head of a dandelion. He ate no other plant food except the centers of dandelion heads until a couple of weeks later.

Obadiah's conceptions of the universe are for the most part unknown. It would seem that he must have recalled a burrow as a place of refuge, dug out in the ground. At least, some such hereditary idea might have been expected to come down to him from his burrowing ancestors. But no such dry definition hampered him. He was an opportunist and regarded a refuge as a burrow and to be appreciated as such, whether it ran up or down, whether it was empty and walled with earth or partly filled with a squirming human limb and walled with serge or tweed. In brief, he climbed trouser legs with great facility and apparent satisfaction to himself. He by no means despised coat sleeves, although they were less commodious, and one day while thus employed put forth his prematurely gray and serious countenance from my coat collar as I talked with a book salesman. This habit of his rendered him undoubtedly amusing, but I somewhat frowned upon it after I had been obliged to reach after him up the coat sleeve of a semi-hysterical young lady, this performance being staged before an appreciative little group of spectators. The young lady had held Obadiah in her hands and had been amused when he started up her arm.

Obadiah had manifested some dissatisfaction with his sleeping accommodations, and since he showed such a predilection for anything resembling a burrow, it occurred to me to provide him with a sleeping bag. An old sock (once described by an optimistic supply sergeant as O. D., wool, heavy), when its toe was cut off, was undoubtedly in all essentials a burrow. When, after his supper, it was held open before Obadiah on the floor, he immediately recognized it as such and crawled in. It was then laid in his bed, and he, after sundry contortions, which made the sock twist about like a sausage bewitched, managed at length to tuck his nose under his bulging belly and so slept.

Obadiah cared for his cutting teeth in his own way. When he came into my hands, he already had two tiny lower incisors breaking the gums. He employed human fingers in lieu of teething-rings, and the owners at first offered them willingly enough, even after the upper incisors began to show. However, Obadiah's front teeth, if human standards may be applied, soon grew too large for his face. He never seemed to realize the effect of those chisels upon the human skin and continued to employ as his favorite form of salutation and practical joke the seizing and nipping of convenient fingers.

As the weather grew warmer and Obadiah became larger, he was put out on the grass in a bottomless wire cage where he might have been seen on a fine day lying "prone on his back," giving his aldermanic abdomen a sunbath. Soon tiring of the confinement, he trotted endlessly in a circle until the grass was smashed flat, stopping only to try to climb out of his cage, reaching up with his teeth while he clung with his claws. Hoping that the possession of a home of his own would give him contentment, I dug a shallow burrow of what I judged to be the proper caliber for him and encouraged him to employ his energies. He fell to work with a will. He bit mouthfuls of dirt from the side of the hole, thereby justifying those prominent front teeth. He put his head into the burrow, turned his stubby tail to the sky and scratched industriously with his front feet, sending the earth out in jets behind him, meanwhile turning himself in the burrow somewhat like an auger. Now and then he paused in these activities to kick out earth with his hind feet, all this as if it were an old story being done in the most blasé and professional manner. Unfortunately his zeal proved transitory. He abandoned the burrow and dug his way to freedom beneath the edge of the cage, being recaptured in a yard across the street, while valiantly sitting up on his haunches and viewing in a most confident way the approach of a dog large enough to swallow him at a gulp.

He grew so strong and so impatient of confinement that one morning he was set free out of doors, whereupon he dug a burrow beneath a set of stone steps beside the building and late in the afternoon began to carry into it dead leaves and grass. On being presented with an armful of excelsior, he began at once to stow it away in his new apartment. He filled his mouth with excelsior while he was down on all fours and then sat up, using his front paws very cleverly to tuck up loose ends, meanwhile keeping a bright lookout for danger. This burrow having been furnished, Obadiah, who hitherto had been oblivious to photographers, now became as suspicious as a superstitious Indian and would dive into his hole at the click of a shutter. There was also a difference in his reaction to other strange noises, and as he foraged on the lawn an auto back-firing in the street would send him galloping for cover, although on one memorable occasion he withstood the noisy advance of a gasoline lawn mower until it was a few feet away. Even then his panic was short-lived and he soon looked forth again from his den like Diogenes from his tub.

As he grew older his food habits changed. He began to eat clover and lost somewhat his taste for milk, although crackers soaked in that fluid remained his favorite food. He would eat abundantly of such provender, always sitting up on his haunches and stuffing his mouth, showing the whites of his eyes and meanwhile chewing very rapidly like a through passenger in a railway lunchroom.

In a few weeks Obadiah discovered a hole in the foundation of a neighboring house and transferred his residence, mining out endless galleries beneath the building but never too busy to come when called, his muzzle covered with fresh earth, to eat home-made cookies, bar chocolate, nuts and such dainties. He regarded himself as a member of the family, and by pushing aside a loose board in the floor, came into the kitchen for his morning drink of water, following the housewife about and nipping her ankles until his pan was filled. He resented in the same manner too much affection lavished in his presence upon the family cat. The latter, a lanky stripling, had at first made playful overtures to the visitor and Obadiah had responded in kind, according to his own ideas of what constituted play, the same involving a liberal use of those natural chisels with which nature had furnished him. The cat, after losing several mouthfuls of fur, clawed Obadiah's snout earnestly with the accompaniment of feline profanity, and thereafter each went his way.

Autumn came, and Obadiah was caught and transferred to the basement of the zoology building and incarcerated behind wire netting. A crack in the concrete floor served as the starting point for another burrow. The college circus being in prospect, an emissary was sent to secure Obadiah's attendance at that function. Obadiah put his head out of his burrow willingly enough and accepted and ate with appreciation piece after piece of bar chocolate but would not come entirely out of his burrow nor would he allow himself to be touched. Presently, no more chocolate being forthcoming, he retired to his sleeping chamber and was seen no more all winter.

When he once more awoke, it was spring. The snow in the old cow pasture where he was born had melted and run into French Creek. Sap was dripping from wooden spouts into sugar buckets and trailing arbutus blossoms made a quiet appearance in hidden spots. Among dead grass blades in pools of snow water the spring peepers shrilled. Spring is a season when even certain men have been known to use something less than their best judgment. Obadiah escaped from his home, now become an intolerable prison. Whether the motive was romance or just plain ennui, no one knows. How far he traveled and how he fared cannot appear in the record. He was gone a week and then came home to his adopted friends, three toes gone from a front foot and a great wound in his throat. He seemed glad to be back with us, but he lived only three days. And so Obadiah was buried under a cherry tree in a sunny garden.

The Little Brown Jug

George Elwood Jenks and Kay McKay

I FOUND my first little brown jug cemented to the top of a dry wild oat stalk. It was a perfect miniature jug, modeled in clay and about the size of a small marble. A little yellow-and-black wasp was still working on it, sealing it up with a stopper of clay.

Then the wasp flew away, and I never saw her again, nor did I ever find another such jug nest in nature. But the following summer I discovered a few more of these wasps feeding upon the nectar of wild anise blossoms. So I started a small colony of them in an apple-box cage with a glass front. It was late in the summer, however, and nothing happened; no jug nests were built to provide material for study.

The next year I started early and was able to build up a colony of about a dozen wasps. After two or three weeks they began to feel at home in their new habitat, and two of them started to build jugs. I hoped that I would be able to obtain pictures for a complete life story, but then came tragedy. A horde of ants swarmed into the cage one night and wiped out my entire colony.

A similar fate came to my wasp colony the next summer, and then came World War II. War work called me and I had to abandon any wasp investigations. But with the coming of victory I turned back to my wasp studies. So, the seventh summer after my first encounter with the jug nest of the wild oat stalk, our luck held good. We were able to complete the story of the little brown jug and the little wasp that is such an expert at pottery. These years of trying to get the story will explain why, in the series of pictures that follow, we have used several different jug nests in order to show clearly all of the successive stages of construction. The species presented is known among entomologists as *Eumenes xanthogaster*.

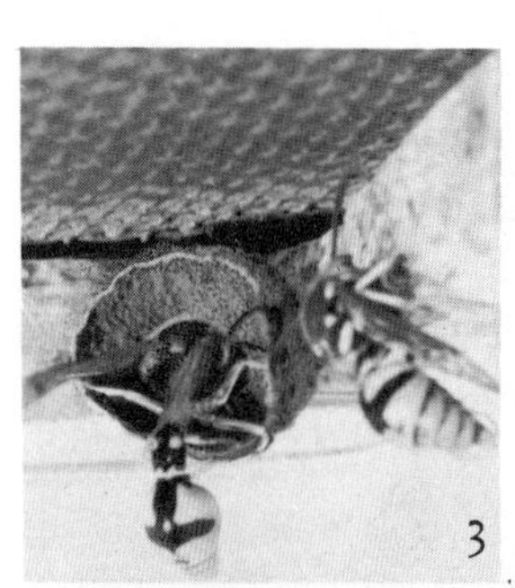

1. *The little wasp first lays a rough floor. She finds it easier to use the clay cement from the walls of a nearby abandoned jug than to dig up fresh clay.*

2. *Here the floor is finished and the side walls started, but there is not too much left of the old jug nest.*

3. *The jug nest is built in the manner of a cistern, with thin, delicately modeled walls of cement that is a mixture of clay and saliva.*

4. *The walls rise higher, the wasp carefully holding the soft clay in place as she adds to the height, usually modeling the clay cement between her "forearms" and her "chin."*

5. *Now the wasp is beginning to "draw in" the walls to start the circular, arched roof.*

6. The opening grows smaller as the dome approaches the "bottleneck." Apparently the male wasp is just a back-seat driver during most of the building operations, leaving the real work to the female.

7. Here the skillful little sculptress is modeling the bottleneck.

8. Not satisfied with simply leaving an opening, she finishes it off with a circular lip, or flange.

9. The female wasp is laying an egg. As she rests on the flange, her telescopic abdomen enables her to reach into the interior of the jug nest.

10. When we violate the privacy of the jug nest, we find a single egg, which is attached to the wall with a strong thread.

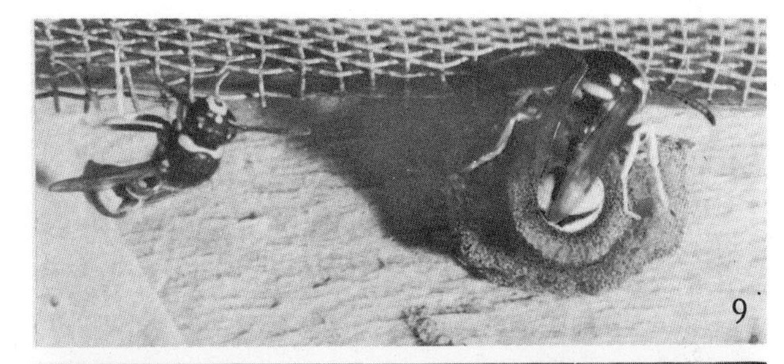

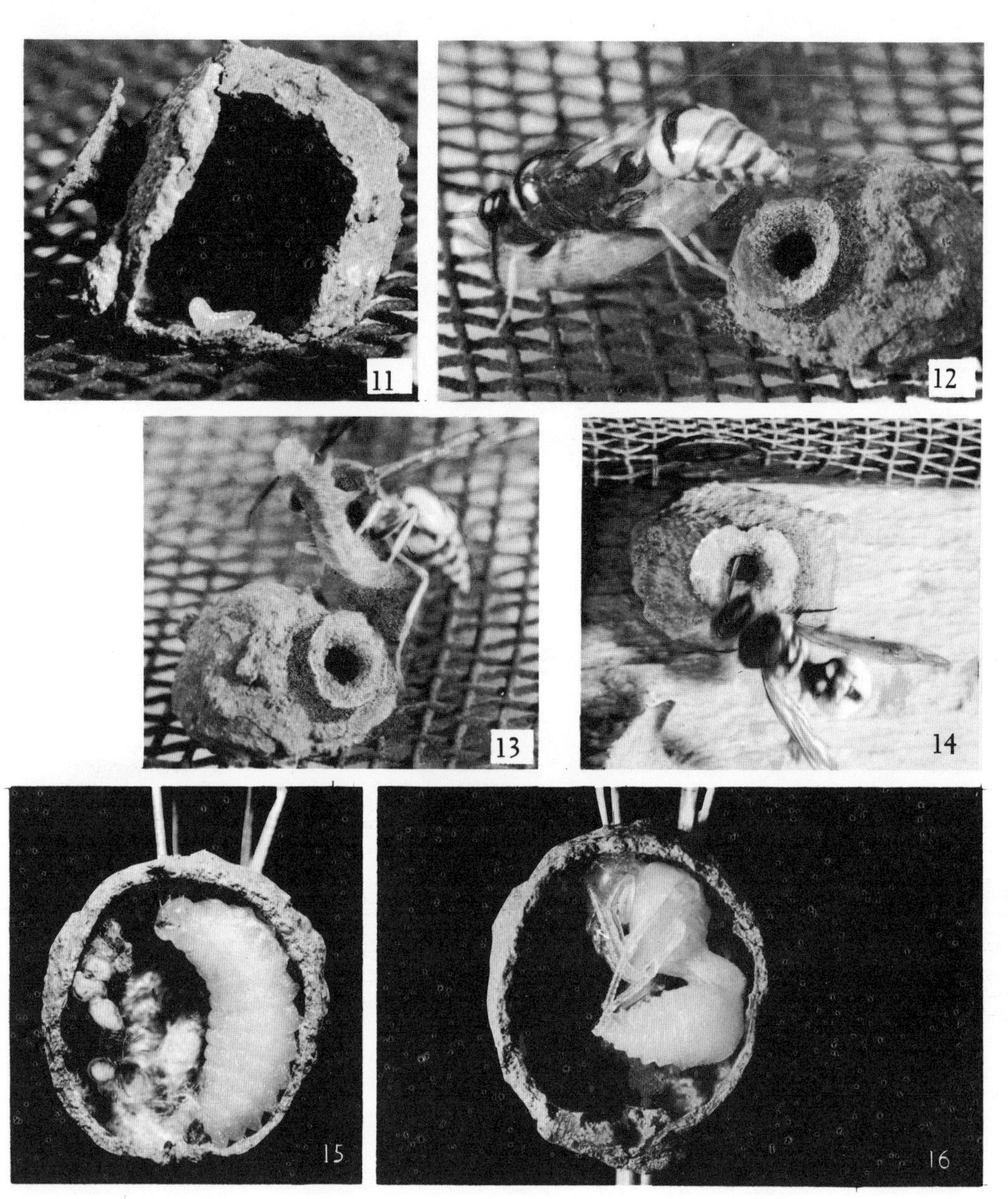

11. *In a few days the egg hatches. Meanwhile the mother wasp has been cramming the brown jug with food.*

12. *She catches small caterpillars and paralyzes them with her sting, which only stuns them and keeps them in "cold storage."*

13. *The caterpillar is limp and helpless, and the wasp is getting ready to poke it into the jug. (She does this so swiftly that it was never possible to photograph her in the act.)*

14. *Here she is testing the interior with her antenna to make sure it is well filled with baby food. Then she will cork the jug with clay cement.*

15. *Several weeks pass. The food is low, but the larva is about to pupate.*

16. *First, however, there is another period of inner development and the final molt.*

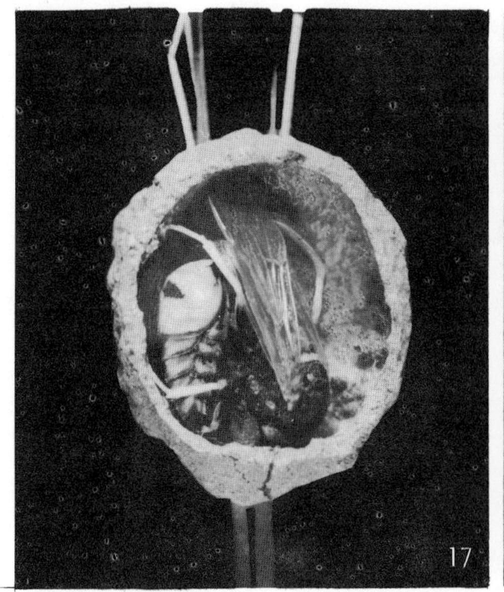

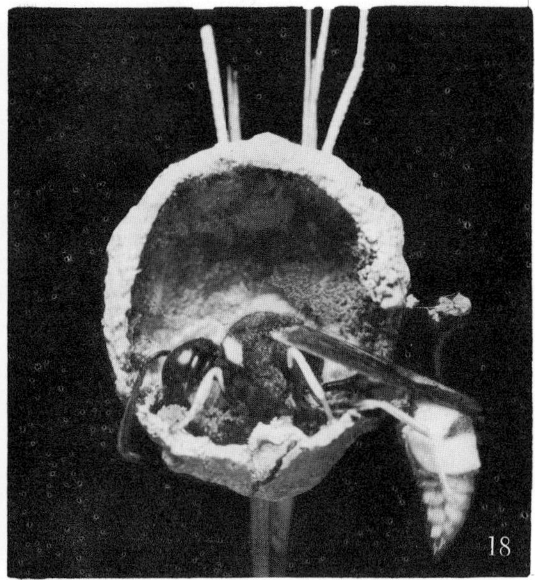

17. *It would seem that the wasp-to-be has been sitting on the end of its spine so long that it will never be able to straighten its back. At last the pupa has turned into a wasp, although still a rather topsy-turvy one.*

18. *It is ready to kick a hole in the thin, fragile wall and back out.*

19. *A few hours of drying off in the sunshine, and the new wasp, now a strict vegetarian, is ready to take off in search of some nectar-laden flower, and, perhaps, to build some little brown jugs of her own.*

Strange Animal Friendships

J. Frank Dobie

IT WOULD NOT startle me to see a lion and a lamb lying down together—provided each had been cut off from its kind, and the lion had made the acquaintance of the lamb while not hungry. Some animals, of course, are notably more gregarious than others. I shall never forget the cry of distress I heard one late winter evening from a little blackbird that for a minute or two had become separated from a flock of thousands that was shifting about in a field. On the other hand, the lone wolf may be tracked for months without finding where he has joined his mate. Nevertheless, nearly all animals yearn for companionship, and when they cannot consort with their own kind they sometimes form fast and fiercely devoted attachments to creatures utterly foreign.

The otter of Britain is usually harried by dogs and men, but Lockwood Kipling tells how a Scottish gamekeeper once trained an otter to run with his dogs, which formed a friendship for it. It was the best "hound" in his pack.

A ranchman out on the Frio River in Texas used to have a pet buck that had been raised from fawnhood with the house dogs. It formed a particular friendship with a massive mongrel known as Old Blue. The two were inseparable. The buck would paw other dogs away from food while Old Blue gorged himself. When the pack hunted, sometimes five and six miles out from the ranch, the buck would accompany them, leading in the chase after wolves or other animals. When he was four or five years old, the buck took to ranging far away and alone, being gone for weeks at a time. The only way to entice him back to the ranch was to lead Old Blue to his vicinity. Once he sensed the dog, he would go straight to him and accompany him back to the ranch, there to stay until the call of the wild tolled him forth again.

I have heard of a javelina, or peccary, raised as a pet by Mexicans, that took up with the dogs and became a hunter with them. I know one peccary that, captured as a pig and suckled by a goat, became as vigilant a caretaker of a herd of goats as any shepherd dog.

The dogs used by Mexicans for shepherds are nearly all mongrels out of rangy blood. They could have become sheep-killers, yet because they have been suckled as pups by nannies or ewes, and because the goats and sheep have become used to them, they are as one with their charges. I know of a kid that was taken from its flock and raised as a pet with some ranch dogs. The dogs had each other for company, but they seemed to love the goat, as it grew up, like a brother. When they rushed out at night barking at mocking coyotes, the goat would rush with them, as brave as a lion.

W. H. Hudson, in *Idle Days in Patagonia*, tells of a wild heifer that broke away from a herd being driven along the coast and swam to a small island inhabited by wild hogs. She was considered lost, but about a year after her escape a native who went to the island to cut rushes came upon the cow stretched out asleep with the whole herd of hogs, twenty-five or so in number, piled and heaped around her, each one, apparently, ambitious to pillow its head against her. She was almost covered up. On various other occasions the cow was seen, always in close company with the hogs who had adopted her.

Almost any creature taken away from its kind and from its habitual environments will readily take up with another form of life. Billy the Kid set out on one of his desperate rides on a wild horse that had never before been saddled. After he had kept the animal a day and a night in strange mountains, cut off from all other creatures, it would follow him like a pet and was uneasy out of his presence.

These unusual attachments are at times, no doubt, motivated by the instinct for self-protection. On the plains of Kansas, about 1870, a traveler named W. E. Webb observed a feeble old buffalo bull, an outcast from his own herd, keeping company with a band of mustangs. The wild horses probably tolerated him more than they loved him, but in their company he was safe from wolves. On the other hand, Buffalo Jones, who did much to preserve the buffalo from extinction, came into possession of a two-year-old colt—probably a cut-off from some band of mustangs—that had been ranging with a particular herd of buffaloes for about a year.

When I was a boy living on a ranch thickly populated with bobwhites, a certain quail took up one summer with our chickens, going to roost with them in the evening in a chicken house, although it is the nature of quail to roost on the ground. To see this plump little bird cuddled on a pole beside a ponderous Plymouth Rock hen was a comfortable sight. Morning and evening, while bobwhites were calling on every side, he, apparently oblivious to his kind, stayed close to the chickens. I do not know what became of him, but thirty years after he had gone the way of all flesh I learned that a solitary bobwhite, in a region replete with bobwhites and in a county adjacent to mine, had taken up with a flock of young tame turkeys. It was sleeping with them in a tree by night, and by day following them about, eating grass seeds while they caught grasshoppers.

There is a mothering, protective instinct in a great many animals, stronger in certain individuals of a given species than in others, that often leads to remarkable associations. An orphaned calf out on the range is occasionally adopted by a cow. Usually the dogie will try without success to suck first one cow and then another; once in a while, however, a cow that it approaches will allow it to share her milk with her own offspring. It is on record that in 1934 an orphaned moose calf in Wyoming was adopted by a milch cow.

Mules are notorious for their insane passion for company. A mule will all but break its neck in order to get with the bell mare. Sometimes mules, particularly young mules, will run a calf or colt to death—not, apparently, with intent to kill, but from desire to get it to take up with them. One of the most passionately devoted foster mothers I have ever known of was a mare mule that had been adopted by a Brahman calf. Both were owned by a friend of mine in southwest Texas. One day while riding on his ranch he came upon the calf sucking the mule, and soon discovered that the mule was actually giving milk. The calf's mother had died. Whether it or the mule had begun the association nobody could say. Exercise of the mammary glands induced a flow of milk in the mule. She raised the calf and it went on sucking until it was far past the usual age for weaning. The mule was simply fanatical about it. I read recently about a similar case in another part of Texas. In this latter instance, when the rancher approached the calf the mule kicked him on the jawbone, breaking it.

Just as in human beings, there are in animals all sorts of opposing tendencies, dual inclinations, or contradictory instincts. A dog with nursing pups pursued a female coyote to her den and helped kill it. The coyote had pups, and when they were brought out of the hole, the old dog whined and nosed them in a most sympathetic manner. One little coyote was saved and put with the dog's puppies. She nursed it and "flead" it along with her own young, and it grew up a boon companion to the dogs. However, its propensity for killing chickens finally proved its ruin.

H. I. Dillaway of California reports that on one occasion when a mother doe was killed by a train he took the fawn and placed it near a setter that had lost her pups and was still heavy with milk. As the fawn began scenting near her, the setter rolled over as an invitation for the fawn to feed. It immediately began to nurse. Thereafter it had a devoted foster-mother that often fought other dogs away when they seemed to menace her adopted baby.

I have seen cats stalking squirrels and I have no doubt that if a young squirrel came within reach of a hunting cat she would devour it. Yet a California mother cat nursed and licked some young orphan squirrels that a man slipped in among her kittens.

On fox farms, cats deprived of their kittens are commonly used as wet nurses for little foxes. The convicts on a state farm in east Texas knew nothing about this when they raided a squirrel's nest and captured some little squirrels to feed a pet tabby that had just kittened. When they gave them to her, she promptly adopted them and soon had them feeding along with her own infants.

At the village of Oakhurst, Texas, a family of children had as their chief pet a female dog that had not had puppies for about a year. One day someone gave them three tiny squirrels. They were overjoyed at the prospect of raising them with medicine dropper and bottle. First, they lugged in a good-sized box and shut the squirrels inside. Before they knew it, their pet dog was inside also, claiming the little squirrels as though they were her own offspring. They suckled her and she gave milk. She reared them successfully. Before the squirrels arrived, she had been on the best of terms with a cat, but after she adopted them she ceased all comradeliness with the cat and would drive it away in a fierce manner if it came too near her adopted ones.

Although no one would believe that the

she-wolf suckled Romulus and Remus, parallels to which persist today in the traditional lore of India, there is in the story nothing foreign to the mothering nature of many animals. Kropotkin, the great Russian social philosopher, wrote a book called *Mutual Aid* in which he adduces scores of cases exemplifying friendly co-operation between animals, principally between individuals of a given species; but the relationships we are considering are of a different character. Nor do they belong in the category of uncommunicative, often resented, associations whereby one animal uses another for advantage, the coyote, as I have seen, dogging the badger to catch rats the latter runs out of holes, and the crow following the wolf in the hope of getting a morsel from its kill.

Some animal friendships are not to be accounted for either by the theory of protection or the theory of isolation. They develop, like many human friendships, through accidental propinquity. I have read of a hen that took to roosting in the stall of a stallion. She would roost nowhere else, and if she were removed the stallion would grow restless and fierce. The two were devoted to each other.

In 1933 a resident of Duncan, Oklahoma, who kept a cow that was often barked at and tormented by dogs and that he staked out by day on vacant lots, discovered a neighbor's dog trying to sleep on the straw in the cow's shed. At first the cow tried to hook the dog, Buck by name, and keep him away. Finally Buck had his will. Then he took to keeping company with the cow while she grazed. If a strange dog appeared, he would chase it away. The dog and the cow grew to be inseparable companions, the dog leaving her only long enough to go home for his meals.

One of the prettiest sights of nature in my memory is of a spotted fawn and two kittens lying on Bermuda grass in the sunshine. The fawn would stretch out its delicate head along the ground, and on either side of it, cheek by jowl, the kittens would stretch out also, all three cat-napping. They would drink milk together, the felines laping from a saucer while their mistress held a bottle for the little deer to drink from. When the fawn nibbled grass, the kittens would place their forefeet up on its legs and shoulders or on its head. As a captive the fawn had no other playmates; the kittens wished for no other cat society.

On a California farm a Canadian goose and a lamb recently took up with each other, the lamb coming to the goose's honk and the goose responding to the lamb's bleat. Forest rangers discovered a jackrabbit near the Grand Canyon keeping company with a doe.

A Texas rancher some years ago raised a litter of hogs and a litter of dogs together, the pigs and pups playing with each other promiscuously. One day he trapped a fox, tied up his grown dogs, and then released the fox, which was uninjured, for the pups to follow. At first it took to a tree. Then it jumped out, the pups chasing hard. When one caught up with it, the fox turned suddenly to fight. One pup let out a yelp for help. It happened that three of its playfellow shoats were rooting nearby. Hearing the cry, which persisted, they came running, attacked the fox, and were killing it when the rancher pulled them off.

In 1847 an Englishman named John Palliser came to America to hunt and to gather a menagerie. He accumulated several buffaloes, a pet bear, an antelope that the bear considered a friend, and various other animals. When he reached the docks at

New Orleans, as he relates in *The Solitary Hunter*, he sent a man ahead leading the antelope, he himself following with the bear. Suddenly a huge mastiff sprang for the antelope. The bear lunged forward, slapped the dog over, and would surely have killed it had it not managed to get away.

The bear's protection of the antelope and the rush of the hogs to the distressed pup are essentially no more foreign to nature than a dog's guardianship over a child belonging to his master. If dogs, elementally predaceous toward sheep, become their protecting shepherds, we need not be surprised that a lioness was so devoted to two dogs belonging to a Michigan policeman that she pined away and died after their death. Given the opportunity, almost any combination may develop between one kind of animal and another, just as between man and any kind of animal. It seems to be part of nature's plan.

Feathered Personalities

John Lindsey Blackford

SOME COOL SWEET MORNING in late March or early April, if you chance to tread the the dank places of the woods, you may hear the varied thrush, often called the Canadian or Alaskan robin. He is an artist in whose soul must rest the consciousness of immortality; lyric perfection such as his was never intended for a brief existence. And if you are wise and follow those rare moments with a further acquaintance, you will come to rejoice in his friendship. You have, in fact, met one of the wildwood's feathered personalities.

Personality, although it remains undefined, unless it be by the undefinable third person singular neuter, is recognized by all. And even though it may wear feathers, as in the case of our bird friends, its charm is certain to captivate the rest of us. Indeed, so marked in individuality are the feathered folk, that whether we have made them the subject of life-long study or know them only from an occasional jaunt over field and across stream, we leave them feeling that our acquaintance has been all too brief and fleeting. Surely one cannot listen long to the varied thrush without wishing he might capture the experience for all time.

Scarcely have soft chinook winds scattered the snow patches when, on waking some morning, you hear his vibrant note. Like the twang of a zither or the ringing note of a chime, his music possesses something that adds an elusive tone of eerie mystery. Pitched low or high in a minor key his notes awaken an answering vibration in the heart of his hearer; henceforth your enthusiasm for this songster cannot be understood by one who has not as yet come under the spell of his enchantment.

Of him Louis Agassiz Fuertes has written: "His song is most unique and mysterious, and may be heard in the deep still spruce forests for a great distance, being very loud and wonderfully penetrating. It is a single long drawn note, uttered in several different keys, some of the high pitched ones with a strong vibrant trill. Each note grows out of nothing, swells to a full tone, and then fades away to nothing, until one is carried away with the mysterious song. When heard nearby, as is seldom possible, the pure yet resonant quality of the note makes one thrill with a strange feeling, and is as perfectly the voice of the cool, dark, peaceful solitude which the bird chooses for its home as could be imagined. The hermit thrush himself is no more serene than this wild dweller in the western spruce forests."

In size the varied thrush is somewhat smaller that the western robin and trimmer in shape. His markings, however, are striking and beautiful. Across the brilliant burnt orange of his breast extends a crescent of black, while his back is dark bluish slate, the wings banded and edged with brown. A strip of orange brown lightens the dark slate of his head. The movements of the bird are quick, and until his alert shyness has worn off he is difficult of approach.

Always he seems to have a passion for spring. And like a lover he follows her northward each year. In the cool northern forests and high mountain meadows, where summer is but a blush upon the face of Earth, he finds her lingering in July and August. There he nests for a brief season, and, with the change of the year, drifts southward to the rainy coasts of Oregon and northern California. To me he is so much a part of spring that his ringing notes are the theme song of bursting buds, bright sunshine and showers, and soft spring breezes. Since I can remember he has been associated in my mind with the "Spring Song" of Mendelssohn. I have always thought that surely the great composer was inspired by the song of some European thrush when he wrote those notes of liquid melody. And if I am often tempted by one or the other to follow spring into the woods and mountains, it is because the song of spring is in the hearts of us all.

And though spring's lavish beauty is all about us bringing renewed life and hope, one cannot but have a poignant feeling of regret, even in this season of rejoicing, when the varied thrush goes northward. Perhaps it is because we are not quite consolable that another feathered friend arrives to delight us with a voice of incomparable sweetness.

He is the hermit thrush, a celebrity to nature lovers, and the delight of all who hear him. His shy nature, however, and the fact that his habitat is always in the depths of the forest have given him the reputation of a recluse. But, like many another artist of rare ability, his retiring habits have failed to keep him from the public eye, and he is widely famed for his virtuosity. Truly a Meistersinger, he is credited with being the finest songster of the continent.

"Three birds stand out in my life experience," writes Dr. Charles Pease. "The first is the hermit thrush; the only time I have heard him was close to evening by a small river in New England—that unforgettable purity of unbelievable melody!" And he continues: "The thrush in his many varieties belongs to the highest type of bird life. This gifted group leads me sometimes to wonder if man may not have blundered in conceiving himself as the topmost form of life. To be given the power of flight and the gift of song comes close to the apex of Nature's largess."

The species in its several variations is distributed from coast to coast; in the West the Alaskan hermit, the dwarf, the Monterey, and the Audubon hermit are distinguished by ornithologists.

The latter, whose range covers the Rocky Mountain region from near the northern border of the United States south to Guatemala, east to Texas, and west to the mountains of Arizona and the southern

Sierra Nevada, is best known to the writer. The adult bird is some seven or more inches in length, upper parts grayish-brown, chest mottled, and its tail of a rufous color. In summer he is abundant in northwestern Montana along the south watershed of the Kootenai, and his vesper song at twilight is a most enriching experience. From the damp fastnesses of the forest where black birch, willow, and mountain maple crowd one another for the light that comes down through the tall tamaracks, his notes come sweetly, seeming not to break the hush of nightfall. How reassuring after the hot, tiring day! How restful and calm. What lessons of faith and hope might he not teach us!—that voice so full of certainties, so changeless in its serenity.

Almost never has a description of nature been written comparable to the reality, but in her *Birds of Western United States* Florence Merriam Bailey, writing of the hermit's song, rivals her subjects in the beauty of her words. She tells us:

"As you travel through the spire-pointed fir forests of the western mountains, you know the thrush as a voice, a bell-like sublimated voice, which, like the tolling of the Angelus, arrests toil and earthly thought. Its phrases can be expressed in the words Mr. Burroughs has given to the eastern hermit, 'Oh, spheral, spheral! oh, holy, holy!' and the first strain arouses emotions which the regularly falling cadences carry to a perfect close. The fine spirituality of the song, its serene uplifting quality, make it fittingly associated with Nature's most exalted moods, and it is generally heard in the solemn stillness of sunrise, when the dark fir forest is tipped with gold, or in the hush of sunset, when the western sky is aglow and the deep voice rises from its chantry in slow, soul-stirring cadences, high-up-high-up, look-up, look-up."

Thoreau proclaims that, whenever and wherever a man hears it, there is a new world and a free country, and the gates of heaven are not shut against him.

Wandering up the watercourses of the western mountains mid fern and bracken and golden mimulus, one is often mindful of a slate-colored wren-like bird whose uncommon antics and clear melodious voice soon gain for him a place in your heart. The water ouzel, or dipper, is a boisterous, cheery little chap, a gay bundle of personality plus. He dashes into and out of the water, perilously close to the strong currents, and teeters up and down on some wet rock amid the flying spume. He can walk on the bottom with swift running water over his head and come up dry as a duck. With a splash he dives beneath the surface to bob up here and there and then go off in swift flight over the foaming rapids. But soon you overtake him and hear him singing, adding sweet overtones to the music of rushing waters.

Springtime and fishing weather! Morning air with a cleansing fragrance of pine and balsam, and the jolly little dipper is that extra touch that makes a day complete.

Perhaps you can discover his nest, a fairy dream house, behind the gossamer curtain of a waterfall. Where the site is to his liking it nestles on a rockshelf, drenched by rainbow mists. It is a beautiful sphere of living moss, braced with twigs and well cemented. If the stream be small the nest is yet artfully placed near the water and the birds have been seen to sprinkle it themselves. They do it by diving into a pool, then going to the top of their wee hut and shaking themselves violently.

Unless you are familiar with the habits of

the water ouzel you would be amazed should you revisit the spot in winter. There he is along the icy brink of the cascade, a picture of urchin enthusiasm! Watch how he splashes about in the eddies or behind miniature waterfalls! Now he clambers upon a snow-capped boulder in midstream or explores some crystal grotto fashioned by the frozen spray. You may see him carried beneath the ice and feel the impulse to go to his rescue, but in a second he pops out at an airhole! Apparently he has left the weather out of his worries and you can find him at home in all seasons from the Yukon southward to the Isthmus of Tehuantepec.

The adult bird is nearly a uniform slate gray, a trifle lighter below, and the head and neck are tinged with brown. He is about as large as a robin, but the abbreviated tail gives him a "chunky" look. His family is allied to both the thrushes and the wrens although in their aquatic habits and covering of down they differ from all other perching birds. Consequently, we sometimes think of them as having joined the shore species.

John Muir, who found the wonder of the High Sierras a lifetime inspiration, has told us much of what we know about the water ouzel. He says in his *Mountains of California* that the ouzel sings all winter and never minds the weather; and that so fond of water is this droll little fellow that he never goes far from the stream. Always he flies close over the brook and follows its windings. His presence in the deep canyons or in the remote wilderness lightens that sense of loneliness and depression which the high solemn peaks are apt to cast over the wanderer despite their grandeur.

When next you behold this surprising bit of feathers, dipping and bobbing before you in friendly curiosity, drop your cares and follow him for a delightful hour or two. He is a perfect host and will show you all the sequestered haunts of the brooklet, the torrent, or the mountain tarn of which he is so proud.

It was near my home, about which is grouped a stand of virgin timber, that I had the opportunity of studying another of these feathered personalities. An elderly pine had lately succumbed to the larvae of the boring beetle, and my guest announced his arrival by a slow deliberate knocking upon its naked trunk. From my window I could observe him as he gravely inspected his find, prying here and there in the crevices of its bark and testing the toughness of the wood. He was, of course, of those species which we have unceremoniously dubbed "the woodpeckers," but he was a lord of the tribe, a pileated woodpecker or logcock. This bird often measures eighteen inches in length and appears like a large hen to the astonished eyes of one seeing him for the first time.

Presently his "bugle call" brought his spouse to my dooryard. She came with powerful bounding flight and alighted near him. At my first approach they were shy and wary, keeping the tree between us, and flying when they saw what I looked like at close range. But as I was a persistent caller and the infested pine a perfect cafeteria, they became accustomed, and at last indifferent to my presence.

It was a revelation to me to see them at work. Among the Mexicans the ivorybill is known as *el carpentero*, a name quite befitting, but I doubt if any other member of that trade could do as much with a single tool.

Upon locating a satisfactory place to begin operations, this arboreal craftsman sets diligently to work. A few preliminary pecks, a moment when, with head cocked back, he measures the distance, and then a steady pounding that makes the chips fly. The broad wedge-shaped bill is adze, hammer, and probe all in one. And the bird's long neck swings in such a wide arc that the head seems in danger of coming off. Nevertheless, the blow is well directed and the bill comes down with malletlike force. A chip is cut out and then flecked off. Later I could find a little hole at the bottom of the larger cavity from which the worm had been extracted.

Two busy weeks it took to chisel out all the delectable young borers and then my friends departed. But they left me in a mood to find the removal of four wheelbarrow loads of bark and chips from our yard a light task.

The nests of this species give further evidence of their strength and skill as woodworkers, being cut in the solid trunks of trees. After reaching a depth of several inches the hole is driven downward for a foot and a half and the large white eggs are laid on a bed of fresh chips.

It is regrettable that the striking size and coloration of these birds have led to such a diminution of their numbers by human vandals, but if one can locate a pair early in the season they will afford many interesting hours of observation and study. A good set of binoculars may not disclose the secrets exchanged between the couple by means of the drumming, which they do upon some dead branch in lieu of a love song, but the glasses are a most valuable aid in getting "close-ups." And when the awkward youngsters appear you may share the comics of the nursery without worrying mother woodpecker overmuch. Altogether you will find these crimson-crested aristocrats among the "famous people" you want to know.

Early mornings in late October are of those experiences that cause us to regret the swift passing of time. Perhaps the fascination of these days of the autumn month lies in the fact that nature is about to reset the stage in her drama of the seasons. The chill air holds a threat of winter and the expectancy of change grips all the wild folk, sending geese and ducks southward, while grouse scatter, and deer and elk begin their herding. It is then too that the cold rudely awakens every sleeper who ventures into the woods overnight without a plentiful supply of blankets, and wet gray mists penetrate to the bone. But if you are in the mountains and awake to see the dawn light as it brightens, sending long silver shafts to the zenith and illuminating the dim forest floor, you will not complain much of the cold and may even linger in the making of a fire to watch the greater one building in the east. Quickly the mists are rising too, swirling down the long forest aisles and gathering in low wispy clouds over the deep valleys. It is at that hour, when the wild futuristic notes of the cock-of-the-woods are flung far out over the treetops, that one seems to come nearer the truth and to an understanding of things.

Secrets in Tree Rings

Henry W. Schramm

PHOTOGRAPHS BY HAROLD J. NISNOFF

TREE DIAMETERS, the circular segments cut from felled trees, are telling a tale to foresters that may some day mean larger and healthier forests for lumber, for recreation, and for wildlife. It is the story of the effects of outside forces on the life of a tree, and vividly bears out the forester's contention that wise forest practices mean bigger, healthier trees.

The key is in the study of annual rings. These, by their shape and distance apart, give clues to the environment and problems encountered by the tree during its life span.

Each year trees grow with great vitality in the spring. At this time, thin wood cell walls appear. These are light in color. The annual growth is concluded with thicker cell walls, giving a denser, thus darker, appearance. The annual ring is composed of a light and a dark portion, enabling us to distinguish one annual increment from another.

This means of measurement of a tree's age and activities is most useful in the temperate zones. In the tropics this decisive annual separation does not usually occur because of the continuous growth in such climes.

At the State University of New York's College of Forestry at Syracuse, students learn the "whys" of tree development from an exhibit of ring diameters. Some of the trees shown grew with rings in elliptical shapes to compensate for leaning positions on hillsides. Others indicate the effects of disease and insect infestations. Past histories show up irrefutably in the diameters.

One tree, in mature form, was discovered in an Adirondack bog. It was only eighteen inches tall. A close study of the tree diameter, seven-sixteenths of an inch wide, showed forty annual rings spaced only 1/180th of an inch apart.

The results of tree growth under proper forest management procedures, including thinning, are compared, in the collection, to those of trees that were cramped and shaded throughout life. Tree rings truly reveal the written biography of the tree.

Opposite: *Inset on the 15-inch diameter of a 12-year-old southern pine is a cross section of a 40-year-old spruce that measures only 7/16 inch across.*

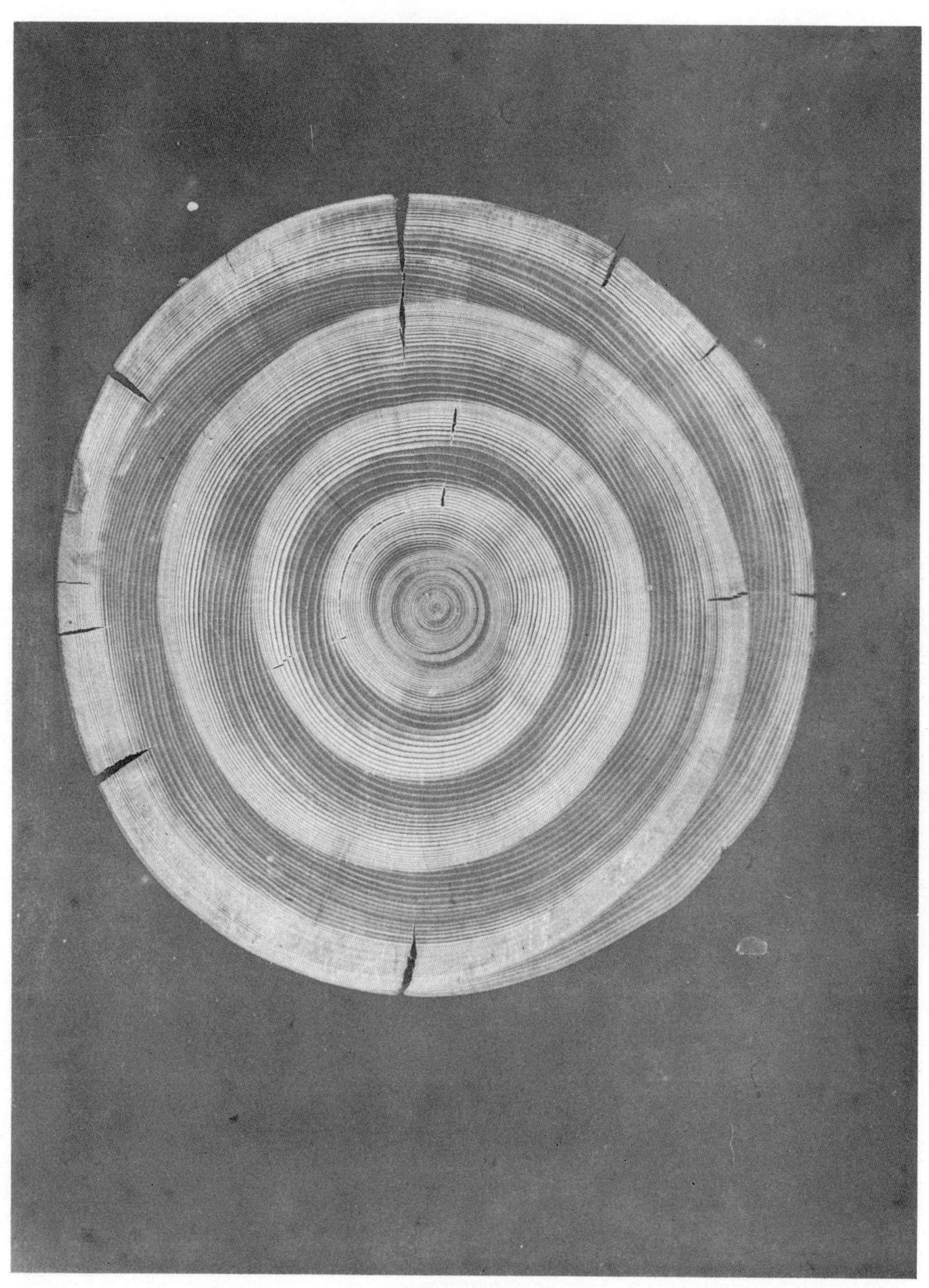

This unique spiral pattern of tree rings leaves forestry experts scratching their heads for an answer. The spiral continues from the core of the tree right to the outside, in an unbroken line. So unique is this that it was featured in a Ripley cartoon.

Top: An apple tree, the diameter of which is shown above, grew near Syracuse, New York, and is an example of the need for protecting trees against open wounds. A branch broke off during its early years. Healing began, but infection occurred. The disease spread and centered near the tree's heart. Still alive, the tree was attacked by insects, probably through the gap left by the wound. Near the diseased area, these insects built a series of galleries. The tree fought back; healthy outside rings covered the wound, but could not remove the rot which gradually occupied the center.

Bottom: Cross section of white pine shows the results of wise forestry practice. Tree grew in a plantation where all the trees were planted during the same season. For eight years the rate of growth was good. Then other trees competed.

Virgin timber is represented in this diameter of a 440-year-old eastern hemlock from Fourth Lake, New York. Toppled by a windstorm, the tree recorded its slow growth in close-together rings that reveal a cramped space caused by too many trees occupying a limited area.

Eccentric growth is shown in this diameter of a basswood tree that grew near Syracuse, New York. The anatomical center, or heart, is off to the right side because the tree grew on a steep hillside, leaning badly downhill.

Wee Tim'rous White-Foot

William Byron Mowery

ONE BITTER January Sunday in the woods, we came upon a little, furry, mouse-size creature sitting half-frozen in a spice bush. It was just sitting there.

Its big ears and bright fawn color told us it was a white-foot, and we wondered why on earth this nest-loving, nocturnal animal was perched in a bare bush in ten-below-zero weather, on a dazzling white day.

Its queer behavior was all the more a mystery to me because I had known White-Foot so long and well. A friendly, dainty little thing, it is one of the commonest wild creatures of our woods and fields. Farm boys everywhere know and like the intelligent little rascal, and give it a special place, as with the cardinal among the birds. It is not merely harmless; around sheds, gardens and groves it is highly useful.

Our first guess was that hunger had driven this white-foot out to forage. Some Promethea moth cocoons dangled from the spice twigs, and moth grubs, including several injurious species, are an item in the white-foot's diet. But then we were surprised to see that this white-foot had four half-grown young clinging tightly to her, and we knew she would never have burdened herself with nestlings on a food hunt.

Plainly some enemy had driven her out of nest and home, and she had courageously taken her young along. But why had she not sought safety in some dark niche of her feeding grounds, in the white-foot way? Why had she fled into the open and climbed a bush? Answers to such questions do not come easily.

There were no weasel prints in the inch of snow, or enemy signs of any kind, and we decided to look into this mystery.

But first, White-Foot had to be given a hand. Cold, homeless and burdened by the four young, she was in a bad fix. As we eased close, she sat quietly, merely twitching her nose at us. When we presented her with the open end of a wool mitten and nudged her with a twig, she crept into the warm, dark haven quite readily.

I tied the mitten shut and put the babies in my pocket, to take home—mostly because I did not know what else to do with them. Certainly I had no foreknowledge of the odd tricks they were to show us, or the fascinating glimpses they gave us into the ways of all animals that flee instead of standing and fighting. Also, I felt I had long owed the white-foot tribe a debt, reaching back to boyhood days on a hill farm. Often in winter I would come to a rabbit den, all tracked up outside, and would be thoroughly exasperated to think of the four or five rabbits sitting safe and sound in the depths of the burrow. On such occasions I would hunt up and capture a white-foot, usually at the nearest fodder shock, and put it into the den. When it went scampering back in, the rabbits would think it was some kind of a miniature weasel, and without caring what kind, just so it was a weasel, they would come boiling out of there bug-eyed because of the intrusion.

With White-Foot safe in pocket, we backtracked her to where she had come up out of a run, and by following this run a few feet we found her nest, at the base of a small stump. Considerably larger than a double fist, the nest was warm, dry and well constructed. The outer layer was of cedar bark stripping to shed the weather, the bulk was of grass, and the lining was the downy fuzz from sycamore balls.

At the nest we found no trace of the unknown enemy; or of a mate, anywhere. This latter was surprising. Almost always the white-foot is found in pairs. The union is one of the closest I know of, and my observations lead me to believe it is permanent.

From our white-foot's nest several runs led out to her nibble gardens. By uncovering these runs we found the enemy at last. It was a shrew.

Although shrews are fairly common, they seldom appear in the open and are usually mistaken for mice, so a few words about them here may be in order. The shrew is no rodent at all but an insect-eater, and it comes from the same ancient stock as the monkeys. It can be distinguished from the mouse by its long, fleshy snout and its hand-like foot and digits. The American pigmy shrew is the tiniest mammal that ever lived. It is no bigger than a good-sized peanut.

The shrew is an incredibly high-strung bundle. Holding one in the hand is like holding a wad of electricity. But its outstanding feature is its incredible appetite. A shrew will kill a mouse of its own size with one explosive onset and eat it on the spot. I have had several shrews, including Florida pigmies, in the observation cage, and the amount they eat is downright fantastic. Like the ground mole they will die in a few hours if deprived of food.

We could reconstruct White-Foot's story easily enough. When the shrew entered her home grounds, the mouse had packed up and fled at the first whiff of the musky intruder. From long racial experience of her kind with the shrew tribe she knew that the voracious shrew would follow and kill her if she stayed anywhere under cover, and that she could save herself and young only by the extreme measure of fleeing into the open and climbing a bush.

That was why we found a white-foot perched in a bare spice in ten-below weather, on a dazzling white morning in the middle of winter.

At home we emptied the mitten on the living-room rug and sat around to watch, keeping quiet and a few feet away. White-Foot could have dragged her young off to a dark corner, but oddly she was not a whole lot afraid of us big Brobdingnagians. She would rise up kangaroolike and sniff at us, then fall to licking the human taint from her four fuzzies, but she made no attempt to flee.

We had leisure now to examine her more

closely. There are *seventy* different species of white-foot in America, with certain variations in size and color, but the type description holds for all, with no need to split hairs. The white-foot has soft fine fur and white feet, paper-thin ears, and the large, shoe-button eyes typical of any nocturnal creature. The fawn-colored back and sides are set off by a sharp line from the pure-white throat and belly. This protective pattern of darker above, lighter below, extends even to the birds of the air and the fish of the sea. With White-Foot the pattern is given an extra twist—the tail also carries out this two-tone scheme. It is fawn-colored above and white below clear out to the tip hair!

After a while one of us reached out carefully and gave White-Foot a shred of coconut. She ate it at once, and then took a second one from the fingers. Mind you, this was a wild creature half an hour after her capture. It illustrates the native tameness and camaraderie of this little thing. In my book the white-foot is the most easily tamed of all American animals, and it also makes one of the most alert, likable pets.

We saw that White-Foot was famished, what with herself and the four nestlings to eat for, and we presented her with a feast of almonds, corn bread and more coconut. She ate mannerly, taking small nibbles and pausing to lick her paws, but she kept at it steadily.

In its daintiness and cleanness, as in so many other respects, the white-foot is as different as day and night from the domestic mouse, that unclean and destructive foreign pest. Nearly all our native American species, like the jumping, harvester and grasshopper mice, are attractive little animals, of amusing ways and soft sleek fur.

In a short time the food that White-Foot ate was transformed into sustenance for the four fuzzies. When they got completely surfeited they dropped off one by one and lay around on the rug on their sides, sound asleep. Now White-Foot was free and could have streaked for a dark corner, but she merely retreated into the mitten, refusing to abandon her young and also showing oddly little fear of us. So little fear, in fact, that we were puzzled and ran a few simple experiments on her, while the fuzzies were asleep, to get a line on her flight instincts.

We discovered that she was much more afraid of the human hand than of the whole human. Also, when a person walked past her at a distance of five feet she was much less alarmed than when a clothesbrush was dragged across the floor at a distance of five feet. A rough explanation of all this was that we humans were *too* big for her to comprehend very clearly as foes. In nature her chief enemies were weasel, snake and shrew, and her escape instincts were rather sharply tuned to foes of that size. To her we were only vaguely threatening, like an overtowering hill or the rumble of thunder.

A fine example of this sharply focused fear can be seen in the common toad. When we roust out a toad, he is not much afraid of us; he may take a few hops but that is all. But put a stick or hoe handle down on the ground and slide it toward him, simulating his chief enemy, the snake, and he will light out for the next county.

We fixed up a cage for White-Foot and the four fuzzies, although they spent more time out of it than in it. In a few days White-Foot was tame enough to be taken into the hands and fed. As for the fuzzies, which grew almost visibly, they were taken over by the younger generation, and carried around in pockets and blouses. One of the four, whom they named Wouse, was supposed to have extraordinary talents, a very wonder of a mouse, although I personally could never see much difference between him and the other three. All of them were good acrobats, tame and friendly, and the equal as pets of any golden hamster, spinning mouse or such-like foreign oddity that I have ever seen.

At night we kept them in the cage, in an alcove outside my study; and as the young became nearly grown I began hearing a queer noise out of them when the house quieted down. The noise was a dull *sn-ii-pp,* repeated at about ten-second intervals and kept up almost endlessly. I tried to find out what it was by snapping on the alcove light and by sneaking up with a flashlight, but I had no luck until one night I placed the cage by a window so that the moon struck it full, and watched from behind a bookcase.

The curious antic that caused the noise went like this:

The four young white-feet, distributed around the cage, would be sitting tense and quiet. Suddenly, and for no visible reason, they would all give a jump, all four at the same instant, and then they would be somewhere else. This sudden leap was the dull *sn-ii-pp* I had been hearing. The word "jump" poorly describes the flashlike quickness of their move. It was too quick to follow. A white-foot would be sitting quiet on the floor and in the next instant he would be sticking up against a side or the ceiling.

It was like some outlandish backfield shift—a silent, quaintly solemn procedure. What the signal was for the shift I do not know yet, but all four jumped at exactly the same split-wink. Perhaps the signal was a squeak too high-pitched for the human ear, and perhaps it was the super-talented Wouse that gave it.

The fact that White-Foot took no part in the antic was the key which finally unlocked the puzzle for me. *The four young were playing.* However solemn and unplaylike it looked, that was what they were doing, with zest and exhilaration. The play of all young creatures is an earnest preparation for adult life. With fighting animals like the dog, cat and bear, play takes the form of cuffing and biting among the litter mates. But with fleeing animals, play takes the form of evading enemies. That was what the four young white-feet were playing at in the cage, hour after hour—the game of "Freeze! Jump! Freeze!" In the dark night woods, with weasel, snake and shrew to elude, the difference between life and death would often lie in that expertness at being in one spot one instant and somewhere else the next.

White-Foot deserted us; one of the fuzzies met accident, and a pair were presented to friends; but Wouse, the super-duper, was with us until May.

We kept him in the cage at night, and I often took the cage into my study. His acrobatics were amusing and he was always tremendously busy at something or other—acrobatics, eating, just messing around, and making his thorough, scrupulous toilet. If I would open the cage and sprinkle a cup of birdseed on the rug, he would spend an hour, busier than a jug of bumblebees, picking up every seed and toting them all to his hoard placed in the corner of the cage.

Like Mary's lamb, Wouse went to school one day—a university instructor in zoology took him to class as an animated example of protective coloration. According to all accounts, Wouse made a hit. He sat kangaroolike on the instructor's desk, galloped along the lab table, and was photographed to show the equalization of direct light on a dark back and reflected light on white underparts. In fact, Wouse did his stuff so well that the instructor, handing him back to me, remarked disgustedly:

"That mouse with its two-tone tail taught those students more about protective coloration that I'd done in an hour's lecturing!"

Before he deserted us, undoubtedly looking for a mate, Wouse paid for his room and board with a valued service. Our big old house was so situated that we had trouble keeping it free of domestic mice. But Wouse kept it free. Whether he killed them or they cleared out ahead of him, I am unable to state, but it adds up to the same figure. I have seen this same thing happen a dozen times, and others have reported it—our white-foot will not tolerate the common mouse anywhere around.

This is one reason—among several good ones—why the white-foot should have our friendly protection. It is never destructive, never flocks together in plague proportions, like the lemming; and the garage or shed with a white-foot pair in it is safe from the foreign pest. White-Foot seems the "better mousetrap."

Revenge in the Meadow

W. P. Hubbard

IT WAS MIDMORNING of a beautiful June day. I was riding in the high country near the Carson National Forest in northern New Mexico. Suddenly the canyon trail opened into a small mountain meadow. Leaving my horse in the shade of some spruces and aspens, I walked across the meadow to a spring at the base of a low bluff. Fifty feet from the spring, and about twenty feet above it, I stretched out to rest atop a flat boulder that was shaded by overhanging aspens and pinyons.

Between myself and the spring, and directly in front of me, was an open, sandy clearing that absorbed the spring water after it had flowed only a few yards from the bluff. To my right, a jut of timber extended out from the bluff. To my left, a dense stand of pinyons cast their shadows on the clearing, and, in front of the pines, at the edge of the clearing was an old, fallen tree, partly concealed by deep, yellowing grass. Beyond the clearing, the gradual upward sloping meadow stretched out for a hundred yards.

As I gazed over the meadow to the edge of a spruce slope, a sharp "Obble, Obble, Obble" cut the still, thin air. Moments later, a big turkey gobbler, followed by three hens, emerged from the brush across the meadow.

Suddenly, although there was no wind blowing, the tall, thick grass about the four birds came alive with movement, and instantly I realized its swaying was caused by poults. I could not see the youngsters because of the distance, their size, and the blending and coloring, but I knew by the swaying grass that there must be thirty or forty of the little fellows. Soon a poult exposed itself as it jumped high for an insect. Others popped up thus from time to time. The poults seemed to be about six weeks old.

The flock fed slowly and cautiously toward the spring. The gobbler was a giant. Now and then he made a running leap, his wings half opening, as he dashed after a grasshopper. One of the old birds was always alertly watchful while the others fed. When about halfway across the meadow, the troop changed course and drifted toward the mouth of the canyon. I felt sure that if they caught sight of my saddle horse they would take flight. Suddenly the birds turned again toward the spring, but when they reached the jut of timber they all stopped at a commanding "Putt-Putt-Putt" from the gobbler.

Beyond the clearing, the trees, grass and underbrush were bright in the sunlight, and the deep purple heads and the sheen on the bluish, black-brown bodies of the four adult birds stood out in vivid contrast against the yellow of the meadow. After a brief halt, the gobbler slowly turned his head and looked about. Apparently satisfied that all was well, he issued a sharp "Purt-Purt," and the tufts of grass came to life as the flock continued their advance.

Several poults emerged from the deep grass into the clearing. One, hopping and scrambling, climbed up on the fallen tree. It spread its immature wings and ran toward the far end. A foot from the end, without warning, the silent, dirty yellowish-brown form of a timber rattlesnake shot upward from the grass at the edge of the tree and knocked the poult to the ground.

I shall never forget the startled sensation that went through me at sight of the rattler. My whole body jumped, and how I failed to give my presence away I will never know. Perhaps the turkeys were too excited to notice me.

As the poult fell from the log, it gave a terrified cry. This brought the gobbler, gobbling sharply, bounding to the clearing. The hens, with alarmed "Purts," hesitated until the other poults retreated from the clearing. Then all but the gobbler hastily moved farther out on the meadow. There a hen issued a series of commanding "Putt-Putt-Putts," and the poults froze, to remain camouflaged in the protecting shelter of the deep grass until the hens returned for them. The hens, in turn, zoomed upward and across the meadow with a roaring of wings, then glided gracefully down over the spruce slope, disappearing from our view.

The stricken poult, crying shrilly and pitifully, ran toward the grass, then suddenly staggered, shook violently, and fell forward, dead. The gobbler, still gobbling excitedly, ran toward the dead poult, just as the rattler slithered through the grass at the end of the tree and came into full view on the clearing. The gobbler arched its wings, leaped high in the air, and landed, feathers ruffled in defiance, head straight forward, facing the rattler, which had coiled and was buzzing angrily, about five feet away. The dead poult lay midway between the two.

The gobbler raised one foot and took a cautious step toward the poult; the rattler weaved a little, aiming to strike. When the bird started another step, the rattler struck with lightninglike thrust. At the same time, and just as swiftly, it seemed, the gobbler shot upward, thrashing the air with his great wings, fanning a film of dust from the ground under him. While in the air he threw his legs up and forward, then pulled them back and downward with terrific speed and force in an attempt to drive his upcurved, daggerlike spurs into the rattler. He also hammered viciously with his beak at the snake's head. When the gobbler landed he was beyond another strike by the enemy.

Before the dust cleared, the rattler had moved forward and coiled beside the poult. The old turkey began to circle his adversary with quick, short steps, first toward, then away from it, but all the time edging a little nearer. At every move, the rattler buzzed in warning rage, and kept turning its head and part of its body so as to face the fearless bird.

When the gobbler edged a little closer the rattler struck, missed, and struck again, its fangs and head hitting the turk's beard a glancing blow, and causing it to fly sideways with the impact. At every strike the gobbler's spurs came as close to the rattler as did the rattler's fangs to the turkey.

Part of the reptile's body was now coiled over the poult. When the gobbler began to circle, the snake again turned slowly, its tongue flicking out wickedly. The gobbler took a sudden step toward the snake, which struck back in savage retaliation, only to miss again. The powerful downsweep of one of the gobbler's wings straightened out the rattler's remaining coil, turning the snake completely over. The gobbler rushed into the thin cloud of dust, and either flipped the poult with his beak, or kicked it into the grass a good six feet away. When the dust settled, the rattler was coiled, weaving its head from side to side, and buzzing in frenzied rage. It struck again and missed.

After the third or fourth strike the rattlesnake seemed to slow down each time it coiled, and its strikes did not seem as swift. And the gobbler kept circling, moving just enough to keep the rattler from getting set for an accurate strike. Suddenly the bird turned, opened his wings, and stepped toward the snake, which lashed out. The rattler's open mouth shot dangerously close to the fleshy, upper part of the gobbler's legs, and there was a feather sticking from between its jaws as it drew back its head. Before the snake could get fully set, the turkey repeated the movement, and again the rattler struck—to its misfortune, for it was off coil. The strike was wild and wide, and, as it drew back, one of the gobbler's spurs caught the reptile a few inches behind the head and tore a gash in its side. The big bird landed clear, but the snake, stunned and trembling violently, left a thin trail of blood on the ground as it drew slowly back to a half coil, then, reviving, completed its coil.

The gobbler again circled. The snake, infuriated, buzzed continually; its body twitched and quivered. Twice, as the bird circled closer, the rattler lashed out, but both strikes traveled only about a foot and ended with a jerk. Whipping back, the snake struck at the gash in its own body.

Now the gobbler must have sensed his advantage, for he suddenly stopped circling, cupped his wings, and took a step toward the enemy. Then, head low, the turkey stood tense and motionless in a pose of defiance and challenge, alert for the rattlesnake's next move. Momentarily I expected the snake to strike; instead, it slowly raised the forepart of its body until it was a few inches above the rest of the coil. Then it curved the raised portion into a weak "U" formation and moved its head from side to side, making two or three short, false strikes. As the gobbler moved a leg, the snake cut loose with a furious buzzing. The turk's head was now within easy striking distance of the rattler. The bird raised a foot; the rattler made its last strike. It was a sluggish thrust, and as the turkey went high in the air the snake shot under him. As the rattler drew back, one of the gobbler's curved spurs caught and firmly hooked the rattler at the base of the head; and the spur came through the top of the head. At the impact the snake's body straightened out in a rigid line, and, as the bird hit the ground with a thud, his knife-like beak pounded into the snake's back with the rapidity of a triphammer.

The rattler's body quivered a moment or two. Then came terrific commotion as the rattler, its head still hooked on the gobbler's spur, began to thrash about. The turkey gave a startled "Obble-Obble," leaped into the air, and beating his wings kicked in savage confusion in an effort to release the snake. For a few seconds the air was full of wings, flying legs and feet, feathers, a thrashing snake, frenzied buzzing and surprised, frantic gobbling. On the third or fourth trip skyward the gobbler kicked the rattler loose, then rushed at its thrashing form and pounded it with his beak. A few seconds later the rattler again became rigid, this time in a slightly curved position, shuddered weakly and relaxed in death. The old gobbler, issuing sharp, mad, nervous "Putts," backed off and stood eyeing his enemy.

Presently the bird spread his tail in fan formation, dropped his wings, and, as he came into a full strut, burst forth with a throaty "Obble, Obble, Obble" that was a mixture of challenge, victory and defiance. His call resounded across the meadow to the bluff and came echoing back. Then the gallant old bird strutted in all his glory, as he issued that peculiar humming sound of strutting turkeys. He took short quick steps until he came to the rattler. There he proceeded viciously to drive his beak into the snake, after which he kicked it a few times in a contemptuous manner, then turned and strutted to where the dead poult lay in the grass.

He was eyeing the poult when a not-too-far-away, short, inquiring "Obble, Obble," penetrated the stillness. In the excitement of the battle I had forgotten the hens and poults. After looking warily about, the gobbler gave a deep, reassuring answer. It was not long before the hens appeared at the edge of the meadow above the spruce slope, where they took wing and sailed toward me. Their heavy bodies landed with a thud-thud-thud, as they alighted in the clearing. There was still not a movement from the hidden poults.

Now the gobbler began to strut in an elegant fashion as he moved proudly among his hens. As they looked on he moved over and around the rattler—but the hens did not go near the reptile. They were nervous and excited, and soon left the clearing. A few yards out on the meadow one of the hens gave a deep "Putt-Putt—Putt—Putt." The poults broke from hiding and grouped about the hens, who led them at a brisk pace toward the edge of the meadow. The gobbler, dropping his strut, followed watchfully a short distance behind them. A few minutes later they all disappeared below the brow of the slope on their way to the wooded land below.

Examining the poult, I found that the rattler's fangs had penetrated the body just under the wing. The snake had a gash an inch and one-half long high up on its side, ten inches back from its head. The gobbler's spur had punctured the spinal column as it entered the base of the rattler's head, and had then curved up to come out through the top of its skull. In addition to this, the gobbler had broken the snake's skull in five places with his powerful beak, and punctured the body in eleven places on the back. I skinned out the rattler, later had the skin tanned, and still have the souvenir. It measures four feet, four and one-half inches, and has eight rattles and a button.

The battle had lasted about a half hour. The rattlesnake put up a gallant fight, but, for sheer nerve and dauntless courage, I think the gobbler deserves greater credit. After kicking or flipping the poult clear, he did not have to join the battle again, but he did, giving me a view of a thrilling wild drama.

Snooky

Hubert Loomis Smith

SNOOKY CAME into our lives through tragedy. Walking down a street one morning, I found him, half-fledged and gasping in the gutter. Forty feet overhead, from the fringed leaf-tip of a California fan palm, hung a few forlorn wisps of what had been the pendent cradle of the Arizona hooded oriole. Many stones, brickbats and sticks scattered over the sidewalk and pavement told the sordid story of juvenile cruelty.

I could not return him to a nest that no longer existed; he was too young and too sorely hurt to cling to a bare limb. Nor could I bring myself to obey the law, and leave him to a roaming cat. So I became a lawbreaker and took him home. I firmly believe in our wildlife protective regulations. But I believe, too, that where man-made laws chance to be in total conflict with the eternal law of mercy, the latter must dominate.

My foundling was too far gone to open his mouth, but I forced his beak open with my finger nails and gave him a little water from a dropper, following it up with a few drops of boiled milk in which a little white of raw egg had been stirred. We continued to force this mixture into him at frequent intervals through the day, and we wrapped him well in warm flannel at night, cuddling him in a box with a low-watt electric bulb so placed as not to risk scorching.

It was several days before our waif showed much improvement. But finally he became quite normal and ravenous for four or five days, then suddenly relapsed and we lost all hope of saving him. Too weak even to draw his feet under him, he lay on his side with lolling neck and legs limply extended. Yet I persisted in the forced feeding, and in about a week he was well again.

Never was a recovery more miraculous or more thorough; from that time on, Snooky was the healthiest of birds. He happened to be our only pet at the time, and having been snatched from death with such labor, he was humored and fondled like a first baby. Indeed, we scarcely thought of him as a bird, but treated him as a member of the family.

Perhaps it was Snooky's upbringing that made him so different from all other birds

I have known. More likely, he was temperamentally different by nature. Every aviculturist knows that there is a marked difference in disposition and intelligence between individuals of the same species, and it seems logical that at rare intervals a veritable bird genius should be hatched. Snooky was such a one; and his was the genius of happiness. It was as though he had sensed that his life would be brief, and had determined to fill every fleeting moment of it with gaiety.

For a large part of every day the bird had the freedom of the house, which, in practice, meant freedom of the room in which some member of the family happened to be—for he would never voluntarily lose sight of his human friends for a single moment. If forced to do so, his bubbling spirits were visibly dampened, although not wholly subdued.

Snooky's curiosity was insatiable. Every article in the room was examined with the intent gaze of a watchmaker, every crack probed, and every small movable object shifted, or overturned by a thrust of the bill, while each mischievous idea that entered his sleek head was welcomed with the gleeful *ee-ee-ee-ee* of the oriole. A book fascinated him, and his efforts to separate the pages often stayed his devastating course for many minutes. This probing was without doubt the insect-hunting instinct in action, but I am sure that food was far from Snooky's thoughts while he was so engaged.

Most tame birds are shy with strangers, if not actually afraid of them, but Snooky was hampered by no inhibitions or inferiority complex. No visitor had time to sit down before Snooky was engaged in an earnest exploration and probing of the hair, eyebrows, ears and the intriguing crevasse between collar and neck. His opinion of what he found must have been unflattering, for he paused frequently with his bill half-opened in a ludicrous silent laugh, or chuckled his *ee-ee-ee* in undisguised mirth.

Snooky had a tiny blue butter plate in which special food treats were usually given him. He always recognized this as his own, and seemed to have an affection for it. His appetite was enormous and as versatile as a crow's. There was almost nothing that he would not eat. Toughened by adversity in his infancy, his health seemed indestructible.

The young oriole was fond of peaches, and the process of peeling them for preserving held so much of gustatory and technical interest that his services as aide-de-cook were offered freely, and with persistence. The table where bacon was being sliced in the morning also was replete with entertainment and material reward. He loved to stuff himself with thin slivers of the raw bacon fat, and never failed to show up at the proper moment.

But the food of foods, in Snooky's opinion, was boiled cabbage. He always seemed to know when cabbage was being cooked, and he waited eagerly for his little blue butter plate to be filled. Boiled-cabbage days were red-letter days to Snooky. Hotcake batter and biscuit dough were not particularly enjoyed, but a few sips or nips were always taken, perhaps out of courtesy to the cook.

In fact, Snooky partook regularly, if sparingly, of many things for which he had no craving at all. Ink, for instance. As a beverage, he detested ink; yet his philosophy seemed to dictate that everything should be tried at least once a day. So, every afternoon when the ink pot was opened, he reached gingerly in, tossed off a small snifter, sputtered, and wiped his bill in violent distaste. Yet, on the following day, he would be ready for another "wee drap." Not because of a defective memory, to be sure, for daily he sidled up to the dreaded black bottle, and to me his expression and actions told more plainly than words that he was steeling himself for an act of heroism. Evidently he considered it the sporting thing to do.

But if Snooky's taste for ink as a beverage lacked sincerity, his love of it in other forms was certainly genuine. He delighted in tracking wet ink across the white blotter covering my desk, and would inspect the resulting Hebraic script with a comical expression of amusement. The oriole is the only bird I know that actually smiles, and Snooky, with his mouth half-opened in a silent laugh and his beady, black eyes twinkling, was often the very picture of roguish glee.

The act of writing greatly mystified the bird. Edging close, he would lean forward, watching the pen move over the paper, apparently puzzled by the sudden appearance of wormy, black lines where none had been before. If permitted, he would apply the tip of his bill to a line and, pushing it ahead of him like a plough, would solemnly march in a tipsy course across the paper, as he retraced the convolutions of the inked words.

Snooky also was interested in the printed word, and would scan the columns of a newspaper with, I thought, considerable gravity. The illustrations in a book or magazine aroused vast enthusiasm. When the pages were rapidly turned he would perch on my wrist and watch eagerly for a picture to appear. When it did, he would open his mouth with excitement, and hold up one foot in a detaining gesture that obviously meant "Hold it!" and was one of his most endearing mannerisms.

On my desk was a little red-and-white celluloid ball that Snooky prized as a personal belonging. Chuckling to himself with many an *ee-ee-ee,* he would roll it back and forth until it fell off the edge of the desk—a result that always evoked a great show of mock surprise, although the twinkle in his eye and the gleeful opening of his mouth showed that this was according to plan. It was his little joke, and almost daily he played it with undiminishing relish.

But the pinnacle of Snooky's day was the dinner hour, and it was then that his quaint little personality seemed most human. For a long time Snooky was barred from the family board, as we conjured up visions of overturned cream pitcher, spilled coffee, drilled butter, scattered meat and vegetables, and tracks outlined in gravy across the table cloth.

Nothing could have been farther from the truth. Certainly his table manners were a trifle crude the first few times he invited himself to the meal, but it took only a few thumps of the finger to discourage such lapses, and in a short time his deportment was that of an avian Lord Chesterfield. We fell into the habit of letting him into the dining room for every midday meal. Always he took his place at the table by his own little blue butter plate, just to the right of my own plate, and never would he stir from this position as long as the meal was in progress.

Once he had learned his manners, Snooky never reached into my plate, no matter how tempting the food, but would intently follow the upward course of each forkful, with tilted head and shining eyes.

If anything looked particularly good, he would raise one foot high with extended toes in a sudden detaining gesture, for all the world like a policeman halting traffic, and the drollest thing imaginable. This was a sign that he wished that morsel to be deposited in his little blue butter plate, where he could sample it—but, to tell the truth, he did usually take a nip from the fork before the transfer was completed. Usually, he had a tiny bowl of milk from which at intervals he sipped politely; but he was not at all finical, and did not mind drinking from *my* glass if it was near him.

In spite of his activity, Snooky was fond of his cage. He voluntarily spent much time in it, especially during the drowsy heart of the afternoon, which was passed in a musical reverie as he learned to warble the note-tumbled, lilting song of his species. But he was not contented in his cage—or out of it—unless one of the family was in sight; so we formed the habit of riding him on a finger from room to room as the social center of gravity shifted. He was the most obedient of birds, and would invariably mount a finger when it was extended to him. If Snooky wished to be liberated from his cage, he would attract attention with a sharp, insistent little *caw!*, accompanied by the detaining gesture of the foot. For that, and his roguish, half-opened mouth, I always shall remember him best.

Unlike most hand-reared birds, Snooky never voluntarily went to roost in his cage at night. He retired at about nine, and, if loose, would invariably crawl under my coat, worming his way into a warm nook under my armpit. And always he was very petulant when dragged from his snug sleeping place, struggling and biting my fingers. At all other times he was singularly sweet-tempered and tractable, never showing resentment when we spoiled his "best laid plans" by shutting him in his cage, or in any way displaying the wilfulness one learns to expect in very tame birds.

In strange contrast to a complete lack of fear of anyone, or of anything that might happen within the house, Snooky was mortally afraid of the outdoor world. He loved to perch on the shoulder of anyone moving from room to room. I attributed this partly to his fondness for riding, and partly because of the new fields for scientific research such journeys opened up to him. Yet if the one on whom he rode passed close by a window—even a closed window—he would run around to the far shoulder and cower down, or else fly away, to resume his ride only when the opening to the terrifying outer world had been safely left behind.

Late in the winter Snooky changed his modest olive for the glistening gold and ebony of the adult male, and the jostling ecstatic notes of his song grew louder and mellower. As the days grew warmer, we turned him loose during the day in a spacious screened veranda, open to the sun and air of the desert; a veranda oasis lush with a great variety of plants in pots and urns.

Pleasant as this was, Snooky hated his daily expulsion, and although he lost his terror of the outer world, he never missed an opportunity to slip back into the house. While this was easy at first, the prank grew more difficult as I grew more wary, and circumventing me came to be a game with him. Watching sharply from a distance as I approached the door, he would pretend to be interested in other matters. Then, as I stepped through the doorway, he would dart through with me like an arrow from a bow.

On the porch, his time was spent largely in frolicking with a small lizard that ran about on the outside of the screening, while Snooky scampered neck and neck with him on the inside, his sharp little claws interlocking with those of the peeved reptile, his staccato *ee-ee-ee* ringing close in its unwilling ear.

We planned, when summer came, to give Snooky full freedom of choice regarding his future, and talked of cutting, high on the screen, a Lilliputian doorway into the garden always to be open for his exits and entries. And there would be another private entrance from the veranda into the house, so he could visit his cherished folks at will.

Yet, deep in our hearts, something told us that our little spirit of gladness was too perfect for permanence, and would flit away before long. And so it was—for as he came into our lives, unexpectedly and through tragedy, so he went out.

It was early spring, and the day predestined for the curtain-fall in the merry little drama of Snooky had arrived. No warning cloud shadowed his morning, or ours. I had been working in the garden by his porch, and he had been in unusually exuberant spirits, fluttering against the screen in mock attack as I moved about just outside the wire, *ee-ee-ee-ing* and cawing to attract my attention. I suppose his nose or his sharp little eyes had told him, too, that this was to be a red-letter day, a day of boiled cabbage; and when just before dinner an errand took me out on his porch, I could see that he was twinkling with anticipation, and more than usually impatient to get into the house. He was at the far end of the long veranda, pretending as usual that he was not interested in doors; but the roguish light in his eye told me that he planned to play the daily game. Still, the distance from little Snooky to the door was so great that no accident seemed possible.

I opened the door and quickly closed it behind me. There was a little scream, the soft, sickening thud of wood and tender flesh and tiny bones. My heart stood still! In consternation I swung about in time to see the door rebound slightly and release a little bundle of feathers—gold and ebony. I expected Snooky to fall dead, but his small body had been caught well behind the most vital organs, and he was denied the mercy of instant death.

Instead, the stricken birdling flew to me; to his pal, his life-long refuge—and clung to my sleeve. I took him in my hand, and he fixed his eyes on mine; those elfin eyes, so roguish a moment before, now filled with unfathomed anguish. Falteringly, beseechingly, he raised one little foot in the old, endearing gesture. That pitiful, imploring, little foot! For years it has haunted me. Snooky was only eight months old. Just a tiny tyke in deep trouble, and he wanted his pal to hold him close.

Gently I closed my fingers about the wee, frail body, and he nestled in my palm. All pain seemed to leave him now, but I knew that hope was vain. For a few seconds his bright eyes gazed up at me in numb wonder. Then, without sign of suffering or death-struggle, he grew limp, with not a single gay feather in disarray.

Tenderly I laid the little prankster on the desk pad by the little red-and-white ball, on the desk pad with small Hebraic ink-tracks criss-crossing it. I wanted no dinner, and I left the house from which the spirit of gladness had taken flight. As I passed the dining table I saw a little blue butter plate with a bit of boiled cabbage placed in it to cool.

The Eyes Have It

Paul Shepard, Jr.

IF SOMEONE were to put into your hands an animal that you had never seen before and ask you to describe its behavior in the wild, what about it would provide you with ideas?

One of the best organs to examine for clues to the animal's activity would be the eyes. Written in them is the story of the creature's life. And they are also the diary of its racial history, of the habits, food sources and the fears born of the ancestral experience of its kind. The eye is the soul's window—yes. But it is cast in a mold fashioned by particular habits from universal material.

Among vertebrates, the fishes developed the first good eyes, by our standards. These underwater eyes were nearly all alike, in many respects. However, when a land environment was adopted in the process of evolution, eyes became as divergent as the varied demands upon them.

Some eyes were sharpened to perfection by natural selection, only to become debased and feeble through the vicissitudes of geologic time. The fish eye reached an evolutionary end because sight under water is limited. Snakes took their fine reptilian eyes beneath the ground, and nocturnal mammals wasted them in the darkness of night. When the descendants of these animals once again moved into the daylight they were handicapped, and the eye was remolded.

What were the forces of this mold? What has it meant to the eye that some creatures must escape in order to live, while others must capture? Why does the rat see only shadows, while the hawk watches a grasshopper a half-mile away? Why do some animals see color and others not?

In the beginning, ocular raw materials were much the same among all vertebrates, but life has since demanded many modifications, and these in comparatively short periods of geological time. If we assume that a "better" eye is one that resolves an image into greater detail, then a strange classification has come into existence. The development of good sight is not in accord with our system of systematics. "Higher" and "lower" groups, each, have all sorts of eyes. The magnificent eyes of birds are belittled by the inadequate ones of the kiwi, and the blurry vision of mammals is honored in the good eyes of man himself. The

reptiles, amphibians and birds also harbor their paragons of vision and the opposite.

Among various kinds of animals, visual efficiency is in proportion to the importance of sight to the animal's existence. A golden eagle hunting an antelope relies on acute vision. The antelope, too, is a creature of much daylight activity, and is often dependent on keen sight. But the antelope may also *smell* the coyote that stalks it. The coyote may put eyes, nose, and a superior intelligence to work in stalking an antelope, stealing poultry, eating sheep and carrion, or digging up rodents such as the pocket gopher. To elude the coyote, the gopher depends only on tactile and hearing senses. To the gopher, sight has little or no survival value. This animal is at the bottom of the visual scale, the eagle at the top.

Animals at the top of the visual ladder—predator or prey, fish or furbearer—have large eyes; not large in proportion to their heads or bodies, but in absolute size. This is because the seeing cells of the eye, which receive an image on the retina, are all about the same size, whether in bobcat or bison. A big eye is important, then; it holds more such cells, which break down the picture into greater detail. The big eye also increases the distance between the lens and retina, throwing a bigger image on the living screen.

Bright light enables an object to be seen better and at greater distance. Thus, the best eyes belong to animals of daytime and *must* have daylight to function well. To most temperate-zone reptiles, sunlight is the great motivator. What use are eyes that see in the "dark" when nights are spent in immobility? Many mammals, and some birds and amphibians, have developed an eye that works fairly well either in daylight or night. Some creatures' eyes shine in the dark, but the eyeshine is nothing more than a reflective material that helps make the most of whatever light strikes the retina. In daylight some of these animals cover this material in a manner similar to closing Venetian blinds.

Generally, nocturnal animals depend on other senses than eyesight; they have poor eyes. Some find it necessary to see, like the owls, and develop exceedingly sensitive eyes. Most mammals are nocturnal, probably because their ancestors were hunted down in the daylight. It is mostly warm-blooded creatures that seek the cover of darkness for protection, like the mice who efficiently scavenge our kitchens. Early mammals inherited keen vision from their reptilian ancestry—good eyes like those of today's lizards. But in millions of years of "sneak" existence in the dark the eyes degenerated, as is shown by any mole or shrew.

Predators generally have greater stamina, quicker reflexes, or move more rapidly than their prey. High mobility requires good ocular resolving power and rapid focusing to avoid collisions. The size of an animal's eyes is directly proportional to its speed. Without bigger eyes the bass and trout, for example, might be relegated to the food habits of carp and catfish.

Fast-moving animals also need quick adaptation to changes in light intensities. A powerfully muscled iris (which stops down the pupil) provides extensive dilation and contraction for just such reasons. Cats see well in the "dark," but also enjoy sunbathing. This luxury would be impossible without an iris muscle that contracts to a tiny slit and protects the sensitive retina in strong light. A Cooper's hawk, darting from the dark woods into a sunlit clearing where sparrows feed, or out of the midday sky to capture a flicker on the forest floor, flies through drastic changes of light intensity. The same is true of a sea lion diving for squid or fish. Hawk and sea lion are equipped with a flexible iris.

Accurate and immediate estimation of distance is also important to a predator. The striking snake, leaping tiger or diving falcon must judge quickly. Binocularity, or placement of the eyes in the head so that they can be focused on a single object simultaneously, makes such judgment possible. This placement—*frontality*—is characteristic of the predator anatomy. Prey species, on the other hand, have lateral eyes, each with its own field of vision. Many occasional predators, who both hunt and are hunted, fall between the two extremes. Their oblique eyes compromise the values of binocularity with the advantage of a wide visual field.

Every animal falls into this picture somewhere. The cottontail rabbit, a prey species, does not see the grass it eats. *Binocularly* it sees only a few degrees in front and rear —where it may need distance estimation to dodge an immediate pursuer. But with one eye on a side, the rabbit has a total, lateral visual field of 360 degrees. Nor can an enemy approach unseen from above, as the rabbit also sees up without moving its head. Opossum eyes are a compromise. The opossum may capture a small invertebrate one moment and scurry up a tree for its life the next. The cottontail's eyes are 90 degrees off the body axis, the opossum's are 30 degrees off. The lynx, with few enemies to fear, and stalking proficiency imperative, is totally frontal, with eyes in the body line.

Eyes also become dorsal or ventral. The woodcock, probing in the mud for larvae, watches the surrounding undergrowth with large eyes, far back on the head. Although a predator as it feeds, the woodcock has little need of seeing the mud its long bill explores. The turtles, eminently successful through the ages, have little to fear from above. Their eyes are almost frontal and canted downward to scan the bottom for food.

It should be noted that frontality may have other values than for predation. The eyes of primates are frontal presumably because of close-up use of the hands and the tree-swinging habit.

The perception of motion is a complex part of seeing, but one aspect is of special interest regarding food habits. It has been asked how a hawk, sitting in a dead tree, can spot a mouse moving anywhere in the field—unless he happens to be looking right toward it. The registration of movement on the retina is exaggerated around the boundaries of the visual field, as though to compensate for not "looking that way." This seems to be especially true of the lateral periphery. You can demonstrate this for yourself when you are a passenger in an automobile by tipping your head horizontally and watching the road ahead; it seems to rush beneath the car at increased speed.

The value of color vision and its corollary, protective coloration, is a popular topic for debate. Color vision is scattered about the tree of life, without certain connection to predation. But the only groups that use sight *exclusively* for food-getting seem to possess it throughout, as with the birds and lizards. It is also found in the turtles, higher fishes, and the primates. The contrast value of color is obvious. What if all your books were one color! It would seem valuable to a predator that must discern its prey. Yet protective coloration seems to compensate for the increased vulnerability of the hunted animal—which, in many cases, does not see color itself. If such coloration were completely successful it would appear to make color vision in the predator a liability—witness the success of "color-blind" artillery observers who spotted camouflaged installations from the air. Probably the two forces, like the "balance of nature," are never quite adjusted.

Predation and habitat have interworked to produce combinations of eye characteristics. Most of the organ's evolution was completed by the time vertebrates came on land. The terrestrial environment superposed modifications on an organ fashioned under water, in an extremely different set of conditions. The higher fishes have superlative eyes, but the development of aquatic vision is limited by the medium itself. Visibility has a range of about 150 feet in the clearest water, and no change in the eye can alter this. In fish, the lens does all the focusing and the cornea serves only as a protective window. The cornea's refractive index is the same as that of water, so that light rays pass directly through it. But not so in the air. Rays entering the eye bend once at the cornea and again at the lens, enabling the terrestrial eye to develop a small, efficient lens. The bulky spherical lens of the fish bumps against the cornea as far forward as possible, to attain a wide visual angle. It protrudes through the pupil, blocking its contraction. This, as we have seen, puts a limit on light toleration. Only a few fishes, such as sharks, have pupil mobility of the sort that makes cats and seals independent of day and night.

Many animals that feed or live in the water are faced with the necessity of seeing well in air, too. Without compensation, their air eyes are sadly farsighted under water, for the cornea is no longer refractive. The problem is met in four ways.

Aquatic birds utilize the nictitating membrane when diving. It is a thin third eyelid, underlying the regular eyelids, and found in all birds. In these diving ducks the membrane has a clear window of highly refractive material. A canvasback, diving for submerged plants, closes the third eyelid to bring the food into focus. The loons and auks share this device with the ducks. It is supplemented by a powerful iris muscle.

In many creatures a strong iris muscle constitutes the sole means of focusing under water. It is attached to the lens so that, when it contracts, the lens is squeezed out of shape and into focus. The turtles, otters, and cormorants have these soft lenses in the grip of a vigorous iris muscle. This lens-squeezing is typical of all reptiles (except snakes) and birds, although greatly accentuated in the divers. Early in their history the mammals lost this efficient method of accommodation, or focusing. It was one of the penalties for night-prowling. Their iris muscle gradually withdrew from the lens, degenerated, and was replaced by zonular fibers, which guy but do not squeeze the lens. Under this handicap, our limited focusing is based on the elasticity of the lens and contraction of the zonular fibers.

The kingfisher, and at least one fish, show us a third way for air eyes to see under water. The kingfisher possesses two foveal areas, or areas of keen sight where the image is focused on the retina. They are different distances from the lens. The more nasal of the two is closest to the lens and receives the image when the bird is in the air, and the cornea refracting. When the bird plunges into the water for a fish, the focal point shifts to the temporal, or more distant fovea, bringing the prey into focus once more.

A minnow of the genus *Anableps* utilizes both areas of keen vision at one time, as the fish drifts along the quiet surface of brackish waters. The iris is so shaped that the pupil is cut into a dorsal and ventral half, the former riding out of the water and the latter beneath the surface. Images in the air are received through the dorsal pupil on the ventral half of the retina, and objects below the surface are seen through the ventral pupil by the upper part of the retina.

The fourth mechanism is simply a highly mobile pupil, which can be closed to a tiny pin point in the daylight. The "depth of focus" is thereby increased, giving a clear picture at all distances like the old-time box camera. Under water, the dilated pupils of seals, sea lions and walruses focus normally on the retina. In the air, or in bright light, the tiny pupil compensates for the additional refraction of the cornea, and the animal sees fairly well.

Some vertebrates, like frogs and crocodiles, inhabit both media but see well only in one. These two groups are hopelessly farsighted under water but see well in the air. The penguins, on the other hand, see well under water but are nearsighted in the air.

Another problem faces animals that must see well into one medium from the other. A fish, looking into the air at a fly, like the osprey looking down at a fish, must overcome the confusion of bending light rays. Their prey is not where it seems to be for the same reason that a stick that you poke into the water seems to bend. The discrepancy in the apparent location of the osprey's intended victim is obvious to anyone who has ever attempted to shoot fish with a rifle.

The fish, as it looks out of the water at an angle, faces a problem involving trigonometry and the refractive indices of both media. Moreover, the angle subtended by the surface of the water over a fish, through which it can see, is about 97 degrees. Outside that angle the fish sees nothing but the reflected bottom. Crammed through that 97-degree window is the whole bowl of the sky, from shoreline to shoreline. The error involved in determining position has a sliding value according to the object's relative position above the fish. Only a fly directly over the fish is seen in its true position, and the same is true of a fish below an osprey. Probably both must strike from directly below or above to make a successful catch. The value of mobility is again emphasized in predation—and the eyes to go with it.

An extreme example of the problem is faced by the archer fish, a South American perch that shoots a jet of water from its mouth, knocking insects from shore vegetation or emergent weeds. The fish's eyes are under water, its mouth above. The shot is usually at an angle. If the surface of the water is choppy, the problem becomes even more complicated, and would seem almost impossible if the wind sways the weed bearing the prey.

When we consider all of these factors related to eyes and seeing, we come to have a deep regard for nature's ingenuity in providing her creatures with eyes for various special needs, that they may survive.

Mrs. Mouse's Miracle

Helen Hoover

IT WAS APRIL, and I was going about the business of trying to make some headway against the accumulation of wood smoke and dust that our cabin in the northern Minnesota wilderness gathers during the winter. Something was moving slowly across the kitchen linoleum, something that looked like an animated bit of dusty lint. I leaned down.

A deer mouse, her gray coat ruffled, her white gloves and face bedraggled, was feebly creeping along with her hind legs dragging uselessly. She did not seem to be in pain, but she was pitiably weak. Her strongest attempts to bite my finger did not even dent the skin. Apparently, she had been the victim of a crushing accident that appeared to have broken her back and paralyzed the hind quarters. Looking for further injuries, I turned her over. The sad little mouse was a nursing mother.

I called my husband, and explained the situation. "What should we do?"

"I suppose," he said hesitantly, "we should put her out of her misery—" He faltered. "Maybe if we feed her—"

Mrs. Mouse put out her miniature pink tongue, and licked tentatively at my finger. "She might recover," I said. "She's a pretty little thing." Mrs. Mouse tried to prove this by washing her white-gloved hands.

My husband settled the matter. "We'll fix her up behind the stove. Nature is a great healer. I hate to think of the little ones—waiting somewhere—"

She lunched on oatmeal, bread crumbs, and diluted canned milk before she crawled on an old wool sock and went to sleep. By evening she was much stronger, and even moved one of the crippled legs a little. In fact, she moved about with astonishing ease and did not seem to be suffering physically, although her milk-swollen little body must have been acutely uncomfortable. But she spent every waking moment—when she was not eating—in the center of the doorway between the kitchen and living room, half-lying, half-sitting, her head low, her dull eyes half-closed, her soft fur ungroomed.

"She's the saddest-looking thing I ever saw," my husband said. "She looks like she's grieving—overwhelmed with despair."

"Mouse-mothers and human mothers seem to have something in common," I observed. "But she can't tell us where her babies are, and she wouldn't even if she could."

"I wonder how she was hurt?" He looked at the heavy storage drawers under the kitchen counter. "She might have been crawling around in there and been caught when a drawer opened or closed." Hastily he began to peer into the drawers. Then: "Here they are!"

On top of a wide-mouthed jar of crumbs, without its lid, that I had carelessly put into a drawer was a nicely constructed spherical nest, soft as the finest silk, as carefully made as if for winter quarters with a round entrance on top. Lying on the chilly, bare wood of the drawer bottom were four infant mice, not more than three or four days old, that had crawled out of the nest. Were they alive? I timidly touched one. Such a fragile, helpless, little pink creature—and so cold. It squirmed in the way of all baby things, and feebly moved its incredibly delicate limbs, uttering a squeak so faint it was hardly a sound. I touched the others, one by one.

"They're all alive," I said happily. "Do you suppose we can give them back to her without injuring them? They're much too small and frail to just pick up with your fingers."

He handed me a sheet of thin, stiff paper. Carefully I rolled one of the little fellows on it and carried him to the warm sock behind the stove. Then I lifted Mrs. Mouse and set her down beside the sock. She must have been utterly terrified, but she neither protested, moved, nor looked up. Then that whisper of a squeak came again.

Mrs. Mouse's ears perked up. Her eyes lost their dullness. She scurried to the sock and stopped short, quivering all over. Slowly she reached out one paw and verified the reality of what she saw and smelled. Then, squeaking and chirping all the while, she patted her child all over carefully. She licked him clean, and tucked him cozily underneath her for his long-awaited meal. Courageous to the tips of her whiskers, she looked up at our huge bulks as though to tell us that this was her own, and that she was prepared to defend it no matter what the cost.

Hastily we brought the rest of her family to her, and moved the nest nearby. Mrs. Mouse was suddenly quite busy, settling her family, examining her nest, popping over to get a bite to eat.

"I never saw so much happiness in one little bunch," my husband said. "It's like someone had turned on a light down there. "She's—she's—"

"Transfigured is the word. That's what miracles do."

When we finished our dinner, Mrs. Mouse was sitting in her old place in the doorway. Full of mousy high spirits, she was busily working out a technique for washing her face with one paw while she supported herself with the other. Her little eyes glittered brightly at us, clearly saying that if there had ever been a baby mouse in our house it was news to her. She had hidden them cleverly indeed, and had even moved the nest piecemeal while we were not looking.

Now her days were full of housekeeping and mouse rearing, but such free time as she had was spent sitting in the old place in the doorway, calmly surveying the kitchen as though she had not a single responsibility.

Some three weeks later, I awoke in the morning to the sound of outraged and urgent squeaking in the kitchen. Mrs. Mouse's children, all four of them, had fallen into the sink. I rescued them, dried them off, presented them with some cake crumbs, and sent them home. This happened regularly for the next five days, and at the end of that time the small, fat, gray balls were quite calmly waiting for me when I got up.

We partially solved their problem by leaving a short length of board propped in the sink corner, so that they could crawl out. As soon as I appeared, they lined up in a neat little row, and waited to be fed. They liked chocolate cookies, which probably were much too rich for them, and corn bread, which should be fine for growing mice. They soon outgrew the sink game, but came regularly for their morning treat.

At about this time, any onions that are left over from our winter supply sprout briskly. As the snowy season is rarely garnished with any green vegetables, we place the sprouting onions upright in a glass on the window-sill until the tops are big enough to eat. To my amazement, the little mice found onion greens a treat. The height of the shoots posed a problem, but the youngsters managed well. One of them would climb from the window frame to the top of the glass and the onion sprouts, bending them down. Then all four would pounce on the tender tips and nibble.

When they were about nine weeks old and almost full-grown, I was sweeping the kitchen with the door open and they hopped out, to hurry up the hill and go about the business of being independent woods mice. Only then did Mrs. Mouse cease her quiet, diversionary vigils in the kitchen doorway. Without any attempt at concealment, she moved her nest from the old boot where she had raised her family to one end of the wool sock, which she used as a sort of patio. Her hind legs were hopelessly paralyzed, but she put this briskly aside, and scurried about on her front legs almost as rapidly as a four-legged mouse. She hunted eagerly for crumbs that I dropped for her, and occasionally startled a visitor by climbing up the cloth of a slip cover, and appearing in a friendly manner on a chair arm.

She often sat contentedly by her food dish, her head held confidently high as though with the knowledge of a task well done. All summer I kept her supplied with the food and water she was unable to find for herself, and it was not until autumn that her dish at last remained untouched. Mrs. Mouse's brave little days had ended finally.

All in the Life of a Swainson Hawk

George McClellan Bradt

SPRING COMES EARLY to the deserts and mountains of western Texas. But long before the sudden and ephemeral vernal showers have inspired dust-green vegetation to new and miraculous growth, birds are building secret nests. From the middle of March onward, innumerable desert birds sing and mate, brood and rear their young.

It was on May seventeenth that my wife and I discovered the nest for which we had been especially hunting—that of *Buteo swainsoni*, the Swainson hawk. Of all our western hawks few are more completely beneficial or more worth our gratitude than the Swainson. During the long hot hours of the desert day these magnificent winged hunters war upon man's rodent and insect enemies. Yet poor myopic, prejudice-ridden man in many parts of our country still slaughters not only the Swainsons but all the other fast-decreasing and irreplaceable birds of prey—our hawk, owl and eagle allies.

The solitary yucca in which our Swainsons had built their platformlike nest of coarse twigs stood on a great stretch of rolling desert. Close together on the dry twigs lay three greenish-white, faintly marked eggs. Too readily do the Swainsons abandon a disturbed nest, so, after taking a few quick photographs of nest and eggs we withdrew to a distant rise to watch the parent bird's return. Soon, beating low over the sparse ground cover of cactus, agave and creosote, the adult flew straight to the nest and settled herself upon it. Fervently we hoped that ours were the only eyes that thus observed her.

During the next two months we found that a weekly visit was sufficient to record the progress of the nest's occupants, and yet not often enough to frighten them away from us.

On May 24 we made our second visit. The single brooding adult again disappeared into the desert distance, but we caught a fleeting glimpse of the extensive unmarked buffy areas on the under sides of its wings so characteristic of the Swainson, and, with the help of a long lens, got a fair shot of her departure. We found the eggs still unhatched, so spent the short time we dared remain measuring the height of the yucca, and noting that from a vantage point, some twelve feet above the desert floor, the incubating hawk could see

—and herself remain unseen—for several miles in every direction.

May 31, our third Sunday, was claimed by the Army, so hawk and nest and eggs were spared our spying, but June 7 found us again on the way to the distant nest. Not far from the nest we ran into a blinding cloudburst. Coming opposite the yucca we could barely see the sitting parent bird protecting its precious contents from the chilling rain. So heavy was the driving downpour that even a moment's exposure would have meant disaster, so we are still wondering whether or not the eggs had hatched by that date. It seems quite certain that the great event took place no more than a day or two before or after that drenching afternoon.

June 14 finally arrived and we rushed off to the nest site full of eager anticipation. All being well, we knew we should find in it something a bit more exciting than three eggs. When we came within sight of the yucca we began searching for signs of life. Soon we could make out an adult bird standing on the nest edge apparently pulling at something with its strong beak. When the bird saw us it flew from the nest with an ear-piercing scream, and instead of disappearing as heretofore, remained to circle high above us, emitting shrill cries all the while. These actions were unmistakably those of a hawk with young in its nest. Climbing to the roof of the car, we found staring at us with beady eyes two tiny white hawklets. In the nest with these fuzzy babies were parts of a cottontail rabbit and of a young pack rat. It was this food that the parent had been tearing.

After getting a good look at the little fellows and trying unsuccessfully to imagine the fate of the third egg, we set up the ladder and our cameras and photographed the weak and hungry fledglings. Feeling quite certain that the nest would not be deserted now that it contained helpless young, we stayed longer than usual. Apparently we stayed too long, because ten minutes after our arrival both adults, seen together for the first time, began taking turns diving at us. Although they never actually struck us they did fly close enough

Seven days old and still weak. Note the partially eaten cottontail rabbit in the nest.

for their swift wings to whistle only a few inches above our heads. Finally we left, the adults no doubt believing that they had driven us off.

On the twenty-first of June we returned to find the two young birds considerably larger but still too weak to stand. We again photographed them from our insecure position on ladder and car, while the parents either perched on low yuccas and screamed at us, or practiced pulling out of power dives close to our heads.

Sunday afternoon, June 28, was a sad one for both the parent Swainsons and for us. When we drew up under the nest only one little white head and one pair of beady eyes peered over the nest edge at us below. What could have befallen its nestfellow? Had a hungry enemy taken both nestlings? Had it died and been removed by the adults? *Quien sabe?* But whatever the fate of its "brother" the one remaining bird had grown and changed remarkably. Now strong and well able to stand, it had even acquired a few black quills in its wings and in a day or two would have some poking through its ludicrous tail. When we climbed the ladder to get its picture it quickly spread one wing, clenched its yellow feet and hurled at us what was undoubtedly meant to be a defiant scream, but was really a feeble wail.

July 5 was our seventh hawk-Sunday. We found the one remaining nestling finally beginning to look like a hawk. Although retaining much of its natal fuzz it now had many chocolate-brown, buffy-edged feathers on wings and back and even a few

in its short tail. It stood well, could tear its own food, and occasionally would stretch wings or legs as if in the throes of "growing pains." We took a few pictures of the appealing hawklet before turning our attention to the adults, which for so many weeks had gone almost unobserved, so intent had we been on the young birds.

The parents had remained all that July 5 afternoon gliding through the desert air above our heads with their sharp eyes ever focused on the nest and us. Both were beautiful specimens, almost identical in color, size and markings. Their wingspread was probably a bit more than four feet, while their dark, grayish-brown bodies were hardly more than twenty inches long. The immaculate white throats of both sexes gave way to a broad pectoral band, chestnut-colored in the male, grayer in the female. Both had light gray tails crossed with nine or ten dusky bands. These two adults must have been at least three years old since true adult plumage is not worn until the third feather-suit is acquired. Immature birds are almost completely brown, except

Opposite page: An adult in second-year plumage. These graceful birds breed from northern Canada and Alaska to middle Mexico, and winter south of the Equator, mainly in Argentina.

Right: *Partially feathered nestling, probably about four weeks old. Its head is still clothed in its downy skullcap, but a few dark feathers begin to poke through. A little more than half grown.*

for the white chin, buffy undersides of wings, and tawny, drop-marked breast and belly feathers. In the hand the wings of the Swainsons have the three outer primaries cut out or indented on the inner webs near the tips. Even immature birds will not be confused with the red-tailed hawks, no matter what the plumage, if this one fact is remembered, for the latter birds have four primaries so notched.

On July 12 we found the young bird so

Three of the greenish-white, faintly marked eggs of this hawk.

large and so well fledged that we hesitated before approaching the nest. We feared that the bird, perhaps by now able to fly, might take off and leave its nest before it was ready. When first seen it was lying down on the nest, but when it saw us it stood up to watch our approach with its large, dark-gray eyes. We shot a few pictures of the hot and hungry fellow and then left to visit occupied mockingbird and thrasher nests not far distant. The fact that both these nests had young in them caused us to wonder why such easy and toothsome morsels had not long before fallen prey to our pair of Swainsons—so popularly and so erroneously called "chicken- or hen-hawk." Each time we had visited the hawk nest not a dead bird—nor even a feather—had been found, although there were numerous nests close by that contained unprotected young. Cottontails, lizards and wood rats formed the Swainsons' diet as far as could be determined from our observations. *Food Habits of Common Hawks,* by W. L. McAtee, confirms us with the statement: "Swainson's Hawk, eminently a destroyer of ground squirrels and pocket gophers, and of grasshoppers and crickets, thoroughly deserves considerate treatment at the hands of man."

The July 19 afternoon marked the end of our hawk-Sundays. In a very few days the young hawk would leave nest and parents to lead its own life in the great sun-drenched desert. Never again would it have to endure man's presence, no matter how sympathetic. It would be as free as is anything in nature, and concerned with little except getting enough food to satisfy its voracious appetite. Soon it would forget the two strange creatures that peered at it over the nest's edge Sunday after Sunday.

Pollen—Wonder Dust of Nature

Donald Culross Peattie

ALL ABOUT US in the air drifts a miraculous and potent dust of life. Invisible to the naked eye, a grain of pollen yet carries a spark of fecundating life—male life. Some pollens ride the wind to seek their fortune, and you may see them rise in a golden cloud when you tease the curls of a slim alder, or tap the ripe tassels of a pine. Others enslave the dusty bee as she threads her way from flower to flower. But every pollen grain is bound upon a journey, which may be an inch in length, or hundreds of miles, and its destination is a female flower of the same species.

Without pollen no seed would set anywhere in the world, grass would wither, and the fruit tree put forth no fruit. But because of pollen the wheat in the wind bows heavy with its grain, and the young oak rises where the old one fell. For pollen flies across the ever-present chasm of death, and starts the miracle of new life.

Although so potent, pollen is frailer than a candle in a gale. Always it is in danger of dying of thirst or starvation. Unlike a seed, it has no great reserve within itself. A single drop of dew may kill a pollen grain, for water makes the pollen coat swell up and burst, exposing the male germ to the fatal ultraviolet rays of sunlight. A grain of corn pollen can live under natural conditions only thirty-six hours at best. A small proportion of date pollen has been found still alive after several months. But, artificially preserving it in sealed tubes at cool but not freezing temperatures, plant breeders have sometimes kept apple pollen alive for half a year.

Fragile as snowflakes, prismatic as jewels, fanciful as Christmas tree ornaments, some pollens under my lens appear—to make crude comparisons—like chestnut burrs, photographs of the moon's surface, sea urchins, or clusters of those frilly paper cups around bonbons. The basic shapes are dominantly spheres and footballs. But pollen may also take the geometric forms of cubes, tetrahedrons, and pentagon dodecahedrons. The biggest grains, such as those of pumpkin flowers, are only one one-hundredth of an inch thick; the pollen of the alpine forget-me-not is one hundred times smaller!

Pollen experts can identify almost any pollen, so they can distinguish those invisible bombers—pollen of ragweed and oaks, grasses and plantain—that drop their poison on hay fever sufferers. Indeed, there are some seventy observation posts in the United States, keeping watch on these flights—wave after wave of them, as the different types, the seasons around, come over. Specialists inform us that even an office high above the street is not sanctuary against pollinosis—as hay fever is more accurately designated.

Luckily not all or even most wind-borne pollens are venomous. Almost no one, for instance, is ever hurt by pine pollen, although it is extremely abundant in spring, and, provided with big air sacs, it has astounding buoyancy—so great indeed that pine pollen has been found on the snows of Greenland, although the nearest pine forests are four hundred miles away across open sea in Labrador.

Nor is there much credence to be placed in the old wives' tale of "rose colds." For practically all the flowers with conspicuous petals and fragrance are exclusively insect-pollinated. Their pollen is quite unadapted to wind transport, and normally is never recovered from the atmosphere.

Every child today can instruct his parents in the facts of life from the analogy of the bees and the pollen of flowers. Yet only three hundred years ago the wisest scientists did not know that plants have sex. Or, rather, mankind had forgotten it again, for the Egyptians and Babylonians knew it when they pollinated their date palms by hand. So even the great Renaissance anatomist Malpighi informed his classes that plants rid themselves of pollen to purify their sap!

It was not until 1793 that Pastor Konrad Sprengel discovered in Germany that insects transport pollen from flower to flower. Regarding this as God's prettiest little miracle, he spent so much time in the fields studying flowers and bees that he would forget to come to his fashionable church and preach a sermon, so his congregation dropped him. He was so far ahead of his scientific times that scientists failed to recognize his work till Darwin unearthed it sixty years later.

It was Darwin who first showed that many kinds of flowers have elaborate ways of preventing inbreeding by their own pollen. In some the female organ or pistil is actually infertile to pollen grains from one of its own stamens, and will not produce seed when sprinkled with its own pollen. In certain flowers the stamens ripen before the pistil, in others the pistil ripens before the stamens; hence, for fertilization to take place, the pollen must come from some other plant of the same species whose stamens have ripened either later or earlier.

The best all-around pollinator is the common honeybee, which is abroad earlier in spring than any other flower-loving insect, and is the last to leave the field in fall. It has the habit of sticking faithfully to one kind of flower, at least for a while, unlike the butterflies that sip at one kind of blossom after another. The pollen the honeybee carries is therefore likely to arrive at its intended destination—a female flower of the same species. This is important because of the short life of pollen.

A beehive is almost a necessity in apple and orange orchards. The bee is paid for its labors by the large amounts of pollen she carries away to the larval or baby bees in the hive. Although she tucks a great deal of this into a special little pollen basket in her leg, she inevitably becomes dusted with pollen as she clambers around in the bloom, and thus carries a vast amount—sometimes up to half her weight—from one flower to another, inadvertently pollinating hundreds of blossoms a day.

Flowers have almost as many devices for dousing pollen on bees or fixing it to their bodies as there are kinds of flowers visited by these industrious little insects. In the flower the pollen is borne in little tubes called anthers, which open by pores when ripe, and from these the pollen shakes out like talcum powder. Some flowers have little piston systems, so that, as soon as the bee treads among the organs of the flower, the anther comes down like a mallet or piano key and gently strikes the insect, dusting the powder over its body. Others conceal their nectaries in such a way that the bee, to get at them, has to clamber over the anthers and thus scrapes pollen on her abdomen.

One of the most marvelous of all cases of mutual dependence in nature is that of a little moth that lays its eggs only in the ovary of the yucca plant. The hatching larvae eat some of the seeds, then bore their way out and escape. But no seeds will ripen if the flower is not pollinated. The moth herself performs this rite, quite deliberately. Her mouth parts are specially modified for rolling pollen into little balls, and after she has laid her eggs in the ovary she collects pollen from the anthers and carefully crams it down on the stigma, or receiving surface of the ovary. Without the moth the flower would fail to reproduce itself. Without the seeds the moth larvae would die. The act of pollination the moth performs is as expert as if she had a college degree in plant breeding.

This moth was pollinating yuccas at least as far back as the last Ice Age. Yet not until 1717 was the first plant hybrid made by man's hand, when Thomas Fairchild, in England, placed the pollen of a carnation on the female flower of a sweet william. Most of the work of crossbreeding has been done since 1900, for only with the discovery of Mendel's law, in 1866, did breeding become an exact science.

Gregor Mendel was an Austrian monk who spent his life pollinating peas in his cloister garden, and proving that nothing, after all, is so *unlike* as two peas in a pod. To a great extent he revealed the secret of heredity, showing that strains repeat themselves in a regular mathematical pattern, and, by breeding, can often be perpetuated, increased, eliminated, or blended. Thus, by pollinating a rose that has a factor (scientists call it a gene) for ever-blooming, but no gene for fragrance, with a rose that has a gene for fragrance but none for ever-blooming, today's breeder hopes to get a rose that will be both fragrant and ever-blooming.

This and far more important things are done by breeders of all sorts of plants from beans to orchids, working with frail pollen as their strongest tool. It is fascinating to visit a plant experiment station and watch the delicate, swift, accurate technique of the breeders.

The varieties to be pollinated first have their own pollen-bearing organs cut out before the bud opens, to prevent inbreeding. Then the bud is shut in a bag to prevent bees from bringing unknown, perhaps undesirable, pollen to the flower. The breeder now goes to the male parent strain he has selected and collects the fresh, fertile pollen just as the flower opens. This he puts in a little glass dish, marked with the name or number of the bush it came from. He may collect pollen from many varieties at once, and with a whole trayful of dishes he then moves down the row of female parents, each kept immaculate in its bag. Opening each bag, he applies the selected pollen to the stigma of the female flower, closes the bag, and goes on. His work is then complete; he can only await results.

But the pollen grain is just going to work. On the stigma or receptive surface of the female flower it begins to sprout, sending out a very fine tube that grows down and down in the tissues of the ovary, toward the egg cells at the bottom. The distance it may have to travel may be about a thousand times the diameter of the pollen grain, as in the case of the amaryllis. Yet somehow the grain is able to take all this "pipe line" out of itself. For the pollen is actually drawn toward the waiting egg cells by a chemical stimulator called a hormone. This fact has been proved by putting a pollen grain on a moist glass slide, with a tiny piece of the ovary of the same species; the pollen tube grows toward the ovary, guided by the hormone, which has diffused through the water on the slide. So, in the flower, the precious passenger in the pollen grain at last reaches journey's end, and the new life is started.

The result may be a new strain of wheat that will help feed the starving world. It may be a hybrid tea rose, breathing its exquisite perfume in your garden. Or it may be a noble tree to shade the roof of your children's children. Truly, pollen is the wonder dust of nature.

Introducing the Authors

by the Editor

FROM THE VANTAGE POINT of more than thirty-five years of experience we can testify that writers about nature are "something special." They write about the subject they love, which imparts a special quality to what they have to say. It is appropriate, therefore, that they should here be introduced to the readers of this book.

Grand Marais, Minnesota, is the address of HELEN HOOVER ("Mrs. Mouse's Miracle"), although the Hoovers actually live in a log cabin on a Canadian border lake fifty miles from the nearest town. She has been variously a mail clerk, proofreader, editor, chemist, metallographer and a chief metallurgist. A close student of nature, Mrs. Hoover is now a free-lance writer specializing in this field of writing, drawing her inspiration from a region rich in subject matter.

Former editor of *The Fisherman* and writer on wildlife and conservation, GEORGE S. FICHTER ("The Mighty Little Flea") is now a free-lance writer making his base in Florida. When, some years ago, the editor of *Nature Magazine* rejected one of his poems, Mr. Fichter set a goal of "breaking into" the columns of the magazine. This he finally accomplished with his able and entertaining discussion of the flea.

For more than three decades E. LAURENCE PALMER ("Hello! Do You Hear Me?") has been Director of Nature Education of the American Nature Association and a contributor to every issue over that space of years. Emeritus Professor of Nature and Science Education at Cornell University, he has greatly influenced the study of nature in this country as a leading exponent of learning from nature and not from books. He is also author of several books for field use, and a series of more than one hundred special, eight-page educational inserts in the magazine, and innumerable articles, this article being one of these inserts.

Engaged in the general practice of medicine in Lambertville, New Jersey, Dr. PAUL H. FLUCK ("In the Language of Birds") has long been the individual in the vicinity to whom young and old have brought injured wildlife for healing. Birds in particular have received his ministrations, and he is often referred to as "the bird doctor." This activity grew to include his outstanding work at Washington Crossing Park, New Jersey, where, at great personal sacrifice, he has carried on week-end educational work bringing the message of wildlife conservation and protection to thousands of people.

Sit across a desk from ERNEST P. WALKER ("Glimpses of Flying Squirrels") and he is likely to reach inside his shirt and bring out his favorite baby bat of the moment. Or visit his Washington, D.C., home and be prepared for introduction to other bats, hamsters, flying squirrels, a small monkey or two, or other small mammals. Now retired as associate director of the National Zoological Park in the nation's capital, he is working on *Genera of Recent Mammals of the World*, as well as continuing his studies of the language of monkeys, writing about and photographing animals, as he does here with the lovely flying squirrel.

In his position as chairman of the Division of Science and Mathematics at West Liberty State College, West Virginia, M. H. BERRY ("Flowers Tell the Easter Story") finds an avocation in nature photography. Delving into the lore of Eastertime, he has found many fascinating floral associations of the season.

Insects, especially the more minute and uncommon ones, always lured the late GEORGE ELWOOD JENKS ("The Little Brown Jug") and constituted a challenge to him. By painstaking observation and patient photography he ferreted out the obscure life story of various insects, which were only scientific names in the books on entomology. His picture story of the wasp is typical of what others with equal patience and curiosity may do in the field of nature discovery.

Standing today in the front rank of today's naturalist-writers, EDWIN WAY TEALE ("Lucky Bugs, and Others" and "Tail Tales") first was intrigued with life in an insect community. On Long Island he maintained an "insect garden," a wild and natural acreage where he spied upon the goings and comings of its insect inhabitants and, with notable skill, photographed them. These explorations resulted in such books as *Near Horizons, Grassroot Jungles* and *The Golden Throng.*

Field botany and plant exploration have taken WALTER HENDRICKS HODGE ("The Trees that Walk to Sea") to many parts of the world, particularly to Latin America. In between travels he has taught botany and written extensively and entertainingly, especially on plants that he has met in out-of-the-way places. He is head of the Department of Education and Research at Longwood Gardens, Kennett Square, Pennsylvania.

Ardent conservationist and writer on the outdoors, ARTHUR HAWTHORNE CARHART ("It's a Little Dog's Life") makes his home in Denver, but roves widely. He has established something of a record in the number of trout streams he has fished. He is the author of many articles in outdoor magazines and of several books, including *Water—Or Your Life,* a militant plea for water conservation and restoration.

Assistant editor of *Nature Magazine,* PAUL MASON TILDEN ("Rocks that Left Home") finds geology and botany his major nature enthusiasms. Son of Freeman Tilden, Mr. Tilden grew up in a literary atmosphere and was early "exposed" to conservation thinking. He has been a working newspaperman in the West and in New Hampshire, and has a rare faculty of being able to make geology come alive in his writings.

One of a vanishing tribe of field-trained naturalists, the late EDWARD A. PREBLE ("The Mountain Heronry") served for more than thirty years as consulting naturalist and associate editor of *Nature Magazine.* As a member of the staff of the old United States Bureau of Biological Survey, he made several trips to the far North, one with Ernest Thompson Seton, and was the author of a classic mammalogy of that region. Before his death he established a 1000-acre sanctuary surrounding the family farm in New Hampshire, and this article is laid in that area.

When a person writes about Canada geese the devoted monogamy of these birds is bound to be mentioned. This attribute provides the theme of this moving story by GERALD MOVIUS ("So Long, Voyageur!"), which brought much comment from the readers of *Nature Magazine* when it was first published. This boyhood observation so effectively expresses the theme that runs through the selections in this book that it was chosen for first position.

For many years an eloquent editorial writer for the *Portland Oregonian,* BEN HUR LAMPMAN ("The Baron of Cowfoot Lake") had a deep love of nature, of which he was a keen and understanding observer. Most of his writings in this field appeared in the pages of his newspaper, or in *Nature Magazine.* It was often necessary to prod him into writing, but the result was always worthy of the urging. He preferred the fictional approach, and this story—one of only two fact-fiction stories in this book—is typical of the moving beauty of his work.

An active ornithologist and member of the American Ornithologists' Union, A. MARGUERITE BAUMGARTNER ("Ookpikjuak the Lonely") has such a deep understanding of avian life that she is able to write as though she were a bird. *Nature Magazine* has not often used nature fiction because it is so rarely well or accurately done. In this life of the snowy owl Mrs. Baumgartner has written a story so poignant and so full of the "feel of the wild" that it was regarded as irresistible when first published, and it insistently demands republication here.

Adult attitudes toward wildlife usually stem from youthful encouragement of interest in and understanding of our fellow creatures. HELEN ELLSBERG ("Uncle Hoiman") was a mother who realized the importance of bending the twig in the right direction.

Nebraska is the native state of MARI SANDOZ ("Musky") and it provides the locale for this story of a nature experience of childhood. Nebraska also provided the setting for her prize-winning best seller of 1935, *Old Jules.* Novelist, historical writer and teacher of writing, Miss Sandoz is at home both in New York City and Ellsworth, Nebraska.

One of the world's eminent ornithologists, Dr. ROBERT CUSHMAN MURPHY ("The Turbulent Life of the Sand Bug") is especially an authority on oceanic birds, the study of which has taken him far and wide. Now retired as chairman of the department of birds of the American Museum of Natural History, he makes his home on Long Island. Most recently Dr. Murphy has taken a leading part in attempts to check indiscriminate spreading of insecticides because of their destruction of bird life and ecological balances.

One of the early leaders in the nature study movement, EDITH M. PATCH ("Upstream with the Alewives") was a Maine naturalist, teacher and writer. A past president of the American Nature Study Society, she was the author of several outstanding nature books for children, as well as a popular series of elementary science texts. Her story of the alewives is typical of her ability to describe the drama of nature.

Texas is the native state of J. FRANK DOBIE ("Strange Animal Friendships") and he is often referred to as the historian of the Lone Star State. To his credit are several books dealing with the early history of Texas, where he was a professor of English and where he still makes his home, in Austin. Nature, however, has always been one of his abiding interests and plays an important part in all of his writings.

During the 1920s and early 1930s ARTHUR NEWTON PACK ("A Question of Taste"), past president of the American Nature Association and editor emeritus of *Nature Magazine*, in company with William L. Finley, made several trips into wilderness country in our own Northwest, Canada and Alaska. Their goal was the study and photography of mountain goats and sheep, moose, elk, caribou, the great Kodiak grizzly and other wildlife. This article is one of many that resulted from these exciting experiences of hunting with a camera. Mr. Pack now makes his home in Tucson, Arizona, where he is active in civic affairs and directs the work of the Charles Lathrop Pack Forestry Foundation. He was in large measure responsible for the Arizona-Sonora Desert Museum near Tucson.

Active conservationist and teacher, PAUL SHEPARD, JR. ("The Eyes Have It") is a professor of biology at Knox College, Galesburg, Illinois. He earned his Ph.D. at the Yale Graduate School of Conservation under Dr. Paul Sears, and is conservation consultant for the National Council of State Garden Clubs.

Although he is perhaps best known for his many fine novels, the late WILLIAM BYRON MOWERY ("Wee Tim'rous White-Foot") had a deep love of nature and was a keen observer of the outdoors. Indeed, he once observed that while much writing was hard work, writing about nature was a pleasure. His story of the whitefoot mouse is eloquent testimony to that fact.

When K. F. BASCOM ("The Chronicle of Obadiah") wrote the appealing story of the woodchuck, he was teaching anatomy and completing his medical studies, graduating from medical school in 1929. A practicing physician in Manhattan, Kansas, he writes us that 3200 deliveries and more than 3600 major operations have interfered with any writing. Four sons have now graduated from medical school, so Mr. Bascom feels he may find time again to write.

WILLIAM BEEBE ("A Motherly Knight in Armor") possesses a rare combination of talents—those of both able naturalist and accomplished writer. Noted as an authority on birds, especially pheasants, and as a mammalogist, his explorations beneath the surface of the ocean have brought him equal fame. Now past the fourscore mark, he is still active in the field for the New York Zoological Society, with which he has been associated for more than a half-century. His story of the sea horse is typical of the notable nature writing that can be found in the pages of his many books.

DOUGLAS F. LAWSON ("Hidden Beauty") lives in Banstead, Surrey, England, and is a British naturalist with a wide interest in many fields. An area of special interest to him comprises the exciting things of nature to be seen through a microscope. His group of photomicrographs reproduced here proves how fascinating the minute may be.

Once, when writing to ALAN DEVOE ("Mothers of the Wild" and "A Genius in Feathers"), this editor apologized for the necessarily modest size of a check. He replied quickly, declaring that the check did not matter and that he would rather be published in *Nature Magazine* than anywhere else. This response was typical of his sincere love of nature, about which he wrote so eloquently. His untimely and early passing reduced the ranks of nature-writers by one of its most distinguished members.

DONALD CULROSS PEATTIE ("Uncle Sam's Bird" and "Pollen—Wonder Dust of Nature") was a contributor to *Nature Magazine* in its early days in the 1920s. Rereading these early articles, many of them biographies of famous naturalists, one realizes how inevitable it was that he should attain the position of eminence that he now enjoys in the field of nature writing. Although he now and then departs from it, usually into the field of history, it is his first love, for he was a botanist by training.

MARJORIE SHANAFELT ("Just Maggie") was one of those people who somehow seem fated to care for orphaned birds and mammals. She was on the staff of the State Museum of the University of Nebraska. In 1927 she wrote that "one of my self-imposed tasks has been to raise the orphans who have crept, fluttered, or been carried in, pleading eloquently, 'Sanctuary.' " This story of a magpie concerns one of these.

A teacher of writing at Syracuse University for the past twenty years, GEORGE L. BIRD ("Andy, A Mischief-Loving Crane") wrote this article when he was living in Florida. He is the author of a book on writing for the market.

LOUISE DE KIRILINE ("Blackburnians of the Pines") is a Canadian naturalist, with special interest in ornithology. She is also an active and militant conservationist, living at Rutherglen, Ontario.

Tracking HARRIET H. BURKHART ("An Owl in Our Chimney") in connection with her story was a merry chase, leading from Pennsylvania to Los Angeles, to South America, and finally to Barro Colorado Island in the Canal Zone. She is a widely roving grandmother with an unquenchable enthusiasm for nature wherever she may find it. When home, which does not seem to be often, she lives in Union City, Pennsylvania.

WILLIAM L. FINLEY ("The Wit of a Red Squirrel") was a pioneer photographer of nature, field naturalist, lecturer and conservationist. He served for many years as field naturalist for the American Nature Association and took part in most of its expeditions into wilderness areas. His home at Jennings Lodge, Oregon, entertained a wide variety of birds and mammals, from Don Q, a California quail who thought he was "people," to a young antelope and a baby mountain goat that arrived at about the same time.

DALLAS LORE SHARP ("A Wasatch Grizzly") was an outstanding nature writer of the first three decades of the twentieth century. He was also a professor of English at Boston University and an early conservationist. His interests were so varied that they include running for the nomination as United States Senator from Massachusetts, on a pro-League of Nations platform, against Senator Henry Cabot Lodge.

Eminent zoologist Dr. CARL G. HARTMAN ("The Story of the Baby Opossum") has been a member of the faculties of the University of Texas, Johns Hopkins and the University of Illinois. Upon his retirement from the latter, he became associated with the Ortho Research Foundation of Raritan, New Jersey, of which he is Director Emeritus. His studies of the only North American marsupial, the opossum, resulted in this article dispelling some of the misconceptions about this mammal, and, later, in a book on the opossum.

A civil engineer, HUBERT LOOMIS SMITH ("Snooky") describes himself as a "tropical tramp" because of his extensive travels in Latin America. Birds, however, are one of his special enthusiasms, particularly birds that have been orphaned or injured. He has rescued and kept for varying periods many such avian guests, but has never trapped a bird or taken one from a nest. This poignant story of one bird that he befriended is a sincere expression of the author's deep feeling for winged unfortunates.

OLIN SEWALL PETTINGILL, JR. ("Shore Bird Extraordinary") is an educator, photographer, writer, ornithologist and lecturer. He is secretary of the National Audubon Society and a member of its screen tour staff. Dr. Pettingill is author of *Guide to Bird Finding—East,* and a companion volume dealing with the West, among other writings.

When GEORGE MCCLELLAN BRADT ("The Life of a Swainson Hawk") spied upon these birds and took the pictures that record its life history, he was in the army. Since then he has taught elementary science in school, as well as taught teachers at the University of Arizona summer school and in a workshop at Arizona State College in Flagstaff. For the past five years, he and Mrs. Bradt have lived and taught in a little, two-teacher rural school about fifty miles south of Tucson in a region rich in nature and historic interest.